Timberdoodle

FOURTH GRADE

Curriculum Handbook | 2024-2025

Nonreligious Edition

We're So Glad You Are Here

Congratulations on choosing to homeschool this year! Whether this is your first year as a teacher or your tenth, we're confident you'll find that there is very little that compares to watching your child's learning take off. We suspect you'll look back at this year as one that shaped your relationship with your child and made you closer than ever.

On Your Mark, Get Set, Go!

Preparing for your first school day is very easy. Peruse this guide, customize your schedule, browse the introductions in your books, and you will be ready to go.

We Are Here to Help

We would love to assist you if questions come up, so please don't hesitate to contact us with any questions, comments, or concerns. Whether you contact us by phone, email, or live online chat, you will get a real person who is eager to serve you and your family.

You Will Love This!

This year you and your student will learn more than you hoped while having a blast. Ready? Have an absolutely amazing year!

Schedule Customizer

Your 2024-2025 Fourth-Grade Curriculum Kit includes access to our Schedule Customizer, where you can not only plan out your school weeks but also tweak the checklist to include exactly what you want on your schedule. To get started, just visit the scheduling website:

schedule.timberdoodle.com

If you ordered online under the same email address as your Schedule Customizer account, your kit is preloaded and ready to schedule now! If not, use your activation code + order number to gain access now. (See page 12 for complete activation information.)

Your Timberdoodle Activation Code:

N6UZZUG3CAYK

You'll also need your order number. If you ordered from a school district or don't have it handy, call, email, or chat with us, and we will be happy to look it up for you.

Get Support

Are you looking for a place to hang out online with like-minded homeschoolers? Do you wonder how someone else handled a particular science kit? Or do you wish you could encourage someone who is just getting started this year? Join one or more of our online groups.

Timberdoodlers of all ages:

https://www.facebook.com/groups/Timberdoodle

Timberdoodlers with 1st- to 4th-grade students:

https://www.facebook.com/groups/ElementaryTimberdoodle

Timberdoodlers using nonreligious kits:

https://www.facebook.com/groups/SecularTimberdoodle

Contents

Introductory Matters

5   Meet Your Handbook
6   Tips & Tricks
10   Why Use a Weekly Checklist?
12   Meet Your Online Schedule Customizer
16   Your Sample Annual Planner
18   What Is a Lesson?
21   Sample Weekly Checklists
26   Introducing The Reading Challenge
29   Ask Your Student

Item-by-Item Introductions

31   Language Arts
38   Mathematics
42   Thinking Skills
46   History & Social Studies
50   Geography
53   Science
56   STEM Learning
59   Art
64   Learning Tools

Articles and Resources

69   From Our Family to Yours
70   Why Emphasize Independent Learning?
72   What Makes Games a Priority?

71   8 Reasons to Stop Schoolwork and Go Build Something!
76   What If This Is Too Hard?
78   9 Tips for Homeschooling Gifted Children
77   11 Thoughts for Homeschooling Struggling Children
82   Convergent & Divergent Thinking
84   How Do I Fit This Much Reading Into My Day?
86   Help! My Book Says "Common Core"!
88   I Need a Homeschool Group, Right?

Item-Specific Resources

91   Mosdos Ruby Weekly Assignments

The Reading Challenge

97   Reading Challenge Questions & Answers
102 Tracking Your Reading Challenge
104 36 Weeks of Reading Challenges
202 Book Awards & Party

When You're Done Here

205 Your Top 4 FAQ about Next Year
208 Doodle Dollar Reward Points

Get Started

Meet Your Handbook

Simple Is Better

1. The Planning

First up are all the details on planning your year, including your annual planner and sample weekly checklists, which are the absolute backbones of Timberdoodle's curriculum kits. More on those in a moment.

2. Item-by-Item Introductions

We include short bios of each item in your kit, ideal for refreshing your memory on why each is included or explaining exactly what your student will be learning this year. This is where we've tucked in teaching tips to make this year easy and amazing for both of you.

3. Articles and Resources

In this section you'll find our favorite articles and tidbits gathered over 35 years of homeschool experience.

4. Item-Specific Resources

Here you'll find your weekly assignments for Mosdos.

5. Reading Challenge

Last but not least is the reading challenge—a reading log designed to help your child read a huge variety of books this year. We include hundreds of book ideas to give you a head start.

All the Details Included

This Timberdoodle curriculum kit is available in 3 different levels: Basic, Complete, and Elite. This allows you to choose the assortment best suited to your child's interest level, your family's schedule, and your budget. In this guide, you'll find an overview for each of the items included in the Elite Curriculum Kit, along with teaching tips. If you purchased a Basic or Complete kit, or if you customized your kit, you did not receive every item. Therefore, you'll only need to familiarize yourself with the items included in your kit.

Don't Panic—You Didn't Order Too Much Stuff!

We have yet to meet a homeschooler who doesn't have other irons in the fire. From homesteading or running a business to swimming lessons or doctor appointments, your weeks are not dull. As you unpack your box, you may be wondering how you'll fit it all in. We'll go in-depth on schedules momentarily, but for now, know that most of the items in your kit feature short lessons, and not all of them should be done every day or even every week. Your checklist (aka the weekly to-do list) is going to make this incredibly manageable. Really!

Tips & Tricks

Your First Week, State Laws, and More

It Gets Better!

As you get started this year, realize that you are just getting your sea legs. Expect your studies to take a little longer and be a little less smooth than they will be by the end of the year. As you get your feet under you, you will discover the rhythm that works best for you!

Find Your Pace

We asked parents who used this kit how long their students spent on "school." The majority said that they spent 2-4 hours per day using their Timberdoodle Fourth-Grade Kit. That is a wide variation, and it also means some days were shorter or longer than that. Make sure to allow time to find a pace that is right for you and your student!

Books First or Not?

Some goal-oriented students might like to start each day with bookwork and end with fun, hands-on time. Others might prefer to intersperse the hands-on thinking games, STEM, and so forth between more intensive subjects to give their brains a clean slate. If you don't know where to begin each day, why not try starting with something from the Thinking Skills category? It will get your child's brain in gear and set a great tone for the rest of the day.

A Little Every Day, or All at Once?

Depending on your preferences, your child's attention span, and what other time commitments you have (teaching other children, doctor appointments, working around a baby's

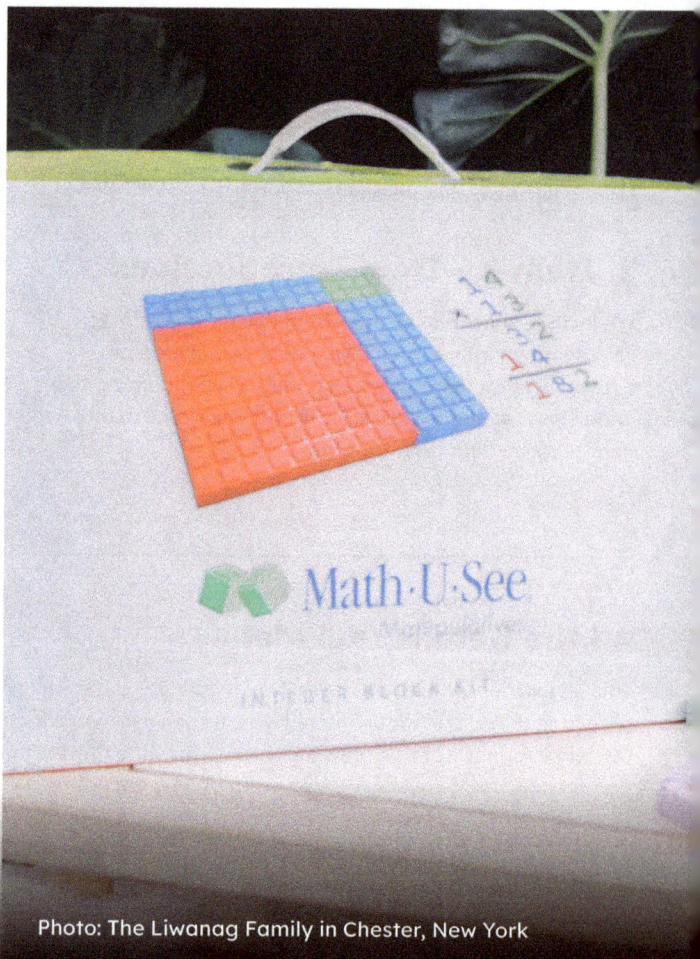

Photo: The Liwanag Family in Chester, New York

nap), there are many different ways to schedule your week. Some families like to do a little portion from nearly all subjects every day, while others prefer to blast out an entire week's work within a subject in a single sitting. Throughout the year, you can tinker around with your daily scheduling and see what approach works best for your family.

Tips for Newbies

If you're new to homeschooling, it might be helpful for you to know that some subjects are typically taught and practiced several times a week for the best mastery. These include basic math instruction, phonics, and spelling.

However, more topical subjects such as geography, history, and science are often taught all at once. Meanwhile, thinking skills, STEM, art, hands-on learning, and games can be even more tailored to the preferences of the child or used for independent learning while you are busy.

What about the Courses That You Don't Work on Every Week?

As you go over your checklist, you'll notice that some of your courses are "2–3 per month" or "as desired." That may leave you confused about how to tackle them. Here are a few options: You could go ahead and do it every week, completing the course early. You could set aside the item for summer. Or you could complete it as suggested, of course!

The Summer Plan

If you're looking at all these tools and feeling a little overwhelmed, or if you just wish you had more structured activities for the summer, feel free to grab a handful of items from the kit and set them aside for summer. Then set a reminder on your phone or calendar about which ones they are and where you stashed them so you won't forget to use them!

Meeting State Requirements

Check https://www.hslda.org/laws to see the most current information on your specific requirements. For many states, it is sufficient to hang on to your completed and dated weekly checklists along with a sampling of your child's best work this year. Some states ask you to add a state-specific topic, such as Vermont history, or a generic course like P.E. or health. We have a summary on our blog comparing your kit to state requirements, but HSLDA is the gold standard for current legal information.

P.E.? Health?

We suggest thinking outside the box on this. Many of the science courses have a health component that meets the requirement. P.E. is a great way to fit your child's favorite activity into the school schedule. Ballet, soccer, horseback riding, swimming...there are so many fun ways to check off P.E. this year.

Put Your Child in Charge

The weekly checklists are the framework of your week, designed for maximum flexibility. Just check off each item as you get it done, and you'll be able to see at a glance what you still need to do this week. (This is true of the daily checklists as well—just on a shorter schedule.) Many students even prefer to get all their work done early in the week and enjoy all their leisure time at once!

Do Hard Things and Easy Ones

Our family provides foster care for kids who need a safe place for a while. This has exposed us to a whole new world of hard days and stressful weeks. If your child is struggling today, you are not failing if you take a step back and have him start with his most calming project. For our crew, often that would be art or the reading challenge. You even have a little slush room in most subjects, so don't hesitate to trim the lessons short during a busy or challenging week or to pause schoolwork today for a complete reset and tackle it fresh tomorrow.

At the same time, you are not doing your child any favors if you never teach him how to work through a challenge. After all, you have hard days as a parent and still get up, drink your coffee, and jump back in. Be aware of your own tendency either to have your child buckle down and push through or to let him ease off completely, then work to provide a healthy balance for your child, particularly if he is in the process of healing.

Pro Tip

If you are using paper checklists, when you first get out a week's checklist, go ahead and check off all the things you don't need to do this week. For instance, if your child did a few extra pages of math last week or you are putting off all art kits until winter, check those off. Doesn't that feel better?

The Sample Schedules

We're including a sample annual planner on page 16, as well as sample weekly planners for each level of your kit, reflecting a typical 36-week school year. This lets you see at a glance how this might work for you, even before you get a moment to sit down at your computer and print your own custom-fitted schedule.

Photo: The Johanson Family

Why Use a Weekly Checklist?

Flexibility and Structure Unite

One of the primary concerns a new homeschooler faces is "How do I know I'm doing enough?" Your Timberdoodle kit gives you the structure you need for the year, but how do you break that down into a plan for your month, week, or day?

Pitfall 1: No Plan

We've seen 2 significant pitfalls over the years. The first is having no plan or consistency at all. Perhaps you start materials at random and then toss them aside if it gets tough or something else catches your eye. You end the year having made undefined progress, and your days often seem like a frustrating blur that leaves you counting the hours to bedtime.

Pitfall 2: Overscheduling

The other pitfall is to overschedule your life:
8:30 song
8:33 storytime
8:40 math lesson
8:50 thinking skills game
8:57 history book

In our experience, this approach makes your life exponentially more stressful. What if the baby has a blowout at 8:30? Or perhaps you finally get the long-anticipated return phone call that you need to take? Or even a scheduled interruption such as a swim lesson or doctor appointment? Any of these scenarios will add stress, which heavily impacts the tone of your school time.

The Cure?

Timberdoodle's checklist system offers the perfect mix of structure and flexibility. You'll go online and build your schedule using our exclusive Schedule Customizer. (More details on how to do that in a moment.) Then you'll work the plan each week.

Start with Blocks of Time

We highly recommend a building-block approach for your homeschool schedule. Think through all the things you want to do: one-on-one school, independent learning, read-aloud books, outdoor time, chores...then create a rhythm that sets you up for success. (Need inspiration? You can read more about our own schedule in the articles and resources section.)

Put Them Together

Now that you have the building blocks in place, you may know you want to tackle one-on-one school topics right after morning chores while the toddler plays. This plan will work well whether morning chores take forever today or your child wakes up early and races through them. It will even work if you're doing emergency clean-up at your normal start time!

Use Your Checklist

Now, grab your weekly checklist and begin checking things off. As you settle into a rhythm, you'll discover whether your child likes to ease into the day with his least intimidating subject or whether he is at his most focused then, so you'll be doing something more challenging. But no matter where you begin, you'll be checking off items from the list!

Check It Off!

Consider having your child check off items as he finishes them. Some students prefer to check things off online or have you do so, while other students thrive with a paper list that they can frequently reference.

It's OK to Stumble

If you are new to homeschooling, expect your first few weeks to be a bit of a blur. Even those of us who grew up homeschooling and are implementing the program we wrote find that it can take a good 3-6 weeks to feel that we've really settled into a new rhythm.

Rewards?

Make this process as fun for you and your student as you can. Our crew loves screen time, so once a week we have a family movie time for those with their school list done. But if screen time isn't your child's motivator, pick something that is. Visiting a special park? A field trip to the zoo? Game night? Dessert? You could even vary it each week. Just make sure that it is genuinely motivating, sustainable, and, ideally, fun for you as well!

Weeks Will Vary

As you settle in, you'll find that your weeks vary. Sometimes the weather is terrible, the lessons are fascinating, and the rest of your crew allows you a lot of time to focus in with one student. Other weeks the newborn has colic, the weather is tempting you outside, and library books must be raced through before they are due back. Don't stress! We suggest checking off the big 3 (language arts, math, thinking skills) each week and allowing the other subjects to shift as needed.

Because you're logging progress online, you'll be able to recalculate easily if you realize you need to redouble your efforts for the last 8 weeks of school. But in the meantime, embrace the flexibility that you have. Outside time = P.E. Library books = literacy. And that colicky newborn? Well, he just might be helping your other students learn to be kind, sacrificial caregivers or even curious learners who find their own entertainment. It's hard to overestimate those skills or pencil them into the plan, so just embrace them when they arrive even if you have to cross off a few of the art plans for the week.

Meet Your Online Schedule Customizer

Getting the Most Out of Your Planner

Newest Feature

Among the many behind-the-scenes improvements already completed and the bigger updates scheduled for spring, there is one new feature on the site that you'll want to know about now: You can now see at a glance which things you skipped in previous weeks. This will make catching up even easier!

Use the Customizer

Beginning on page 21, you'll find sample weekly checklists for Basic, Complete, and Elite kits. Before you photocopy 36 of them, though, take a moment to check out the online Schedule Customizer that came free with your kit.

You can easily adjust your days and weeks of school and tweak the checklist to include exactly what you want. Plus, you'll be able to print your weekly checklists directly from the Schedule Customizer and even log your progress!

First Time?

You'll need to activate your account for the Schedule Customizer to get started. If you ordered from our website, head directly to schedule.timberdoodle.com and log in. Your activated kit will be waiting for you!

If you ordered through a school district or need to activate a different email address, click the button in the middle of the page to submit your activation code from the inside front page of this handbook + your order number and start scheduling!

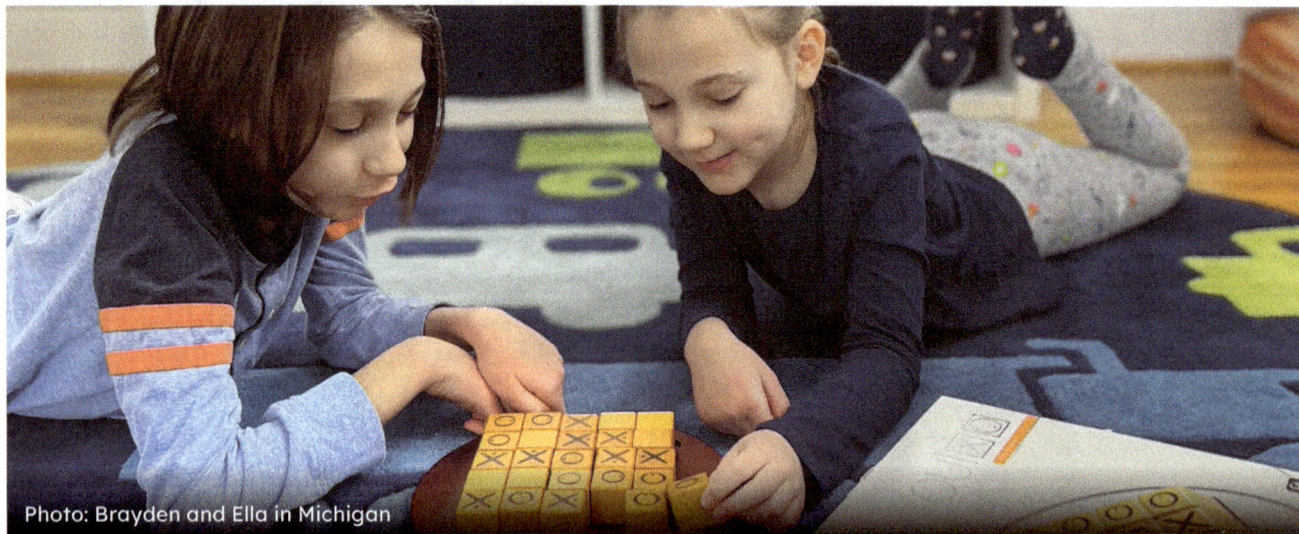

Photo: Brayden and Ella in Michigan

Before you get started, you'll want to know 3 things:

1. How Many Weeks Will You Do School?

A standard school year is 36 weeks plus breaks. Some families prefer to expedite and complete the entire year in fewer weeks—a great option to get this year's school done before a baby arrives, for instance. Or perhaps your family, like ours, prefers to school year-round and keep that brain sharp. Do keep in mind any mandatory school days in your state. Here in Washington we are expected to do some sort of learning 180 days a year (36 five-day weeks).

2. When Do You Want to Start?

Any day is fair game! You may want to match your local school district, but you don't have to.

3. What Breaks Do You Want?

Thanksgiving, Christmas, winter break, spring break…you could also add weeks off for travel, visiting grandparents, or…

If you are using the weekly checklist, you typically don't need to take the time to enter a single-day break since most families prefer to work a little harder on the other days that week and not lose their stride. But if you're using the daily schedule, or if it's easier for you, feel free to add in partial-week breaks too!

Check Your End Date

A standard school schedule is often 40 weeks long, with 36 weeks of schoolwork + 4 weeks of breaks.

What Days Do You Want to Do School?

If you are using a weekly schedule only, don't worry about this setting! But if you prefer a daily checklist, this is the place to set a 4-day week or move all school from Wednesday to Saturday.

Choose Your Items

Now just pop that data into the Schedule Customizer and proceed to the subject-by-subject review. Under each subject, you'll see your kit's items loaded by default, and you'll also find options to add in items you already had on hand, add custom courses, change the subject color, etc.

Edit Items

If you're opting for the daily scheduler, you have some helpful fine-tuning options. Just click "Edit" on any particular course to select which days of the week the course will appear. This lets you do things like schedule history only on Wednesday because that is co-op day. Or you could schedule science only on Tuesday/Thursday and STEM on Monday/Friday so that science and STEM are never on the same day.

Pro Tip

You can also opt to exclude an item from certain weeks. This is useful if you already know that you want to save an art kit for May so that Grandma can do it with Andrew or if you don't want to break out the graphic novel until after Christmas since you've set it aside as a gift.

Front-Load vs. Back-Load

This setting lets you manually tell the Schedule Customizer what to do with lessons that don't fit neatly into the schedule. E.g., if you have 40 lessons to complete over 36 weeks of school, would you prefer to do the 4 extra lessons over the first 4 weeks of school, the last 4 weeks of school, or spread evenly throughout?

Each will default to "spread evenly," but there are 2 cases where it can be helpful to change it. If it is a course that increases in difficulty as your child progresses (e.g., a Smart Game), then it can make sense to front-load so that he doubles up on the easiest possible lessons. Or if it is an item that builds on other courses (e.g., Daily 6-Trait Writing's 25-week course), then back-loading can make the most sense so that your child has completed as much of the other introductory material as possible before beginning.

Add Custom Courses

Your course list is limited only by your imagination. Perhaps your friend created a custom curriculum you want to include, your family band practices weekly, or you need to include ballet since that's P.E. this year. You can add these by using "Add Course" at the end of the subject-by-subject review.

Schedule Summary

Look over your schedule summary and make sure that everything is the way you want it, then click "Save & Continue." Congratulations—your schedule is complete!

Go to Your Dashboard

Click "Checklist" to print your checklist or log your progress. More about that in a moment.

Make More Lists

If you have 1 student and 1 teacher, feel free to buzz past this idea. But if you have an extra teacher—perhaps your spouse, a grandparent, or even an older sibling—then this may simplify your life! Instead of putting all of your child's work on a single list, you could put only the subjects you will teach on your list and the remaining subjects on "Grandma's list" for her ease.

If you have twins or multiple students at the same grade level, you can also make multiple lists to best meet each student's needs.

Print Your Lists

From the checklist section you can choose to log your progress on the screen or print your checklists. (We prefer a printed checklist for ease of reference, but some of you may find electronic tracking easier. To print, click "Schedule Overview," then set your view options and either download or print your lists.

Here are a few settings you may tweak:

1. Weekly or Daily?

As we discussed already, we generally prefer a weekly schedule for the simple reason that our weeks are rarely without some anomaly. Off to the dentist Tuesday? You won't fall behind by taking a day off. Or perhaps you have Friday Robotics Camp for a couple of weeks and need to get all the week's work done over 4 days instead of 5. No problem! This approach also teaches time-management skills. (See the article on independent learning at the back of this handbook.)

However, we've heard from many of you that having a daily schedule, especially for the first month, is a real lifesaver. The daily option of the Schedule Customizer is programmed to split up the work as evenly as possible over the week, with the beginning of the week having any extra pages or lessons. (We all know that end-of-the-week doldrums are a real thing!)

2. Show Unit Range?

This feature sounds very data-y and not super helpful, but we think you just might love it. Instead of saying that you need to do 7 pages of thinking skills this week, check this box to have it remind you that you're on pages 50–56 this week. If you prefer extreme flexibility, leave this box unchecked. But if you're afraid of falling behind without knowing it, this box will be your hero.

3. Large-Font Edition

Want a large-font option? Just check the box. If you don't like how it looks, you can always come back and uncheck it.

That's It!

Click "Download" or "Print," and you'll be ready to get started in moments! We've heard from a number of you that you prefer to print out your entire year's worth of schedules and spiral bind them at the local print shop. This is a brilliant idea, but we suggest using the checklists for a few weeks first just to make sure you've fine-tuned it as you wish so that you can avoid doing that more than once!

Log Your Progress Online

You now have the ability to log your work as you go. Click "Progress" and log what you've done. As you complete portions, you'll see your progress bars fill in, showing a more tangible representation of your progress this year.

Your Sample Annual Planner

Curriculum	Lesson or Pages	= Per Week
Language Arts		
Language Smarts, Level E	363 pages	10 pages
Mosdos Literature Ruby	36 weeks of work	1 week's work
Spelling You See, Level E	36 weeks	10 minutes a day
Daily 6-Trait Writing	25 weeks	1 week's work
CursiveLogic U.S. Presidents & Citizens	69 pages	2 pages
Math		
Math-U-See	30 lessons	1 lesson
Before Personal Finance	10 lessons	1/2 lesson
Thinking Skills		
Building Thinking Skills 2	367 pages	10 pages
Titanic	48 challenges	1-2 challenges
Quixo	unlimited	once a week
History & Social Studies		
The Story of the World 4	42 chapters	1-2 chapters
24-Hour History	5 stories	1 a month
True Stories of War	set of 3 books	1 a month
Geography		
Skill Sharpeners Geography, Grade 4	132 pages	3-4 pages
Flags of the World	nearly 200 flags	as desired

Science

Discover! Science 4	75 lessons	2+ lessons
Dr. Bonyfide 2	108 pages	3 pages

STEM Learning

ROBOTIS OLLO Spark	12 weeks of work	1 model, lesson, or experiment
My Crazy Inventions Sketchbook	50 activities	1-2 activities

Art

Tropical Forest 3D Painting	4 paintings	20 minutes a week
Sketching Made Easy	30 lessons	1 lesson
Have I Got a Story for You!	12 lessons	1 lesson or its projects
Studiostone Alabaster Polar Bear	1 project	15 minutes a week

Learning Tools

Test Prep	128 pages	end of school year

What Is a Lesson?

Item-by-item specs

Beginning on page 31 you'll find a detailed overview of each item, including information about how we scheduled the work and why. If you're looking for a quick reference page to refresh your mind on what exactly "one lesson" means for any of your materials, then here you go!

Language Smarts

You'll find 363 colorful pages to complete. Have your child complete 10 a week to stay on track. Since some pages have more writing than others, your child might be more successful completing 2 pages a day than he would be finishing all 10 on Friday.

Mosdos Ruby

Do 1 week's work as found in the 36-week schedule beginning on page 91 in this handbook.

We suggest completing the bulk of the workbook pages but skipping the writing since you'll be covering that with Daily 6-Trait Writing.

Spelling You See E

There are 36 lessons, each of which includes 5 days of work. Two tips: Your day's lesson is complete after 10 minutes of work—your child does not need to finish the whole chunk. Also, if you're using a 4-day week or don't get to all 5 days of work in a week, it is expected that you will still count that lesson as complete at the end of the week and move on to the next one.

Daily 6-Trait Writing

The course is split into 25 weeks of work. We suggest starting after 11 weeks of school to allow you to ease into the year.

CursiveLogic U.S. Presidents & Citizens

You can split this course by lessons or pages, but the easiest way seems to be pages. Completing 2 pages a week will have you finishing the entire course this year with very little stress on your student's part.

Math-U-See

You'll find 30 lessons here, each with 7 worksheets. You'll be completing only as many of the worksheets as your child needs for mastery per lesson. Since completing 1 whole lesson a week keeps the instructional portions predictable, we suggest this schedule instead of a certain number of worksheets. If you use that method, know that you can spread a tricky lesson over 2 weeks up to 6 times this year without messing up your schedule.

Before Personal Finance

There are 10 lessons to complete, so we suggest aiming for 1 about every 2 weeks. Alternatively, you could complete 1 every week, or spread the course over the entire school year.

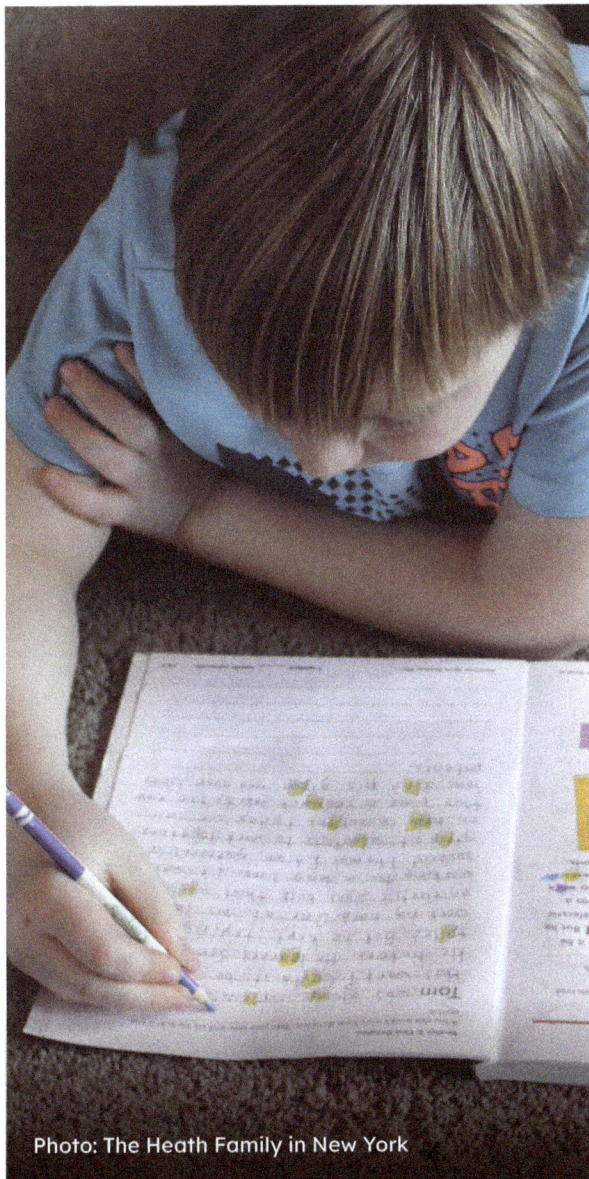

Photo: The Heath Family in New York

Building Thinking Skills 2

You'll be working through this book at about 10 pages per week. If this pace is overwhelming for your student, don't hesitate to drop back to 5 pages a week and use this course for 2 years.

Titanic

Just do 1-2 new challenges a week.

Quixo

This game is unlimited. We suggest breaking it out at least once a week and playing a few rounds.

The Story of the World 4

With 42 chapters, you're going to want to do 3 chapters every 2 weeks. Or, if it's easier, just do 2 chapters one week and 1 chapter the following week. Add in as many activities as you have the time/interest for.

24-Hour History

These books cover the events addressed in Story of the World chapters 28, 29, 35, and 36 (2 books for 36). You may either want to wait until you reach those chapters or release them to your child at any point for free reading.

True Stories of War

Either time these to be used with chapters 5, 20–21, and 28–29 of Story of the World or distribute them early like 24-Hour History. These books are captivating!

Skill Sharpeners Geography

Doing 4 pages a week will get you through this year. Keep in mind that you're free to skip the writing assignments and elaborate activities, but if your student has the time and energy, these will really serve to reinforce what he's learning.

Flags of the World

As you read around the world this year, mark your progress by having your child add the pertinent stickers to this map. You will not find this on your schedule each week, as it is a supplement to the reading challenge rather than a stand-alone task.

Discover! Science

Complete just over 2 lessons a week in order to finish this year. Each review is also labeled as a lesson; a fact that is helpful to know when scheduling.

Dr. Bonyfide

Completing over 3 pages a week will take you through this year.

ROBOTIS OLLO Spark

Ollo Spark is structured as a 12-week course. You have the option to spread out the program by completing one-third of a "week's work" each week. Alternatively, you can do the workbook assignment one week and build the model the following week for a more balanced pace.

My Crazy Inventions

With 50 activities to complete, we suggest doing 1-2 per week.

Tropical Forest 3D Painting

With 4 paintings to complete, we suggest working at this kit 20 minutes every week until they are all done.

Sketching Made Easy

Do 1 of the 30 online lessons each week.

Have I Got A Story for You!

The *Have I Got A Story For You!* course is truly one-of-a-kind art program. It is designed with 12 lessons, and each lesson includes a video as well as art assignments. We suggest watching the video one week and completing one of the related art projects on the two following weeks. Some fourth-graders will want to repeat the video at least once more, so feel free do that as time allows!

Studiostone Alabaster Polar Bear

Your child will carve and polish his own unique bear this year. Since each child will work through this kit at a different pace, we suggest setting aside 15 minutes a week to continue making progress.

NeeDoh Nice Cube

Unlimited. We suggest making up at least 1 tin in the first week of school so that your child has a fidget accessible.

Test Prep

We usually save this for the end of the year to refresh your student on all the skills he'll need for annual testing. You won't find this on your schedule unless you add it.

Sample Weekly Checklist

Basic

Curriculum	This week	Check it off!
Language Arts		
Language Smarts, Level E	10 pages	☐☐☐☐☐☐☐☐☐☐
Mosdos Literature Ruby	1 week's work	☐
Spelling You See, Level E	10 minutes a day	☐☐☐☐
Math		
Math-U-See	1 lesson	☐☐☐☐☐
Before Personal Finance	1/2 a lesson	☐
Thinking Skills		
Building Thinking Skills 2	10 pages	☐☐☐☐☐☐☐☐☐

Sample Weekly Checklist

Complete

Curriculum	This week	Check it off!									
Language Arts											
Language Smarts, Level E	10 pages	☐	☐	☐	☐	☐	☐	☐	☐	☐	☐
Mosdos Literature Ruby	1 week's work	☐									
Spelling You See, Level E	10 minutes a day	☐	☐	☐	☐						
Daily 6-Trait Writing	1 week's work	☐	☐	☐	☐						
Math											
Math-U-See	1 lesson	☐	☐	☐	☐	☐					
Before Personal Finance	1/2 a lesson	☐									
Thinking Skills											
Building Thinking Skills 2	10 pages	☐	☐	☐	☐	☐	☐	☐	☐		
Titanic	1-2 challenges	☐	☐								
History & Social Studies											
The Story of the World 4	1-2 chapters	☐	☐								
24-Hour History	1 a month	☐									
Geography											
Skill Sharpeners Geography, Grade 4	3-4 pages	☐	☐	☐	☐						

Science

Discover! Science	2+ lessons			
Dr. Bonyfide 2	3 pages			

STEM Learning

ROBOTIS OLLO Spark	1 model, lesson, or experiment	

Art

Tropical Forest 3D Painting	20 minutes a week	
Sketching Made Easy	1 lesson	

Sample Weekly Checklist

Elite

Curriculum	This week	Check it off!
Language Arts		
Language Smarts, Level E	10 pages	
Mosdos Literature Ruby	1 week's work	
Spelling You See, Level E	10 minutes a day	
Daily 6-Trait Writing	1 week's work	
CursiveLogic U.S. Presidents & Citizens	2 pages	
Math		
Math-U-See	1 lesson	
Before Personal Finance	1/2 a lesson	
Thinking Skills		
Building Thinking Skills 2	10 pages	
Titanic	1-2 challenges	
Quixo	once a week	
History & Social Studies		
The Story of the World 4	1-2 chapters	
24-Hour History	1 a month	
True Stories of War	1 a month	

Geography

Skill Sharpeners Geography, Grade 4	3-4 pages	☐	☐	☐	☐
Flags of the World	as desired	☐			

Science

Discover! Science	2+ lessons	☐	☐	☐
Dr. Bonyfide 2	3 pages	☐	☐	☐

STEM Learning

ROBOTIS OLLO Spark	1 model, lesson, or experiment	☐	
My Crazy Inventions Sketchbook	1-2 activities	☐	☐

Art

Tropical Forest 3D Painting	20 minutes a week	☐
Sketching Made Easy	1 lesson	☐
Have I Got a Story for You!	1 lesson or its projects	☐
Studiostone Alabaster Polar Bear	15 minutes a week	☐

Introducing the Reading Challenge

Fourth Grade: Read Around the World (Modern World History)

The Reading Challenge for kids will get you and your child reading a broader variety of books this year while covering essential topics.

Your reading challenge introduces 36 different weekly topics to explore together. Choose a book off your library shelf and check off the subject, or go deep with multiple books and activities. Do whatever works for you this week, flexing for at-home weeks with more time to fill and on-the-go weeks that need no extra activities.

At this grade level, your child will read some of these books independently, and you will read many together. Don't be too eager to lose the one-on-one reading time either. Many sources recommend that parents continue reading to their children well past the time they become accomplished readers, and we agree!

Reading Together

Most of us probably have a deep sense that reading to kids is a good choice. But do you know why?

There are dozens of appealing reasons, but let me just remind you of the 3 highlighted by the American Academy of Pediatrics (AAP):

1. Strengthen language skills
2. Build literacy development and interest in reading
3. Create nurturing parent-child relationships, which are "important for a child's cognitive, language, and social-emotional development"

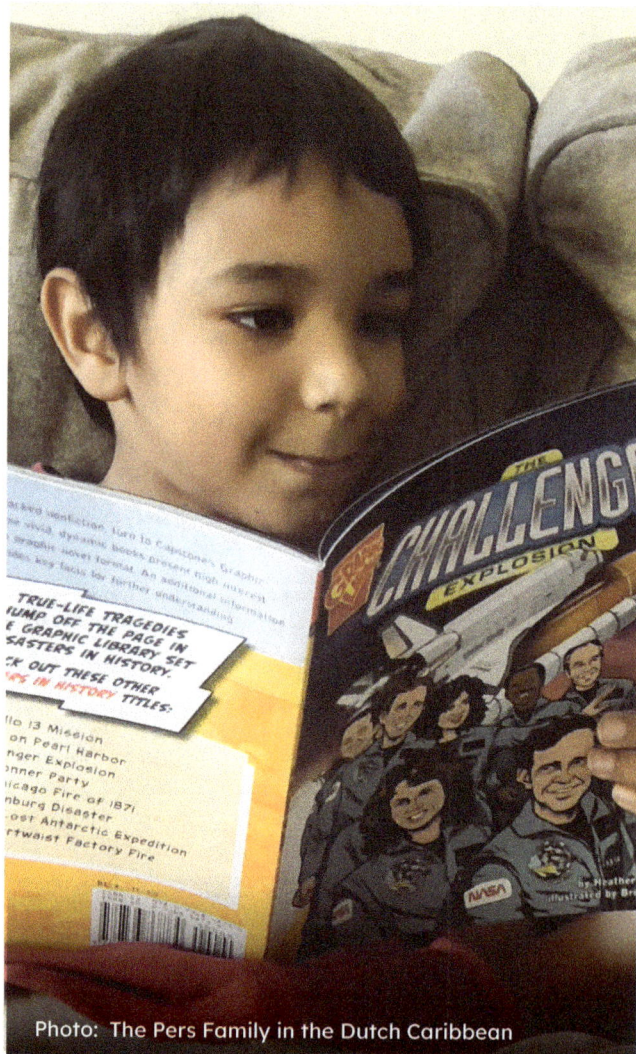

Photo: The Pers Family in the Dutch Caribbean

1. Language Skills

Reading exposes your child to familiar and unfamiliar words, scenes, and feelings as you give words to each of them. As he gets older and the books become more complex, he'll also be learning syntax, pronunciation, rhyming, and more!

2. Literacy Development

Your child is seeing that books are engaging and important to you. You are also demonstrating that they are interesting and a worthy use of time. This is such critical knowledge!

3. Nurturing Parent-Child Relationships

Surely we aren't the only ones who have stared at our darling child feeling like we have already done all the things and wondering how in the world we will fill the remaining time in the day. What if instead of screen time or pleading with him to play by himself, you reached happily for a book? Can you imagine how much bonding and conversation could fill in the gaps of your day?

Now, we know all too well that there are moments when children do need to play independently, for both your sanity and theirs. And if you're blessed with more than one little one (as our family is), you can't sit and read as much of the day as you'd prefer. But every minute of reading you squeeze in cultivates your relationship with your precious child without much in-the-moment effort on your part!

4. Emotional Intelligence

We've added this point to the AAP's list. Emotional intelligence is a critical skill yet challenging to teach. Reading together is an easy way to teach emotional intelligence in an unlimited variety of contexts. This not only helps your child become more fluent in his own feelings but also develops empathy and understanding for the people around him.

How It Works

On each week's challenge page (beginning on page 99), you'll find 3 things:
- A list of suggested book titles
- A place to write in the titles you read together
- A chart to track your progress through the reading challenge.

You will set your own pace this year, ranging from 1 to 5 books per week. Choose a reading goal early in the year and set your pace accordingly, keeping in mind what is realistic for your family this year.

Here's the pace for a 36-week schedule:

- Light Reader: 1 book every week (36 total)
- Interested Reader: 2 books every week (72 total)
- Avid Reader: 3 books every week (108 total)
- Committed Reader: 4 books every week (144 total)
- Enthralled Reader: 5 books every week (180 total)

But I Don't Have Any Idea Which Books to Choose!

We have your back! Beginning on page 101 you'll find thousands of book ideas you'll love this year.

If you want more ideas, we highly recommend your local librarian, the Read-Aloud Revival podcast, and the Timberdoodle Facebook groups as excellent starting points. It's also a wonderful idea to peek at the additional reading ideas in your history or science textbooks—particularly if your child found he was fascinated by something his courses recently touched on.

What about Reading Level?

This year we're providing you with a range of titles. Many are are designed for early readers while others range from chapter books designed to be read to your child to picture books to enjoy together. Pick and choose the titles and styles you think will work best for your child, but we'd also suggest adding a few books to your library list from outside your normal selection. (E.g., if your child gravitates to books he can read himself, make sure you also include some more complex books for you to read aloud.) Why? Children rarely enjoy only one type of book. They just may not know what they like yet! In light of that, we highly encourage you to intentionally expose your child to a broad spectrum of literature and see what stands out to you both.

Will This Be Expensive?

It doesn't need to be. You can read library books and e-books, buy used, borrow from friends, and scour your family bookshelves. Don't forget that many libraries have free e-books as well. If you have Kindle Unlimited or Everand, check for these titles there also. It doesn't get much more convenient than that!

Before You Begin

Please note that you do not need to complete these challenges in order! We highly recommend using the seasonal ones as close to the appropriate holiday as your schedule allows. Or if your child is all about reptiles this week, there is no need to wait until week 21 to study them.

It is also OK to skip or substitute topics. Perhaps your child is well-versed in farms but would love to learn about specific artists. Or on a deeper level, some of our young children in foster care would enjoy books about family, while others would find them triggering. It's totally appropriate to substitute a book about wild animal parents or whatever makes it more appropriate and interesting for your child.

Extra Activities

On the following pages you'll find additional ideas our team has brainstormed that may be helpful for your family. If you're looking for field trip ideas, art inspiration, or a theme for the week, use these. If your week is quite busy enough, skip them! They are not essential—just bonus ideas if you have extra time this week or want to meet a field trip goal.

Let's Read!

Pick your plan, choose some books with your child, and get started!

Looking for more reading challenges? Check out RedeemedReader.com and Challies.com for their original versions of this reading challenge. It has been completely remodeled by us over the years but was initially inspired by them and used with permission.

A Fun Beginning-of-the-Year Interview

Have your student jot down his answers here to capture a fun time capsule of his fourth grade year.

What would you want to invent if you had unlimited resources?

If you could go anywhere you wanted in the world, where would you go and why?

What is something you look forward to doing when you grow up? (Driving a car, doing a special sport?)

What problem do you want to solve?

If you could lead an expedition, what kind of expedition would it be and where would it take you?

Your ship is likely to sink at sea during your rescue mission. What are you packing in your emergency kit?

Item-By-Item Introductions

Language Arts

Practice Makes Perfect

Reading is one of the most important skills your child will practice this year, second only to critical thinking. Whether he is a natural reader or not, it is essential to make reading as fun and rewarding as possible.

Our experience indicates that the best way to cultivate an eager reader is to supply him with reading materials that interest him. Future doctors want to read up on anatomy, young explorers are drawn to adventurers, and the child fascinated by babies will be captivated by adoption stories.

Knowing how hard it can be to load the whole family up and get to the library, we're including a brilliant anthology of reading material in *Mosdos Ruby*. With so many excellent selections, every student is sure to find reading that resonates deeply with him and some that he would never have chosen but finds surprisingly interesting. Assign reading as needed, but encourage it at all costs; a child who enjoys reading will find it easier to excel in most other areas of learning.

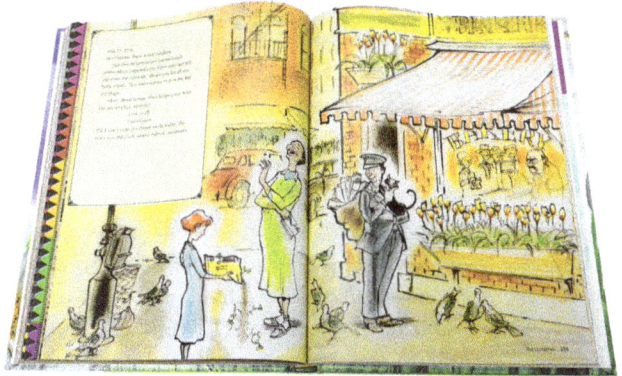

Mosdos Press Literature

Basic | Complete | Elite

Mosdos Press Literature is a complete literature program that cheerily reinforces the universal ideals of courage, honesty, loyalty, and compassion. We found this such a breath of fresh air in comparison to more sensational programs that glamorize evil or present subject matter that is not age appropriate.

Mosdos Press Literature begins with the student readers, which are beautifully illustrated books with a generous number of full-color photographs, color drawings, and black-and-white pictures.

Before each story in the student reader, there is an introduction and an explanation of some facet of literature. That literary focus can include character, theme, internal and external conflicts, setting, climax, foreshadowing, and more. This component is developed and illuminated through the stories. Vocabulary words that might be unfamiliar are presented in boxes on the pages where the words first appear.

The stories are followed by typical review questions designed to assess reading comprehension and also by more complex questions that require thoughtful analysis. Every unit concludes with activities such as writing a short skit, doing a craft, or memorizing a poem. Pick the ones that best suit your child; there are far too many to do them all. Unless your child is a budding author, you can minimize the writing activities. Your child is already doing a lot of writing this year in *Daily 6-Trait Writing* and *Language Smarts*.

Next is the consumable, colorful, and engaging student activity workbook. For nearly every story in the student reader, the workbook contains corresponding vocabulary, creative writing, or comprehension questions that provide extended reinforcement to the literary elements being taught. These assignments help you to evaluate areas of progress or concepts that might require additional work.

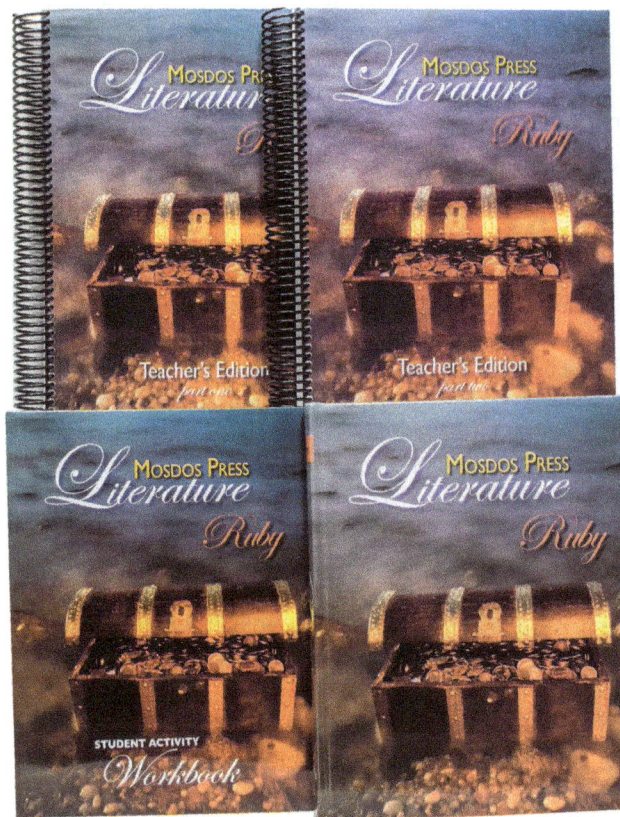

An advantage of Mosdos Press is that the literature, vocabulary, and application components tie together, giving your child a chance to truly understand what was taught.

Through great commentary, plus questions and answers, the teacher's edition will make lively discussions with your child possible. Each page of the student reader is duplicated at a smaller size in the teacher's edition, yet still abundantly easy to read. Information is arranged in the ample margins around these replicated pages, discussing the literary components found in each story with clear, concise explanations. The teacher's edition also includes the answers for the student activity workbook.

Scheduling

Complete 1 subsection per week. Some may find it easiest to have a week's work begin with the Lesson in Literature and include reading until you reach the next Lesson in Literature (unless it's a Lesson Wrap-Up week).

For your convenience, a sample 36-week schedule is included beginning on page 91.

Complete the corresponding workbook pages, but do feel free to skip the creative writing assignments if that best serves your student.

Our family would have chosen to answer the Studying the Selection questions in the readers orally, and if time allowed, select one Focus or Creating and Writing activity to complete for further study. Other families may choose to complete every exercise included.

There are no workbook pages for the poetry unit, so in place of those, students may prioritize writing assignments from the Think about It section.

Busy families may choose to skip the Unit Wrap-Ups, while others who enjoy hands-on activities can complete them as desired.

Language Smarts

Basic | Complete | Elite

Language Smarts is a complete language arts curriculum that will improve your student's reading, writing, spelling, punctuation, and grammar skills. But unlike a traditional workbook, *Language Smarts* also employs both convergent and divergent thinking in its exercises.

Perfect for the child who prefers to work independently, *Language Smarts* pages are brightly colored and contain enough white space to feel easily doable.

About two pages a day will have your student completing *Language Smarts* within a school year.

Language Smarts proves that language arts does not have to be the predictably intensive, tedious, and repetitive activities found in most traditional language arts workbooks.

Instead, *Language Smarts* uses rhymes and riddles, editing challenges, mind-benders, sequencing, and more. The simple, colorful exercises can make this the year your child enjoys language arts.

Scheduling

With 363 pages just complete 10 per week to stay on track.

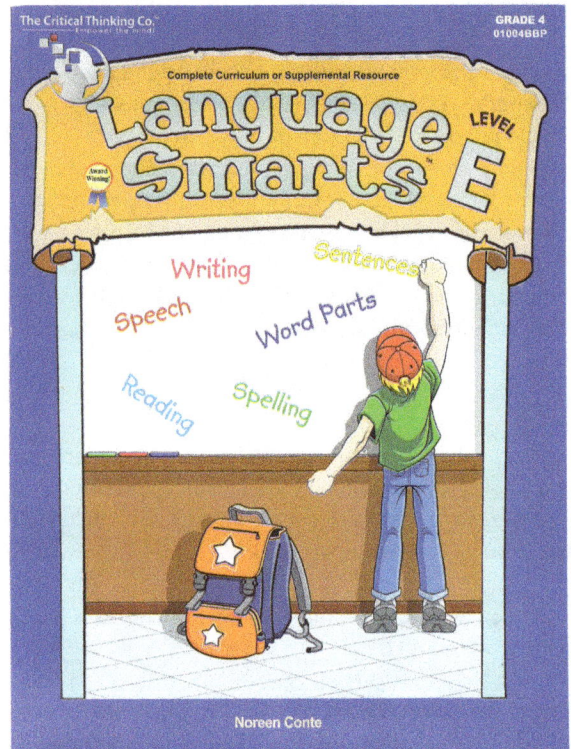

Spelling You See, Level E

Basic | Complete | Elite

This multisensory spelling program will help your child become a naturally confident, successful speller. Because *Spelling You See* encourages visual memory rather than rote memory, there are no weekly spelling lists or tests and very little instructor preparation. Each daily lesson in *Spelling You See: American Spirit* uses real words contextually within nonfiction stories about American history and culture.

Spelling You See: American Spirit is colorful, short, and fun!

Scheduling

The 36 weeks of work, with 5 daily activities each week, are already planned out for you. Just open and go!

Note

Ideally, you will not complete more than 1 short spelling lesson every day for best retention. If your student is at all intimidated by the lesson length, keep in mind that there is enough work in each lesson to teach a speedy writer. A more methodical writer could be overwhelmed trying to complete everything. Consider setting a timer for 10-15 minutes when you begin the day's work and stop where you are when it rings. The next day, just move on to the new lesson.

Also, if you do a 4-day week, you can do the first 4 days' work and skip the fifth. It seems unusual to all of us who feel we must finish every page, but this course is designed to be most effective when used in this way.

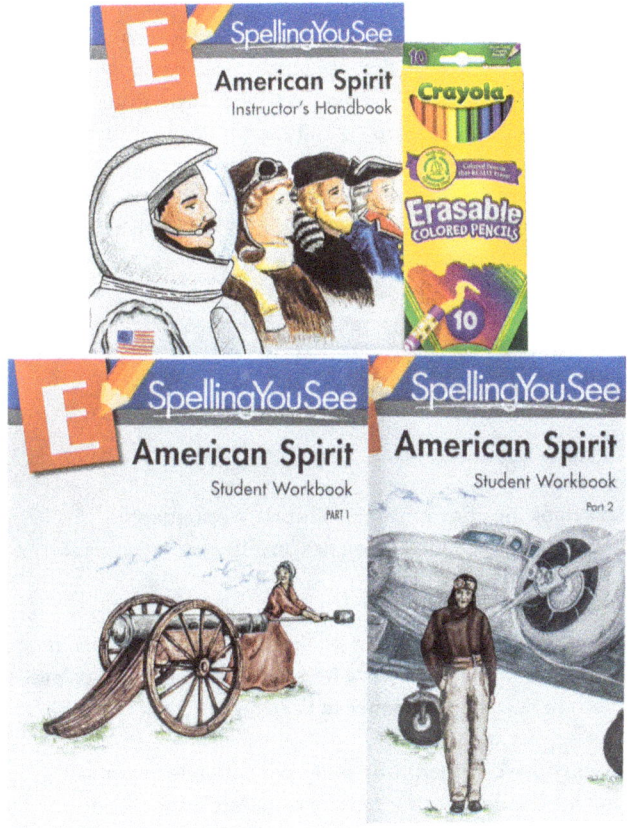

Daily 6-Trait Writing

~~Basic~~ | Complete | Elite

Are you familiar with trait writing? Trait-based writing is an impressive method that educators have developed to determine if a child's writing is skilled. The 6 traits or characteristics that shape quality writing are content, organization, word choice, sentence fluency, voice, and conventions, which include grammar, spelling, and mechanics. It may sound ominous, but *Daily 6–Trait Writing* has made becoming a skilled writer effortless.

These short daily assignments are designed to build skills without being overwhelming. We love them for their brevity but also because they are so thorough!

Scheduling

This book includes 25 weeks of work. We suggest implementing 1 short lesson per day, beginning on week 12 of school.

We also suggest you begin when your student is ready. If you start later in the year, you'll find that the "extra" pages make great review in the summer to keep his brain sharp.

If you have a student who struggles with fine motor skills, you may have more success by completely separating writing skills from motor skills. Most families do this by allowing their students to dictate their writing. You could also use a whiteboard (bigger writing may be easier) or allow your student to use a computer tablet or phone. This enables your child to build fantastic writing skills even while his motor skills are still developing.

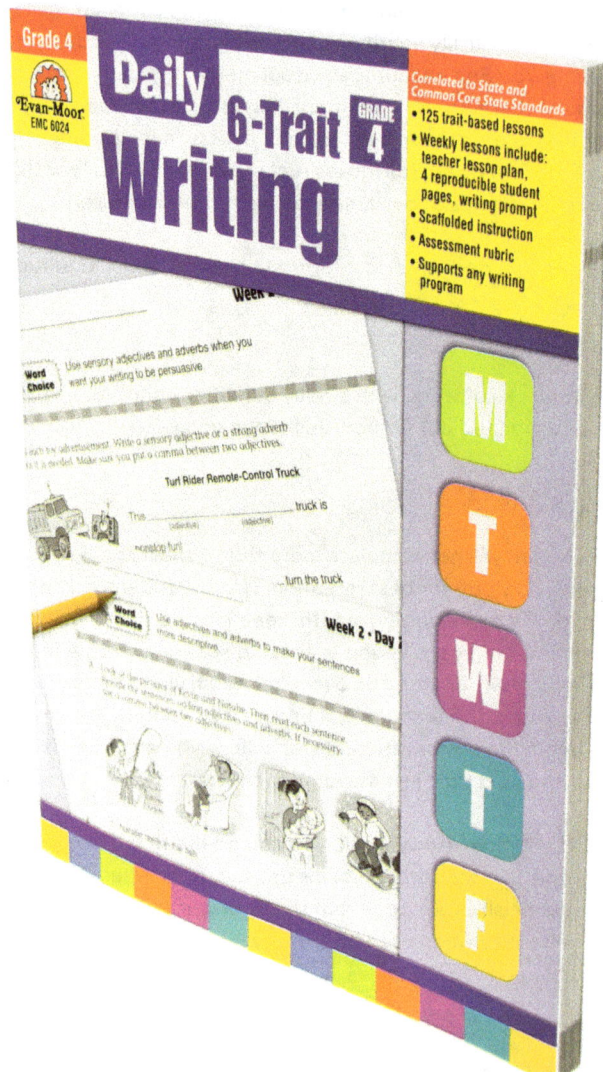

CursiveLogic U.S. Presidents & Citizens

~~Basic~~ | ~~Complete~~ | Elite

This workbook provides additional cursive practice for students who have learned cursive using the CursiveLogic method. *CursiveLogic U.S. Presidents and Citizens* introduces students to distinguished Americans—one born in each of the 50 states.

Selections include expected figures, such as George Washington, but they have also taken the time to include broad and interesting choices such as Ida Lewis, who received the U.S. Gold Lifesaving Medal in 1881. Or Sequoyah, who developed a syllabary that enabled reading and writing in Cherokee and took only weeks to learn.

The *CursiveLogic U.S. Presidents & Citizens* workbook is spiral-bound at the top so that it works equally well for both right- and left-handers.

After a brief review of the CursiveLogic method of handwriting, your student will discover that every lesson includes a full review of the lowercase alphabet and provides students with inspirational quotations to trace and write.

Each page offers an etching of the celebrated citizen, an outline of the state they were from, and the date that state was ratified: all in all, a fascinating method for keeping your student's cursive skills polished.

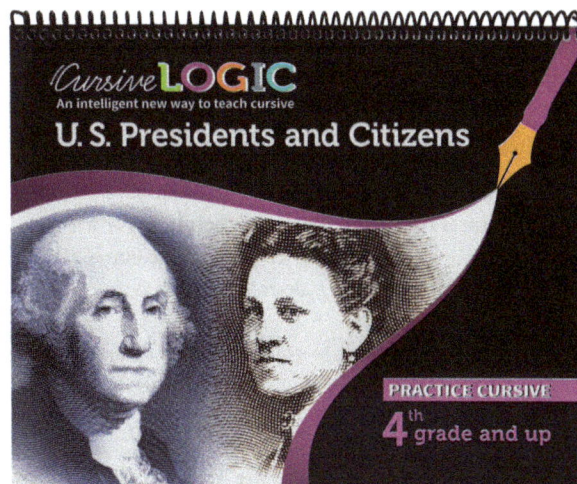

Scheduling

Complete 2 pages a week to easily finish this year. (Each side counts as a page.)

Mathematics

A Fundamental Skill

Basic math is a critical skill for your child to master, whether he grows up to be a carpenter, doctor, accountant, or farmer. But all too often math programs rely on memorization instead of comprehension, leaving the student at a disadvantage.

That's not going to happen to your child! The real-world math problems posed in Math-U-See (combined with the hands-on manipulatives) create an unbeatable math program.

With simple, uncluttered pages, Math-U-See is mastery-oriented, clear, to the point, and effective. In Math-U-See, new ideas are introduced step by step in a logical order, while concepts that have been mastered are reviewed periodically.

Math-U-See's teacher guide and supplemental DVD will teach more than just how to solve a math problem. They will also show why the problem is solved in this manner and when to apply the concept. On the DVDs, each lesson is demonstrated with kind-hearted enthusiasm. DVDs can be played on a DVD player or computer; however, Windows 10 users will need to download a separate video player.

Math-U-See does require a fair amount of parental involvement. At first glance, it can seem overwhelming, but the maker of this math program has bent over backward to make the lesson planning as painless as possible. Still, at this grade, feel free to merely skim the teacher's guide, as it is pretty straightforward.

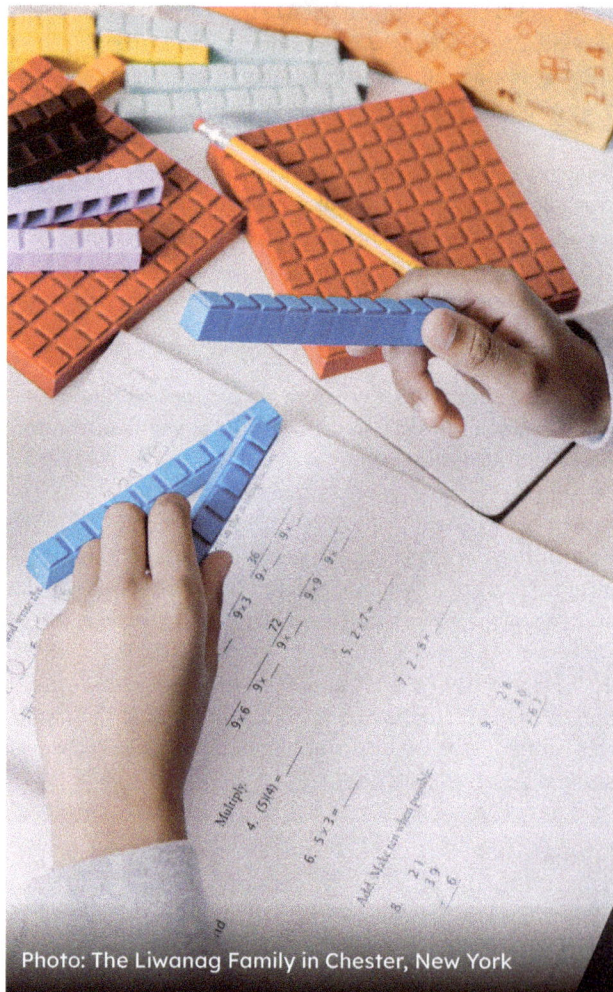

Photo: The Liwanag Family in Chester, New York

Math-U-See

Basic | Complete | Elite

One Math-U-See lesson is designed to consist of several parts:

- A video lesson

- Worksheet A, teaching this lesson's concept

- Worksheet B, teaching this lesson's concept, in case your student needs a bit more practice

- Worksheet C, still teaching this lesson's concept, in case your student needs even more practice

- Worksheet D, review work

- Worksheet E, more review work

- Worksheet F, still more review work, for the student who thrives on repetition or struggles with math and requires the extra practice

- Worksheet G is often a test or optional application and enrichment section. While it is considered honors material, we suggest you do this if you can tackle it without stressing your child!

Some parents prefer to watch the lessons themselves and then teach their students personally. However, most prefer to watch alongside their students, pausing the video, rewinding, and clarifying as needed.

After watching the video lesson or your recreated lesson, your student will complete as many worksheets as you deem appropriate. You will want to decide as you start the year whether your student will be completing the optional "Application and Enrichment" section on each lesson (sometimes considered the honors portion). If these challenges overwhelm your student, you should skip them or offer generous assistance. Otherwise, embrace them for the opportunity they provide to help him learn more skills and train his brain to think logically.

It's hard to overemphasize the importance of thoughtfully assigning math pages. Most students should complete worksheets A, D, and G, and that may be enough!

In our crew, we have some students who struggle with math, and for them it is best to complete most of the worksheets and just slow down the pace of the program. This is perfectly acceptable but shouldn't be the norm for every child since the only thing worse than being overwhelmed by rapid-fire challenging concepts is being bored with too much repetition!

Scheduling

You have 30 lessons to complete, so we suggest planning on 1 lesson a week, including the DVD as well as the textbook/workbook portions and any relevant tests.

However, as Mr. Demme points out, some lessons will take you longer than others to achieve mastery. If you find yourself stuck on a lesson, feel free to allow it to take you an extra week. Just don't do that more than 6 times this year!

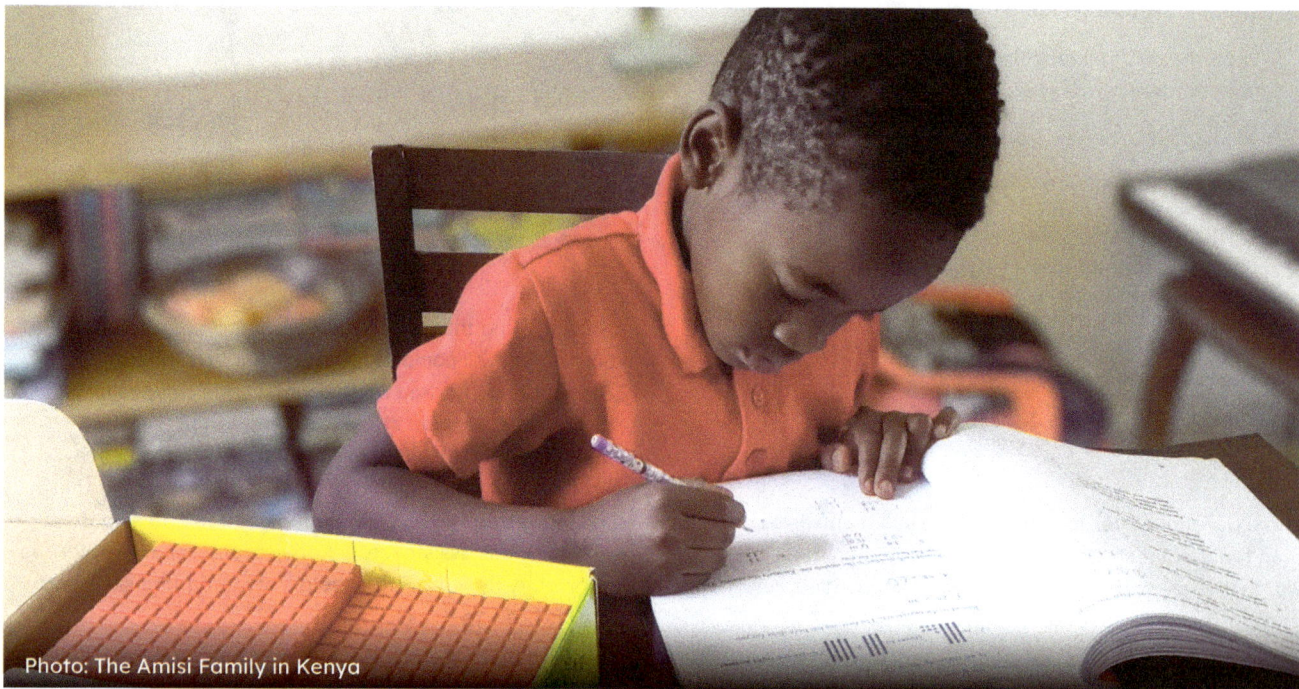

Photo: The Amisi Family in Kenya

Before Personal Finance

Basic | Complete | Elite

As your child approaches the preteen years, his financial savvy must outgrow impulsive spending habits. *Before Personal Finance* aims to provide your child with a comprehensive yet approachable understanding of real-world budgeting.

Each two-page lesson is followed by enriching activities to deepen your child's knowledge. Parents can spread each lesson over a week or have their child complete them in a single day.

Throughout each lesson, your child will explore scenarios in which he is already a teenager and ages one year per lesson. As he navigates through ages 13 to 22, he must make choices on earning, spending, giving, and saving, adjusting his budget to reflect his current financial journey at each stage. The surplus funds from one lesson become the savings carried into the next.

The spin of an online wheel adds unexpected financial twists to each lesson, prompting your child to make strategic choices.

Every lesson concludes with a comprehension quiz, providing an excellent opportunity for students to assess their understanding. Both students and parents can find quiz answers and other essential resources online.

Before Personal Finance delivers an enjoyable, informative experience, serving as a valuable asset for all preteens.

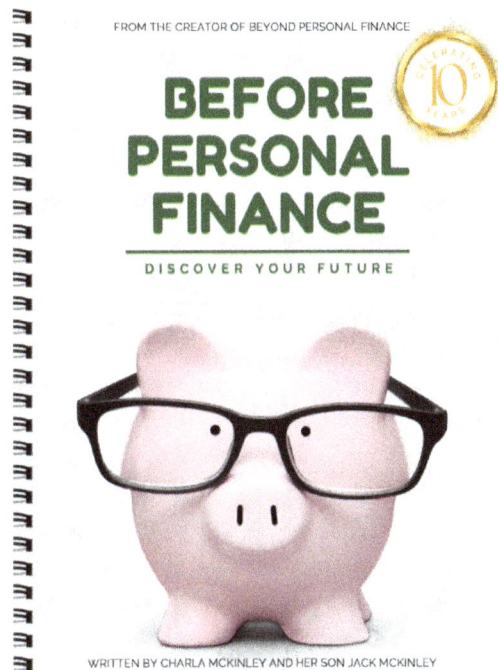

FROM THE CREATOR OF BEYOND PERSONAL FINANCE

BEFORE PERSONAL FINANCE

DISCOVER YOUR FUTURE

WRITTEN BY CHARLA MCKINLEY AND HER SON JACK MCKINLEY

Scheduling

This course includes 10 lessons with a variety of activities. We suggest spreading each lesson over 2 weeks, completing the course in 20 weeks. However, you could also power through the course in 10 consecutive weeks, or take a slower pace to finish in a school year.

Thinking Skills

This Is As Critical As It Is Appealing

In Timberdoodle's curriculum kits, you will find a rigorous pursuit of thinking skills for every child in every grade. This is not an optional skill for your child. A child who thinks logically will be able to learn well and solve problems independently in ways that an untrained brain will find difficult.

You won't have to persuade your child to learn to think, though. He's wired for problem-solving! We're guessing this portion of the curriculum will be the hardest to not race through. After all, who doesn't want to work through a thinking skills puzzle book, navigate lifeboats to the rescue, or challenge an opponent with a riveting wooden strategy game?

Building Thinking Skills 2

Basic | Complete | Elite

This series of thinking-skills books is among our favorites because of their tremendous scope. Studies have shown that students using these books have raised their national test scores significantly in both content and cognitive tests. Not many curricula have been that thoroughly tested.

In this volume your child will develop 4 basic analytical skills (similarities/differences, sequences, classification, and analogies) through both figural and verbal problems. In addition, there are problems dealing with deductive reasoning, map skills, Venn diagrams, mental manipulation of two-dimensional objects, and much more.

Does that sound overwhelming? Don't worry—it truly isn't. When I was a child, these types of puzzles and pages were often a highlight of the day.

You'll work from front to back in the book, studying one skill at a time and building upon it. Pages are perforated—perfect if your student is overwhelmed by the scope of the course and would do better being handed the week's pages.

A note about the writing: Some pages expect a fair amount of writing from your student. If this is hindering rather than helping, feel free to have him type his answers, answer orally, or dictate as you write them. While writing does strengthen brain connections, this is a thinking skills course, not a writing course. We don't want your child to be held back from enjoying this book while still gaining the dexterity needed for writing.

Scheduling

Completing 10 pages per week will get you through the entire book in a year. Most children will love that pace, but if it is too much for your student, feel free to drop it back to 4-5 pages per week and work through it in 2 years.

Titanic

Basic | Complete | Elite

Are you ready to be a hero? Then launch the Titanic lifeboats, patrol the water, and rescue passengers. During a rescue mission, it's challenging to stay in charge of the situation because everybody wants to be saved first.

At the beginning of the game, there are many people in the water, making it difficult for you to maneuver the lifeboats. Get too close, and a desperate passenger will insist on climbing in. However, the number of seats in each boat is limited, and full lifeboats can no longer move, which makes Titanic a constantly changing labyrinth of people and boats.

This beautifully rendered game (the sea has separate waves of different heights) is exclusive to Timberdoodle. Titanic contains 48 icy challenges, a game board with a storage compartment, and solutions.

This life-saving logic game helps develop thinking skills, strategic planning, and visual and spatial perception.

Scheduling

There are 48 challenges, so we suggest doing 1-2 new challenges per week.

Quixo

~~Basic~~ | ~~Complete~~ | Elite

A Parents' Choice Gold Award Winner and a Mensa Select Winner, Quixo is one of the few strategic games played by 2 or 4 players.

In Quixo, the player chooses a cube from the perimeter, places it on the opposite end of the row/column, and shifts the entire row/column until one player manages to create a 5-in-a-row to win.

Because all turns result in a row/column sliding, the playing surface changes with each move. Every play in Quixo can be offensive or defensive, but the best actions are both. This strategy results in a battle of wits, with each player carefully considering the implications of every move.

Quickly learned by all, Quixo is a perfect coffee table game with attractive wooden pieces.

Scheduling

Unlimited. We suggest playing as many rounds as you like at least once a week.

History & Social Studies

Many history curriculum options make the mistake of focusing solely on U.S.A. history. As important as that is, doesn't it make more sense to start with the big picture of history? This year you'll learn about the modern age, covering the major historical events from the years 1850 to 1994. You'll answer questions like these:

- Where was the Crystal Palace?

- Who was the Sick Man of Europe?

- And, of course, how did cow fat start a revolution?

With *Disasters in History*, your child will also get to learn more about history through the true accounts of 8 infamous disasters.

Many families have found that graphic novels provide huge incentives to their budding readers. The pictures will help your student to stay focused and want to understand the written text. With the *True Stories of War* and *24–Hour History* graphic novels, your student will be immersed in the places and times he's studying. What a way to bring the past to life!

The Story of the World 4

~~Basic~~ | Complete | Elite

This curriculum is very easy to use. Just have your child read one section from the storybook, then ask him to tell you what it was about. Afterwards, pick an activity page or worksheet that is appropriate for your child's interest and your schedule.

Did you see how big the activity book is? One of the its biggest advantages is the fact that it offers a wide range of activities for each lesson. Pick the ones that best fit your child's learning style and your family's schedule, but don't try to do them all!

One brilliant way to use this text is to approach it from a notebooking perspective. To do this, you'll want to give your child a blank notebook that he will fill with his recap ("narration") of each chapter. As he goes on, he'll add art, maps, and even photos of more tangible projects that he does. This is a somewhat labor-intensive approach, but if you're eager for your child to have a firm grasp on world history, it is hard to beat this method for helping him retain information.

Scheduling

Completing 3 chapters every 2 weeks is a realistic pace that will get you through the books in just under a year.

If you purchased the Elite kit, you'll love having the audiobook download. It includes the same content as the storybook, but it can be much more convenient. Download the files to your device and your child can listen to his history along with anyone else who would like to participate. What a treat!

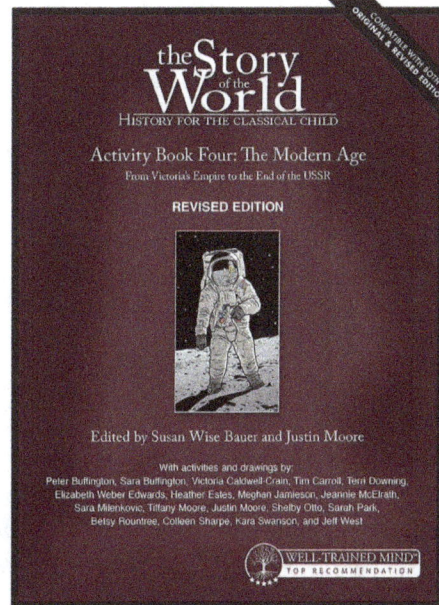

Note

Would you like to coordinate the graphic novel stories in your kit with your readings in *The Story of the World*? Here's where to put them in:

True Stories of the Civil War: chapter 5
True Stories of WWI: chapters 20–21
True Stories of WWII: chapters 28–29
24-Hour History Pearl Harbor: chapter 28
24-Hour History D-Day: chapter 29
24-Hour History Apollo 11: chapter 35
24-Hour History John F. Kennedy: chapter 36
24-Hour History Martin Luther King, Jr.: chapter 36

24-Hour History

~~Basic~~ | <mark>Complete</mark> | <mark>Elite</mark>

In each of the five *24-Hour History* stories, your child will learn key events that happened in a very short amount of time but that still have impact today.

At the end are short biographies of characters, timelines, pertinent maps or diagrams, and a glossary. *24-Hour History* will provide your child with an action-packed introduction to key historical events.

Scheduling

Unlimited. You can spread out the fun by assigning 1 story every month or two, save these books for a dreary afternoon, use them where appropriate for *The Story of the World*, or (perhaps best of all) hand it to your child immediately so he can read and reread it.

True Stories of War

~~Basic~~ | ~~Complete~~ | Elite

Many families have found that graphic novels provide huge incentives to their budding readers. The pictures will help your student to stay focused and make him want to understand the written text.

You'll be thrilled that he's not only enjoying reading but also getting a memorable, insightful look at history. Be forewarned, though, that war is far from pretty. That said, this series does a tasteful job of showing what it would have been like to live through these events without depicting unnecessary gore.

In *True Stories of the Civil War*, he'll read the stories of the people who lived through it. From the first shots on Fort Sumter to the surrender at Appomattox, True Stories of the Civil War will give your child a visual look at the war that nearly tore our nation apart.

During World War I, known as the Great War, many soldiers kept journals about their experiences. *True Stories of World War I* encapsulates six of them, including Alvin York and the Red Baron. Your child will learn of the horror of gas warfare and the tragic sinking of the Lusitania.

Using the unique accounts taken from actual diaries and letters, *True Stories of World War II* tells the stories of five men and women who fought for their countries during World War II. From the Bataan Death March to the sinking of the USS Indianapolis, this graphic novel will open your child's eyes to the horrors of a war that must never be repeated.

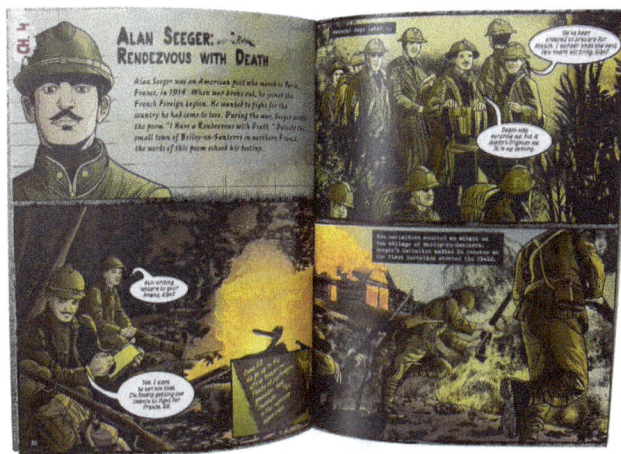

Scheduling

We suggest not assigning these stories but just letting your student read them and see what he thinks. Or save them for when they tie into *The Story of the World*—if your student can leave them alone that long! (That would be in chapters 5, 20-21, and 28-29 of *The Story of the World*, FYI.)

Geography

While The Story of the World teaches the geography of historical events, your child will want to know more about the world around him. The vibrant pages of *Skill Sharpeners Geography* will help him master important geography concepts with a workbook that continually gets rave reviews from families. Flags of the World will help your student retain the locations of the nations around the world as you read about them in this year's reading challenge.

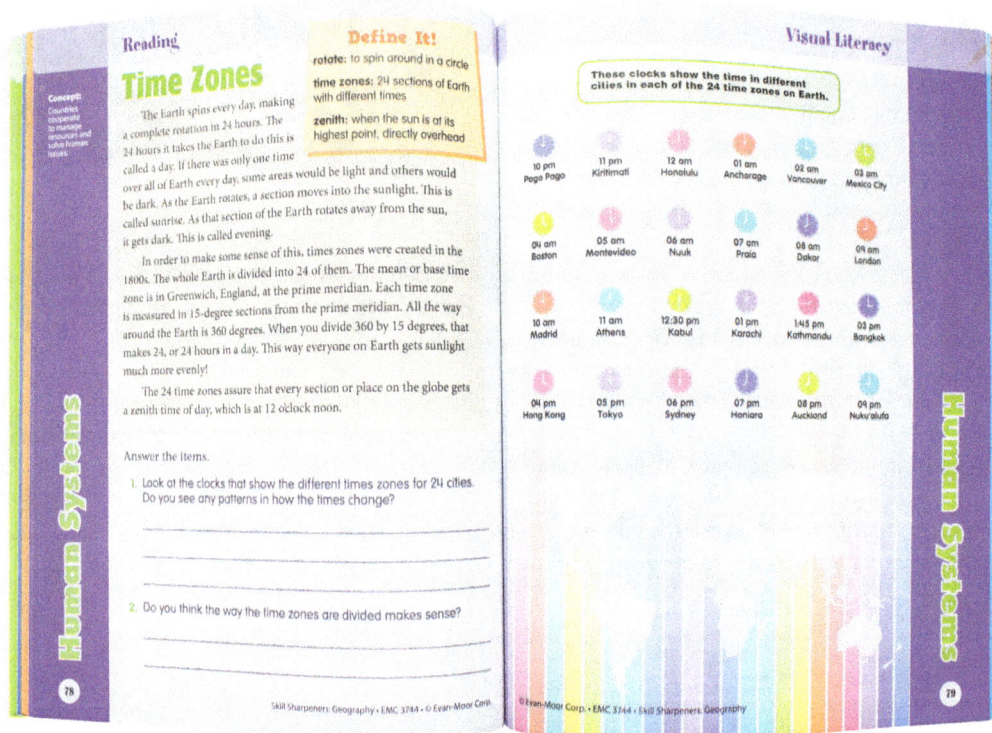

Skill Sharpeners Geography, Grade 4

Basic | Complete | Elite

Skill Sharpeners Geography lets your child explore his world while learning key map skills and geography concepts with little fuss on your part. The cross-curricular activities integrate the most current geography standards, and each eye-catching book is divided into colorful collections of engaging, grade-appropriate themes.

Each theme includes short nonfiction reading selections, comprehension questions, vocabulary practice, and writing prompts.

In this grade, each chapter has a rhythm to it. First, there are a couple of pages of reading, a few questions, and some visual literacy exercises—usually maps or the like. Next is a page of vocabulary practice, using fun tools such as crosswords or word searches. Then you'll find hands-on activities such as designing a passport or performing an archaeological dig. (This is optional; consider it extra credit!) Finally, you'll find a writing exercise. While the prompts are creative, not every student needs this extra writing practice. If it's too much for your child, we suggest having him answer verbally or record his answers on your phone.

Skill Sharpeners Geography takes your child beyond just the basics of geography and includes a smattering of histories and cultures within our world. The colorful illustrations and pages will grab your child's attention, and the handy (removable) answer key in the back allows you to help your student easily check his work.

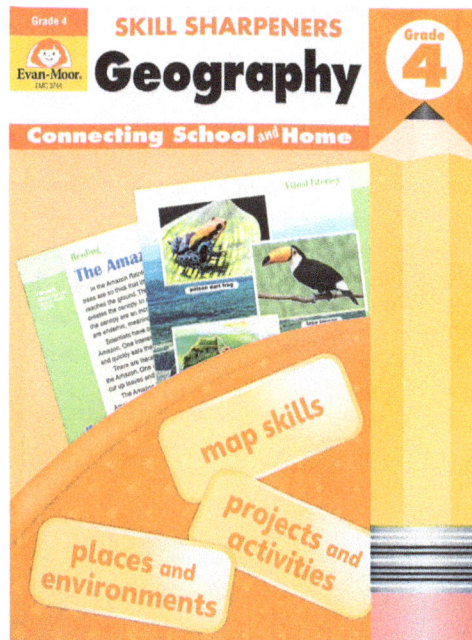

Scheduling

With 132 pages in all, complete 4 per week to stay on track. Add in the activities as time and interest allow.

And yes, you may truly skip the activity and writing pages (with no guilt) if that isn't how your child learns best.

Flags of the World

~~Basic~~ | ~~Complete~~ | Elite

Flags of the World is a large poster with nearly 200 flag stickers that your child should place as he completes a book from that country. What a fun way to learn to recognize all the flags and locate the counties.

The large Flags of the World map was specially designed to be readable by children. Suppose you are unsure where Seychelles, Mauritius, and Eswatini are. In that case, you will be grateful that there is a numbered code to help find each county's location. There's extra info giving the capital of each country, too.

Even before it is complete, the poster makes a super addition to any wall, and it is a great reference tool for homeschoolers.

Scheduling

As you read around the world this year, mark your progress by having your child add the pertinent stickers to this map.

You will not find this on your schedule each week, as it is a supplement to the reading challenge rather than a stand-alone task.

Science

Ready to Experiment?

A foundational understanding of scientific principles is critical for students, but if that is delivered in a dreary way, science becomes a drudgery of facts rather than a joyous exploration. This newly launched science series, Discover! Science, aims to inspire a sense of wonder and curiosity towards the natural world in your child.

Discover! Science instills both a passion for discovery and a deep appreciation for scientific exploration.

A Note on Experiments

While conducting every experiment together would be ideal, we understand that your schedule may not always allow for that. If you have a week where you aren't going to be able to complete the experiments, simply discussing the process and expected outcomes can still provide an insightful experience for both you and your child.

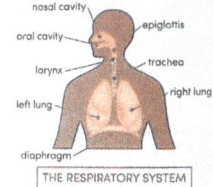

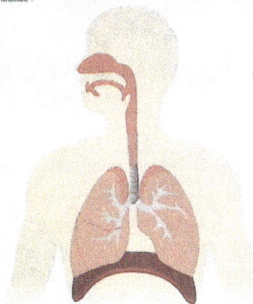

Discover! Science

~~Basic~~ | Complete | Elite

Discover! Science is designed from the ground up for the homeschool environment, giving teaching parents added confidence to teach their children with an academically rigorous science curriculum.

Discover! Science combines beautiful student-driven worktexts and parent-friendly instructor guides to offer a science program that encourages multi-modality learning and critical thinking. The colorful pages have easygoing text and a fresh look, focusing on real-world connections to make learning science more appealing for your child.

Discover! Science is designed to develop independent and critical thinking through challenging questions and creative projects. Throughout the worktext, students will learn, reflect, and apply. Concise yet complete instructor guides provide answer keys, additional activities, and challenges, plus ideas for engaging auditory, visual, and kinesthetic learners.

Scheduling

Complete just over 2 lessons a week in this program in order to set a sustainable pace through the school year.

Dr. Bonyfide 2

~~Basic~~ | Complete | Elite

Dr. Bonyfide is a young person's highly entertaining guide to his own body. You know that if your child has basic information about his body, he is more likely to make healthy life choices. Plus, isn't it natural to want to understand why your body works the way it does?

Developed by a team of educators, health professionals, and parents, *Dr. Bonyfide Presents* will creatively guide your child through the bone structures of his body using kid-friendly jokes, rhymes, puzzles, fun facts, and original comic strips. Plus, a pair of "X-ray vision" (colored) glasses will let your child investigate the bones on special pages. Write-in quizzes and a range of hands-on activities will help you as a teaching parent to assess his progress while simultaneously helping him retain his new knowledge.

Scheduling

With 112 pages in all, plan on doing 3-4 per week if you want to make this course last all year. But be prepared—your child may find it so engaging that he races through and finishes it early!

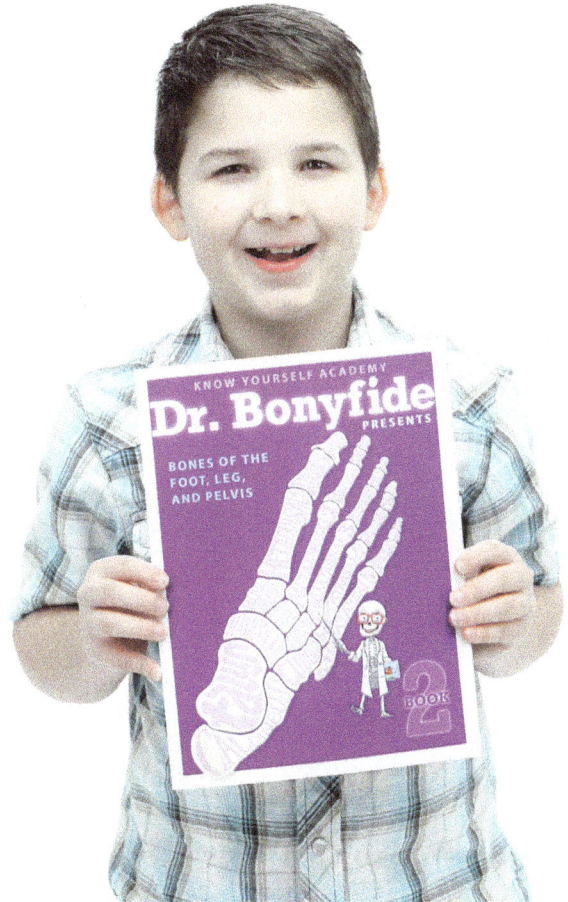

STEM Learning

STEM is Everywhere!

STEM learning is more than robotics and computer programming. STEM tools also include those that engage students in exploratory learning, discovery, and problem-solving that teach the foundational skills of critical thinking and short- and long-term planning.

STEM includes your Titanic logic game as well as your Quixo game, even though they are found elsewhere in this handbook. Anything that goes beyond a read-and-regurgitate lesson undoubtedly falls into the STEM classification. In assembling this guide, many of our products could easily have been classified as STEM, but these tools seem especially appropriate for this category.

ROBOTIS OLLO Spark

~~Basic~~ | Complete | Elite

Get ready to ignite your child's passion for science and construction with the ROBOTIS OLLO Spark.

This fantastic twelve-week beginner's robotics curriculum comes complete with a 108-page colorful workbook that's super-easy to follow—no confusing jargon, just crystal-clear pictures and documentation.

OLLO Spark introduces your child to the world of elasticity, inertia, tumbling bots, and more! It's not just a kit but a comprehensive 12-week adventure integrating a user-friendly block-based programming language. This course will flex your child's mental muscles and sharpen his computer logic and problem-solving skills as he dives into coding.

With the R+Block block-type coding program, the OLLO Spark makes it easy for anyone to code and control their robot. Assembling the OLLO Spark robots is a breeze - just connect the plates with rivets into the plate holes. There are even custom joint parts for complex configurations. The RB88 battery pack has everything you need – built-in motors, sensors, controllers, even extra ports – in one convenient package.

Scheduling

Ollo Spark is structured as a 12-week course. You have the option to spread out the program by completing one-third of a "week's work" each week. Alternatively, you can do the workbook assignment one week and build the model the following week for a more balanced pace.

My Crazy Inventions

~~Basic~~ | ~~Complete~~ | Elite

Inventing is a characteristic of being human, yet surprisingly enough, it is not something that is actively pursued. *My Crazy Inventions Sketchbook: 50 Awesome Drawing Activities for Young Inventors* can change that. With pages and pages of creative prompts, *My Crazy Inventions* will inspire brainstorming, imagining, and, ultimately, drawing.

Each spread contains numerous fun-filled illustrations of real and imaginary inventions and scenarios, plus lots of room for your child's own drawings. "Invent a brand-new candy, a writing tool your friends would like to use, or something that would help you sleep better at night."

My Crazy Inventions has illustrations of actual inventions and is bursting with fun facts about inventions that have succeeded (M&M's) and failed (a car wash for humans).

My Crazy Inventions is beautifully crafted, with thick pages ready for erasers as your child fine-tunes his design. Also included is an application for a patent and a patent certificate, suitable for framing.

Scheduling

With 50 activities to complete, we suggest doing 1-2 per week.

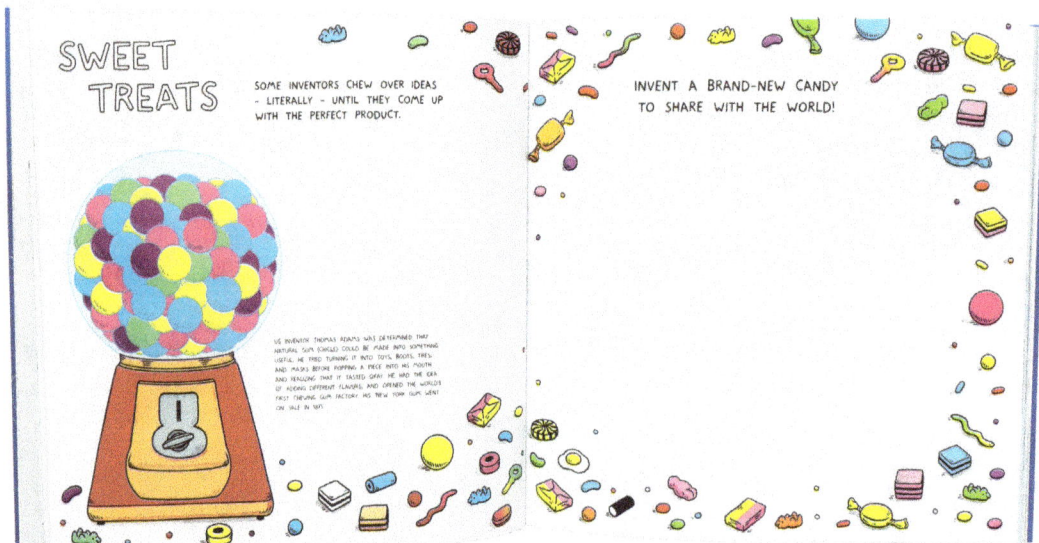

Art

Art + STEM = STEAM

STEM—an acronym for Science, Technology, Engineering, and Mathematics—has been joined by Art to form STEAM! Now the 2 acronyms are used interchangeably in the academic world.

We all know STEM is important, but is the addition of art really that critical? Yes! Art is used to plan the layout of a tower, design a prosthetic hand, and choose colors for the latest app.

In fact, as long as your project is inquiry-based and you have the opportunity to think critically, creatively, and innovatively, then you are looking at a STEAM curriculum.

Because the transition of terminology from STEM to STEAM is still new, we are using STEM for clarity's sake. We list art separately in this handbook. But don't let that fool you into overlooking art this year. It really is a vital skill!

Tropical Forest 3D Painting

~~Basic~~ | Complete | Elite

Embark on a tropical adventure with this vibrant 3D painting activity featuring four elusive rainforest creatures. Your young explorer will unleash his creativity as he wields the tools to craft raised lines and dots, bringing to life a textured, shimmering masterpiece inspired by the jungle's lush foliage and exotic wildlife.

Tropical Forest 3D Painting's specially textured paint creates intriguing 3D effects, while easy-to-grasp miniature bottles with applicator tips ensure precise detailing. Children can experiment with various brush strokes and effects, from iridescent to glittering or matte, effortlessly covering expansive areas of their canvas.

Complete with a handy storage box to keep supplies organized, Tropical Forest 3D Painting promises to ignite imaginations, hone fine motor skills, and provide artistic joy in the heart of the tropical wilderness!

Scheduling

Your student should complete **1 painting a month.**

Sketching Made Easy

~~Basic~~ | Complete | Elite

Sketching Made Easy is an online video course bundled with a PDF workbook that will lead your child into the captivating realm of sketching. As a former homeschooler, the course creator empathizes with parents' challenges in finding quality content for artistic youngsters. Fueled by frustration over the absence of courses blending skill-building and enjoyment, he set out to craft a solution.

In *Sketching Made Easy,* his mission was clear: enabling top-tier art education for all homeschoolers while fostering excitement. Professionally filmed, this course promises an easy-to-use learning journey. With lessons that cover important drawing concepts through a handful of exercises, *Sketching Made Easy* will equip your students with transferable skills for their own artwork.

Flexibility reigns supreme with *Sketching Made Easy'*s online class, allowing budding artists to learn at their own pace and convenience. Accessible from anywhere with an internet connection, it's perfect for busy schedules or areas lacking local art classes. Whether your child is a beginner laying the groundwork or an experienced hand working on refining his techniques, *Sketching Made Easy* adapts to his needs.

Sketching Made Easy's printable worksheets offer hands-on exercises that pair seamlessly with lesson topics, enhancing the learning experience. Embark on a journey of artistic discovery with *Sketching Made Easy*'s online class, which offers convenience and depth for aspiring young artists.

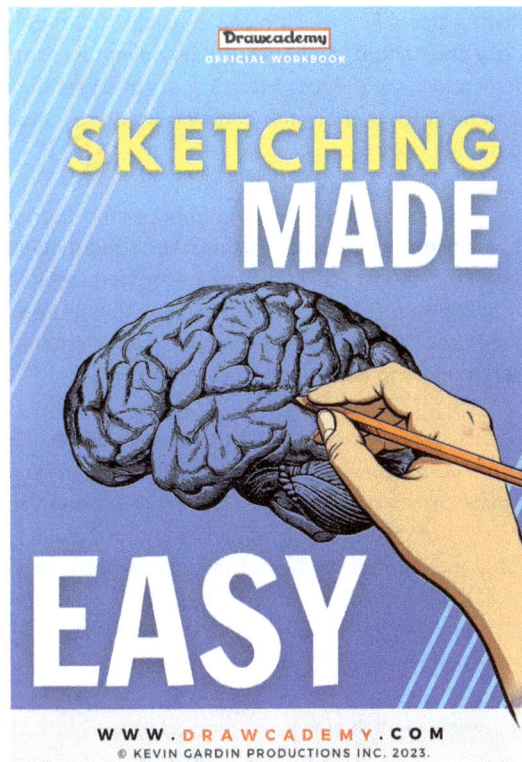

Scheduling

30 lessons are included, so completing one online lesson a week gets you easily through the course this year.

Have I Got A Story for You!

~~Basic~~ | ~~Complete~~ | Elite

Have I Got A Story For You! is a one-of-a-kind multi-child art history course that is part story, part adventure, part art studio, and 100% fun! Used for 13 years at a prominent college preparatory school, this course is now available to you via high-quality videos.

This year your student will study the Impressionist period. He will be introduced to various artists, hear about cultural events specific to that era, and examine masterpieces for style or techniques that make them unique. An animated cartooned drop of paint named Gasfy adds an element of light-heartedness to each episode's journey.

Have I Got A Story For You! consists of twelve 20-30 minutes videos with corresponding lesson plans. Throughout each series, three artists are introduced. Students will analyze the masterpieces of these prominent artists and discuss how their culture, circumstances, and family influenced their art and more. And for those who blush at nudity in art, *Have I Got A Story For You!* is entirely G-rated. This means all nudity has been pixelated out; quite a feat!

Corresponding to each video are detailed lesson plans that include critical thinking questions to engage your students in discussion and generate higher-order thinking skills. The lesson plans also suggest optional cross-curricular age-specific activities in the areas of writing and vocabulary. As a bonus, some lesson plans include geography, history, and even science assignments.

But what your children will love most are the well-chosen art activities. Several are suggested for each unit, each selected

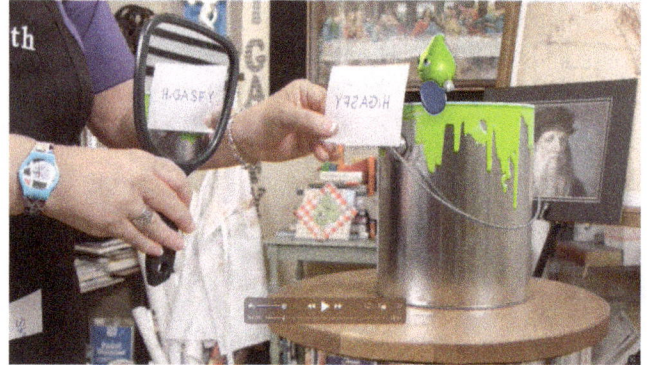

to enhance your child's retention of the lecture material. Most art activities will take about 30 minutes to complete.

Scheduling

Complete 1 lesson every 3 weeks. If you want to invest the same amount of time each week, it will likely work best to watch the video on week 1 and then complete some of the related art projects on weeks 2 & 3.

Our family is using this course for "cousin school" and it works well to have the entire crew watch the video first and then roll right into a related art project.

There is no "right" way to implement this—play with it and see what works best for your family!

Studiostone Alabaster Polar Bear

Basic | Complete | **Elite**

Specially designed for hands-on learning, the Studiostone Alabaster Polar Bear carving kit introduces your child to the centuries-old art of stone carving. It begins with beautiful soft white alabaster. Your child will enjoy the challenge of changing that rough alabaster figure into a more detailed, lushly polished sculpture.

The step-by-step picture-based instructions are easy to follow and will soon have your child carving, sanding, and polishing his very own impressive stone sculpture. Each Studiostone Alabaster Polar Bear carving kit comes with everything your child will need to complete his fist-sized sculpture: a hand-cut alabaster shape, child-safe carving file, two grades of sandpaper, polishing wax, and a tiny buffing cloth.

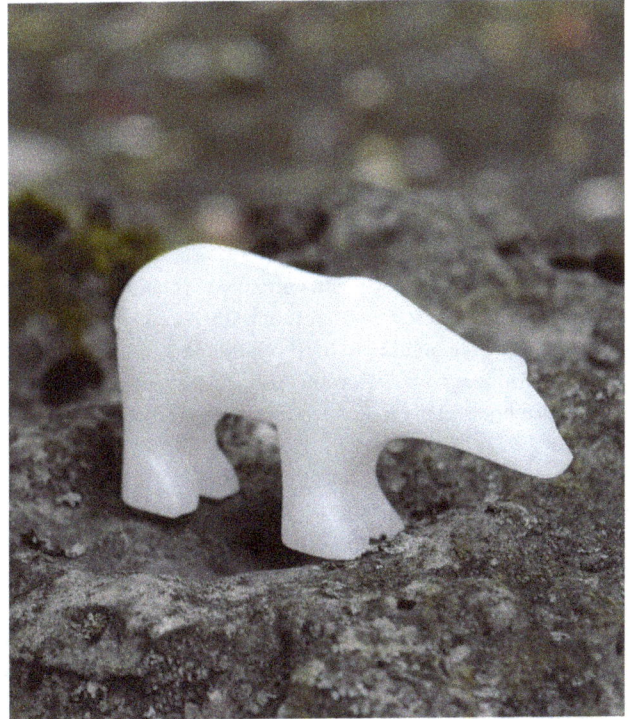

Scheduling

The amount of time your child will invest in this project varies, so we suggest pulling it out once a week for 15 minutes or so until he is satisfied with the finished carving.

Tips

1. To avoid stone dust as you carve, keep your stone wet. If you cannot keep the stone wet, you may be more comfortable wearing a dust mask.

2. Artists suggest spending extra time making your animal round. A few additional minutes rounding the body makes a huge difference in the appearance at the end. If you have an impatient child, he can always do some detailed work and then go back to rounding the body before moving on to sanding.

3. When your student waxes his carving, be sure to get the excess wax off before it dries. To get the highest gloss possible, let the waxed stone cool completely before buffing. If your child is in a hurry to complete his project, you can place the carving in the refrigerator for a few moments, then buff to an attractive sheen.

Learning Tools

Learning Styles and More

Do you know your child's learning style? Most researchers note at least 3: hands-on or kinesthetic, auditory, and visual. Many children are a unique combination of these.

If you don't know which methods equip your child to learn best, you will want to take a few moments to research them. Once you know your child's strengths and weaknesses, you'll be able to focus on methods that help him learn rather than using the approach you've always used. (All students find it helpful to integrate as many learning modes as possible into their studies.)

For instance, if you have a kinesthetic learner, encourage him to move while he learns. Break out the Nice Cube, let him sign keywords to himself, or have him write on a large whiteboard.

If he's an auditory learner, make it a point to have him hear the information he's learning. You could read it to him, encourage him to read aloud, use an audio version, or download a podcast. However you decide to approach it will be better than reading the same textbook silently 4 dozen times.

Visual learners will probably have the easiest time learning. Most information is naturally presented visually in textbooks.

Test Prep: Grade 4

~~Basic~~ | Complete | Elite

Home-taught children who are not prepared for their yearly standardized tests are at a distinct disadvantage to government- and privately-taught children. If you reside in a state that requires standardized tests, you should know that a vast majority of certified teachers teach with the test in mind. In other words, teachers understand the types of questions that will appear on the standardized tests, and they will spend weeks preceding the tests covering the necessary information. If you do not do likewise, your children stand a chance of performing poorly in comparison.

For those of us in a state where some form of testing is required but never scrutinized, preparing is not as critical. But some of you are in states where the test results are not only analyzed but are also used as a basis for whether you may continue to home educate. Why not make sure your children are on a level playing field? The *Test Prep* series offers students the essential groundwork needed to prepare for standardized tests.

Based on subject areas covered by most state standardized tests, these colorful, inviting workbooks provide a good sampling of all the skills required of each grade level. Practice pages, strategies, tips, and full-length practice tests build test-taking confidence and skills in subjects such as reading comprehension, vocabulary, language, and math. The test tips are beneficial, and the information and instructions are super-easy to follow. Developed by a leading educational publisher, Harcourt's *Test Prep* provides a great opportunity for children to review before taking standardized state tests. Engaging, practical, and easy to use, *Test Prep* will help your children face the tests with the same confidence that their peers will have.

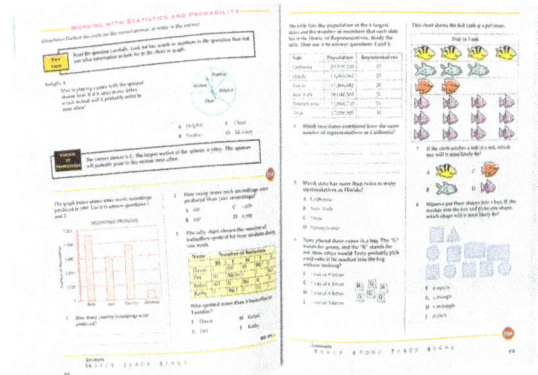

Even if your state doesn't require testing, consider completing the book anyway since test-taking skills are vital across all areas of life

Scheduling

Our family has always preferred to spend the week or two before our state-mandated annual testing working through this book. Keep it low key, and let the change of pace be an enjoyable experience for your child. If you run into a concept he doesn't know, stop and explain it to him; that is why you are doing the prep now!

NeeDoh Nice Cube

~~Basic~~ | ~~Complete~~ | <mark>Elite</mark>

The NeeDoh Nice Cube is a tactile sensation that offers this unique experience: it's soft when slow squished and dense when fast squished, always returning to its original shape to provide endless tactile fun.

Each NeeDoh Nice Cube starts firm but quickly softens as it warms in your student's hands. Once it cools down, it regains its firmness, making it an ideal hand exerciser for fine motor skills and sensory needs. With its satisfying weight, the NeeDoh Nice Cube offers the perfect tactile experience. But this squishy sensation isn't just visually appealing; it's incredibly satisfying to touch. It's like having a giant, squishy, non-melting ice cube at your fingertips, ready to deliver stretchy goodness and endless fun.

Your child can fully interact with this fidget toy by pulling, squeezing, or smushing it to his heart's content. As he engages with the NeeDoh Nice Cube, he'll experience a delightful sensory sensation that aids in calming restless hands and enhancing focus and attention.

More About NeeDoh

While learning new things is always exciting as your child works to get his head around a new concept, general anxiety is also a common experience. NeeDoh, is the ultimate stress reliever that will help your student become calm. Its tactile surface and soft yet solid interior provide endless enjoyment. NeeDoh is known for its durable squish that allows your child to relax and regain composure. Parents of neurodivergent children, those with ADHD, OCD, autism, anxiety, and more, will find that NeeDoh helps children focus and pay attention with each squeeze.

Each NeeDoh is filled with a non-toxic, dough-like compound created from a PVA glue compound, making it safe for kids. Even after a session of rugged squeezing, each figure always returns to its original shape. It's small enough to fit in the palm of your hand, making it the perfect companion for those moments when you need to decompress.

A simple wash with soap and warm water, followed by air drying, will keep it in tip-top condition. Please note that colors may vary, but relaxation and fun are guaranteed.

Grip Colored EcoPencils

~~Basic~~ | ~~Complete~~ | **Elite**

Whether for artwork or schoolwork, Faber-Castell's Grip Colored EcoPencils are a good fit for elementary students. The Grip Colored EcoPencils feature an ergonomic triangular barrel and a patented grip zone for fatigue-free, comfortable drawing. Not only that, the triangular design of these pencils helps prevent rollaways.

Artists will enjoy having 24 colors to incorporate into their pictures, while students will appreciate the selection for color-specific workbook assignments. The rich pigmentation of the core makes the Grip Colored EcoPencils' colors vibrant. What a great set of pencils to equip your young artist!

Schedule

No need to schedule these pencils. Just pull them out whenever your child's worksheets or art projects would benefit!

Articles and Resources

From Our Family to Yours

39 Years of Serving You

In 1985, we were a family of 5. I was the oldest of 3 toddler girls with a mom who absolutely excelled at educating us at home. This was during the "Dark Ages" of homeschooling, and online searching was still a thing of the future. Our mom, Deb, was (and is) a voracious reader and an avid researcher. We girls were thriving academically, and other moms were naturally interested in using the same curricula Deb had found.

That same year, she and Dan, our dad, repurposed the business license originally intended for their world-class Golden Retriever breeding operation, which had come to naught, and she launched Timberdoodle, a homeschool supply company. She created our first catalog, and growth came fast. We shipped curriculum from our laundry room, our grandparents' basement, and finally warehouses and an office. Two more children were added to the family, and we all grew up working in the business from an early age.

Now, decades later, Timberdoodle is still renowned for out-of-the-box learning and crazy-smart finds. Mom's engineering background has heavily influenced our STEM selections and warehouse layout, and her no-nonsense, independent approach has made these kits the award-winning choice that they are today.

All 5 of us children are grown now, and most still work at Timberdoodle in key roles. Our brother and his wife have welcomed 4 amazing little ones in the past 7 years, and we sisters have opened our home to children through foster care and adoption. As our families have grown, we've become even more committed to equipping parents with the best homeschooling resources. The kits we sell are the same ones we use in our own homes, and we hope you enjoy them as much as we do.

In the following articles, you'll hear Deb and others talk about some of the nitty-gritty questions we receive. Do you have a question not answered here? You are invited to contact us at any time—we'd love to help!

Joy (for all of us)

Picture circa 1989, breaking ground for our first warehouse!

Why Emphasize Independent Learning?

The Top 7 Reasons This Is Such a Big Deal at Timberdoodle

1. Avoid Burnout

One-on-one teaching is critical to the success of any student, and homeschoolers are no exception to that. However, we have seen parents become helicopter teachers, micromanaging every detail of their students' education. Is it any wonder that these parents burn out? Independent learning skills provide a natural transition from the one-on-one focus of early childhood to a less teacher-intense educational approach.

2. Cultivate Responsible Learners

There is a lot of (Dare we say it?) fun in teaching. But it is better for your students if they master how to learn on their own. After all, when they are adults, you'll want them to have the ability to pick up any skill they want and learn it as needed. Structuring their education to be more and more self-taught helps them to become responsible independent learners.

3. Special Needs, Illness, and Newborns

Not all parents have the same amount of teaching time. Whether they are doing therapy for a child with special needs, dealing with a chronic illness, managing visits for a foster child, or are blessed with a newborn, there are seasons when homeschooling needs to be more independent for the teacher's sanity!

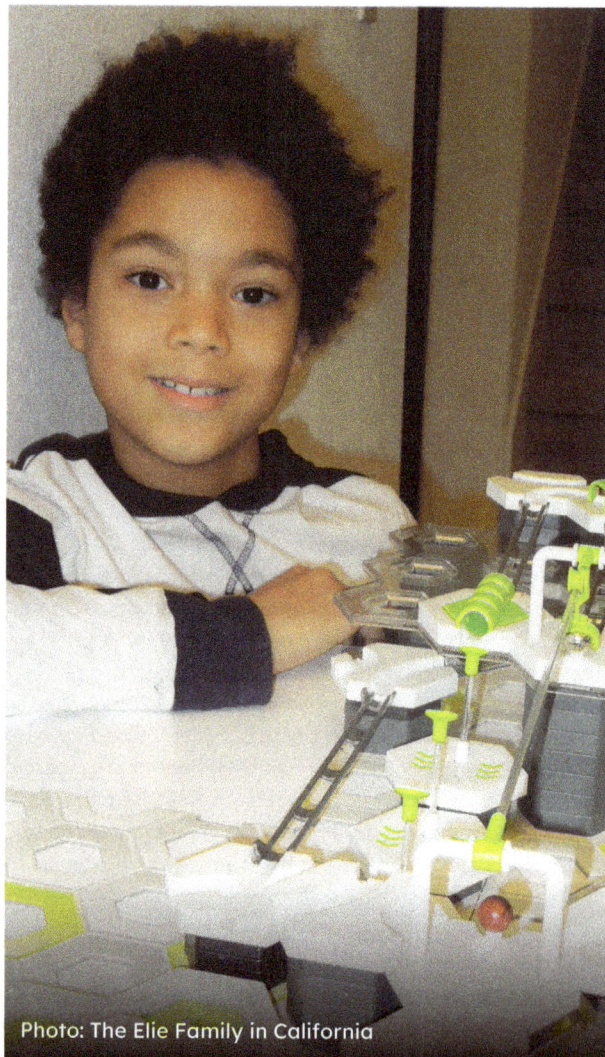

Photo: The Elie Family in California

4. You Don't Have to Love Teaching

As much as no one wants to mention this, we all know parents who struggle to teach. They love their kids and feel strongly about homeschooling, but when it actually comes down to teaching, they are easily overwhelmed and intimidated. If it is an area they are not gifted or trained in, then of course teaching is scary. Independent learning tools can help parent educators get comfortable in their role. Even if they never love teaching, they can still reap the benefits of giving their children a superior education at home.

5. Timberdoodle's Purpose: We Are Here to Make Giving Your Children a Superior Education at Home Enjoyable

Here at Timberdoodle, amid the catalogs, sales, blog posts, videos, Facebook giveaways, etc., we have one primary goal. That goal is to make it possible for parents to enjoy giving their children a superior education at home. We aren't here just to sell you stuff (though we wouldn't exist if you didn't shop!), which is why we have been known to send you to our "competitors" when their product would work better for you. We really just want you to be a happy homeschool family. When that happens, we feel successful! Independent learning is one tool in your toolbox. It is a valuable tool, so use it where it works best for you.

6. Not Either/Or

You don't have to pick between independent and group learning across the board. History and science are typically easy subjects to combine across multiple grades as it is wonderful to have the whole family involved in the read-aloud portion and experiments. Our family has also converted some workbooks into read-alouds. Instead of writing in answers, we took turns answering the questions. If you're seeing that one of your texts this year would benefit the entire family, why not switch it up a little? Just because you want your children to master independent learning, that does not mean you should hesitate to learn as a family!

7. Our Family's Experience

The rule of thumb in our house was that as soon as a child could read, he was responsible for his own education. We each had an annual conference with Mom to set learning goals for the year. We were then given the books for the year—often including the teacher's manuals. Mom gave us each a weekly checklist to complete before Friday Family Night. If we needed help, we asked questions. Otherwise, the responsibility was ours. This also freed us up to do other important things as a family: service, Timberdoodle work, babysitting, elder care, community or church projects, hospitality, farming…

What Makes Games a Priority?

6 Reasons Games Aren't Just for Fun—Even the "Frivolous" Games

You may have noticed there is at least 1 multiplayer game in every Timberdoodle curriculum kit. This is not just to add some levity to your day!

The Research

A quick Google search will net you numerous articles on the benefits of playing board games with your children:

- increasing laughter
- language development
- understanding rules
- grasping fair play
- detecting patterns and predicting outcomes
- learning from experience
- impulse control
- social skills
- increasing focus
- teamwork
- reducing anxiety
- unplugging from technology
- increasing analytical abilities
- setting goals
- patience
- problem-solving skills
- reducing stress
- creativity
- prioritizing steps toward a goal
- self-confidence
- spatial ability

This is a robust and interwoven list, but here are the 6 things that have jumped out at us over the past years and made games a huge priority for education.

1. Social-Emotional Intelligence

Think of your closest and dearest friends outside of your immediate family. What makes them so dear to you? My guess is that it isn't their IQ or ability to speed-solve a complex math problem. A friendship will celebrate those interesting facts, but your friendship itself is more likely rooted in shared interests, time spent together, and an ability to navigate hard situations with grace.

When you spend time teaching a child how to lose graciously, you are teaching a life skill that will translate into all of life and impact his friendships way more than his test scores ever could.

In light of this, the end of each game may be more important than the strategy in the middle. Coach your children in what you expect from the winner and the loser. Around here, a "Good game!" goes a long way, but you decide what is best for your family. Humility is what you're looking for—not the teary deflation of a proud loser or the puffed-up bragging of a proud winner!

2. Strategic Thinking

Obviously, the games we've chosen require age-appropriate logic and strategy. Critical thinking skills are essential, so let's teach them any way we can.

3. Connection

Sometimes it can seem that you spend more time correcting your children's behavior than connecting with them. Then as they grow older, your parenting becomes more and more hands-off. Making games a priority at all ages lets you enjoy each other's company and genuinely become closer to each other. What parent won't appreciate that?

4. Executive Functioning

Are you familiar with executive functioning? It is the ability to prioritize and organize information. The clearest example is the age-old challenge to "guess what number I'm thinking of right now using yes-or-no questions." If you respond by asking if the number is higher than 100, you are using executive functioning. If instead you start rattling off specific numbers, you're not. In games, you're constantly taking into consideration what your opponent is doing, what pieces are still in your hand, which rules apply at the moment while sorting and utilizing all the information to decide what your next game play should be.

5. Regulation

Some articles tie this to executive functioning, but it's worth discussing on its own. Regulation is the ability to control your own emotions. Can you think of a more natural opportunity to practice this than during game play? Calm-down strategies and redos may be implemented as many times as needed until your child is able to endure suspense and even win or lose without outbursts. Whew!

6. Growth Mindset

Some of us, students included, tend to think that either we are good at something or we're not. When our twins were young, this was particularly obvious in our discussions about art. One had a natural inclination for drawing, but one did

not. So the naturally gifted one called himself an artist and proclaimed that his brother was not. It was helpful to come back and discuss that we all learn and grow. So when Mr. Artist set aside his art for several months and his twin worked and worked at it, we had 2 artists on our hands! Game play is a natural place to model that all of us learn and grow. We aren't "born with it," but we learn skills and develop abilities.

Side Note: Think Out Loud

An article from Parenting Science made the excellent point that students don't always naturally ask why a player used a specific strategy. Try to start that conversation by asking why he chose that specific move or explaining that you're starting with this piece because (insert strategy here). This will model the higher-order thinking that you are setting out to teach. It will also model the fact that we are all learners!

So what are you waiting for? Go play some games!

8 Reasons to Stop Schoolwork and Go Build Something!

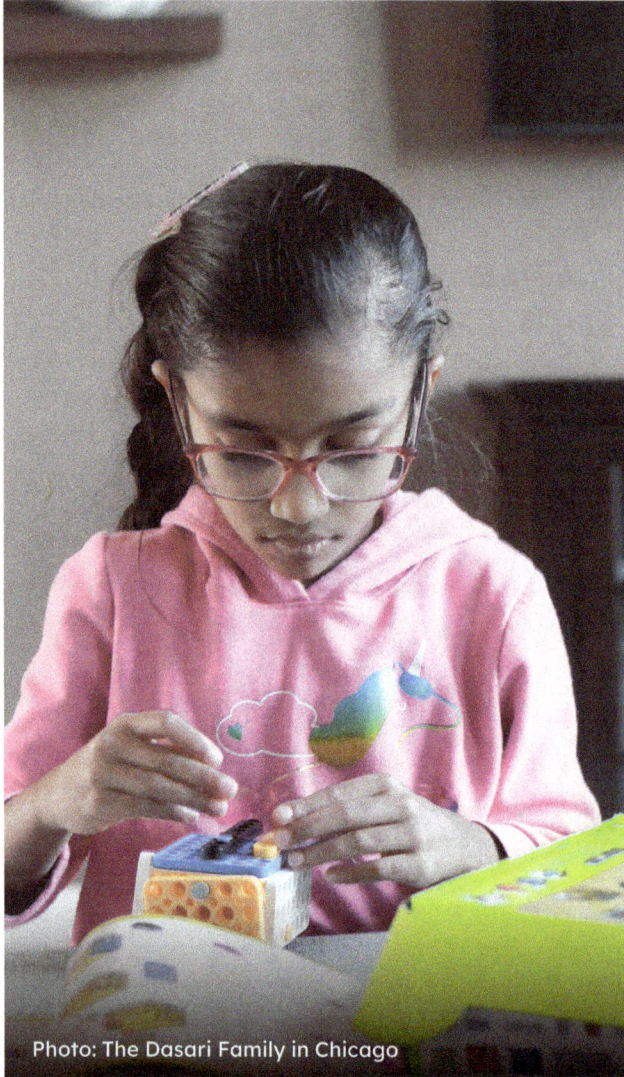
Photo: The Dasari Family in Chicago

Would you like to supplement your curriculum with a program that simultaneously improves your child's visual and spatial perception, fine motor skills, patience, problem-solving, creativity, ability to follow directions, prereading skills, grasp of physics concepts, and engineering ability? Better yet, what if your child would actually enjoy this curriculum and choose to do it whenever he could? No, this isn't some mythical homeschool product guaranteed to solve all your problems. We are talking about the Lego bricks already strewn throughout your house, the ThinkPlay blocks in our preschool curriculum, and the Bioloid robot kit designed for teens.

Construction kits just might be the most underrated type of curriculum ever. It's not just us; research concludes that children learn a lot by designing and building things. Would you agree that construction is one of the most valuable educational processes available? Here are 8 skills your child will learn with his construction kit.

1. Visual Perception

It may be obvious that it takes visual perception to find the right pieces and place them where they belong, but consider that whether your child is reading, finishing a puzzle, or doing open-heart surgery, proficiency in visual perception is mandatory.

2. Patience

Do you know anyone who couldn't use more patience? Construction takes time. Slowing down, reading directions, starting over when you make a mistake or a sibling knocks over your creation…these are all valuable character-building experiences.

3. Problem-Solving

Some children lack the ability to troubleshoot a situation and figure out the next step. Construction sets provide a structured opportunity to figure out what went wrong and to fix it if you are following the directions. If you are designing your own models, you'll have even more opportunities to solve problems.

4. Spatial Perception

Probably the clearest picture of how important it is to be able to mentally convert 2D images into 3 dimensions is that of a surgeon. Knowing where the spleen is on a 2D textbook page isn't nearly the same thing as being able to reach into an incision and find the damaged organ.

5. Creativity

Not every creative person has artistic ability. But construction can open the doors of creativity like no other tool. What if I move this gear over here? Could I build that bridge with only blue pieces?

6. Following Directions

Some children are natural rule followers and need to be encouraged to be creative. Others need constraint to follow directions, at least on occasion. If your child falls into that camp, construction kits are a natural way to encourage him in this skill, with the added benefit of a finished result he can show off.

7. Grasp of Physics

Friction, force, mass, and energy are concepts of basic physics—each much more easily explained and grasped with a set of blocks and a ball than by studying a dry textbook definition.

8. Engineering Ability

Many "born engineers" are not drawn to textbooks. But set a construction kit in front of them and watch them explore pulleys, levers, wheels, and gears. They'll soon go from exploration to innovation, and you'll be amazed at their inventions.

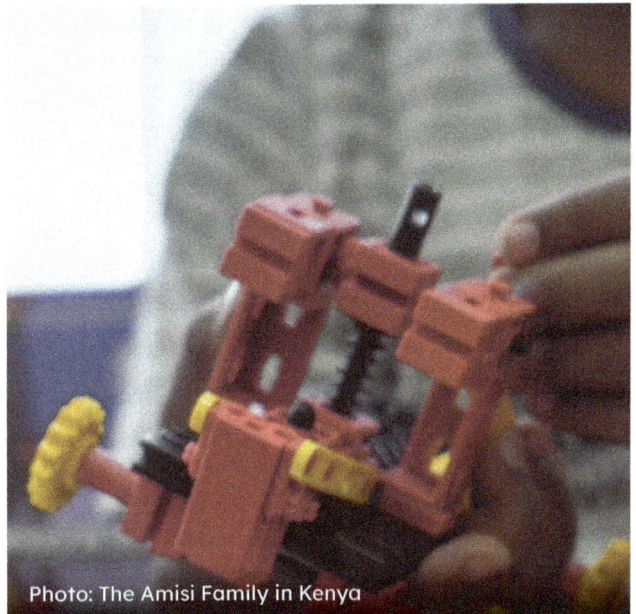

Photo: The Amisi Family in Kenya

What If This Is Too Hard?

9 Steps to Take If You're Feeling Overwhelmed

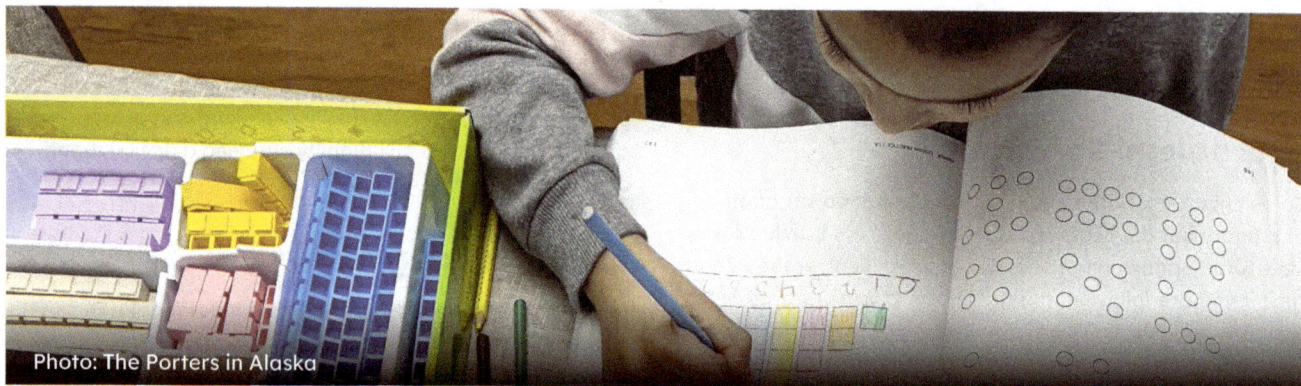

Photo: The Porters in Alaska

Everyone has felt overwhelmed at some point in his education. Whether it's a groan from you as you pull a giant textbook out of the box or the despair from your child when he's read the directions 5 times and the STEM model *still* isn't operating as he wants it to, you will almost certainly hit a moment this year when you realize that an aspect of homeschooling is harder than you anticipated.

So what do you do now?

1. Take a Breath

Just knowing that everyone faces this should help you relax a bit. This feeling will not last—you'll get through this!

2. Jump In!

Ask yourself why you are stressed right now. Is it because something is so intimidating that you have been avoiding it? If that's the case, the simplest solution is to jump in and get started. Could you read just the first page together before lunch? What if you have your student find all of the pieces for step 1 today? Sometimes it's better to muddle through a lesson together than to wait until you're ready to teach it perfectly.

3. Step Back

Perhaps you're too close right now. If you're midproject and totally frustrated by how it's going, try the opposite approach. Close the book for 30 minutes (Set a timer!) and go grab lunch, hit the playground, or swap to a more hands-on project. When the timer rings, you and your student will be ready to try again with clearer heads.

4. Time This

Timers are an invaluable learning tool. If you're becoming distracted, try setting a 10- or 20-minute timer during which you'll do only one thing. Or tell yourself you definitely need to tackle That Dreaded Subject, but only for 30 minutes a day in two 15-minute chunks. When the timer rings, close the text and move to the next thing. Dividing your day into blocks of time can make a remarkable difference in your efficiency level.

5. Level Down

Did your student take the math pretest before jumping in this year? If not, perhaps he is just in the wrong level! If moving to an easier level freaks you out, it may help to remember that you and your student are not defined by his skill set in any field. Faking his way through by blood, sweat, and tears does not help his future self. Taking the time to back up and fill in the gaps, though, will benefit him forever!

6. Simplify

If you are trying to do every possible activity in every course, it's no wonder you're exhausted. By the time your student is in high school, he will need to complete 75% or more of the work in each course to get full credits. We're not advocates of doing the work in name only, but it's OK to watch some experiments online rather than completing each one yourself. It's also appropriate to do only every other math problem in a section if your child is bored to tears with yet another page of addition. Doesn't that feel better?

7. Make Accommodations

What exactly is stressing your student (or you!) out right now? Is it the pen-to-paper writing component? Why not let him use the computer and type his work instead? Or perhaps he can dictate to you and you write for him. Make sure you're doing whatever you can to engage his best learning style.

Encourage Mr. Auditory Learner to read aloud. Or break out all of the favorite fidgets and let Miss Kinesthetic work at a standing desk.

8. Ask for Help

Ask another teacher/parent to work through the issue with you. You may be surprised by how much clarity you gain with a fresh perspective. (Our Facebook groups can be great for this!)

9. Get Professional Help

Check the publisher's website, the book's teacher page, or the kit's manual for contact information. Most of the authors and manufacturers we work with are fantastic about helping and coaching those who get stuck. Not getting the help you need from them? Contact mail@Timberdoodle.com or call us at 800-478-0672, and we'll work with them to get that answer for you.

9 Tips for Homeschooling Gifted Children

From a Family Who Knows This Journey

1. Disdain Busywork

Your child wants to learn, so don't slow him down! If he has mastered multiplication, why are you still spending an hour a day reviewing it? Yes, he does need some review, but we've seen way too many families focus on completing every problem rather than mastering the material. One way to test this is to have him complete every other review problem on only the most essential pages and see how he does. If he can prove he knows it, he doesn't need to be spending quite as much time there.

2. Go Deep

Allow breathing room in your schedule so you have time to investigate earth's gravitational pull or the advantages and disadvantages of hair sheep vs. woolly sheep. Remember that your child is asking to learn, so why pull him away from the subject that's fascinating him? After all, we know that material we're interested in sticks with us so much better than things we learn only because we must.

3. Go Fast

If your child wants to take 3 science courses this year or race through 2 math levels, then why not let him? Homeschoolers can absolutely rock this because there is no one holding us to a "traditional" pace!

4. Encourage Completion

Sometimes it seems there is a touch of ADD in every genius. Give your child as much flexibility as you possibly can, but also keep in mind that you'll be doing him a disservice if he never has to complete something he doesn't feel like working on. Sometimes he may even be surprised to realize that the very subject he dreaded is the springboard for a whole new area of investigation!

5. Give Space and Opportunities

If you can keep mandatory studies to a minimum, you'll give your child more opportunities to accelerate his learning in the areas where he is gifted. Common sense, perhaps, but also worth deliberately thinking through as you plan your school year.

6. Work on Weak Areas Carefully

While you definitely want to help your student overcome his struggles, you also want to be careful that a weakness in one area doesn't impede his progress in other ways. For instance, a child may struggle with writing because his brain works much faster than his hands. While we still encourage working on handwriting skills, we also suggest that his parents try teaching him to type and allow him to complete writing assignments on the computer. This lets him continue to build his writing skills instead of holding him back because of his lack of handwriting speed.

7. Emphasize Humility and Service

We have met way too many children who are obnoxiously convinced that they are geniuses and that everyone needs to be in awe of their abilities. Your child will be much healthier (and happier!) if he realizes these 4 things:

- His identity is *never* found in his brainpower.
- Even as gifted as he is, there are still things that others do better than he does.
- Don't weigh him down by constantly telling him how big his brain is. He is much more than his brain. (Should he lose his edge, he won't lose his worth!)
- His gifts are not for himself alone but for serving others.

Of course, the goal is not to shame, insult, or degrade him but to give him a framework from which he can truly thrive and be free to learn. With a proper perspective, he'll be able to enjoy learning without the burden of constantly assessing his genius and worrying what people think of him.

Encourage his learning, but don't forget to cultivate his character. In 10 years, his response to rebuke will be much more telling than his test score this year, so don't put an inordinate amount of stress on intellectual pursuits.

8. Talk—a LOT!

Talk about what he's interested in. Talk about the theories he came up with today. Talk about his daydreams. Talk about what he wants to study next. Talk about why he may actually need to master that most-dreadful-of-subjects, whatever that may be. Not only will you be able to impart your years of wisdom to him, but you'll also know well the subjects he's interested in so you can link those to his other studies, the places you're visiting next week, or that interesting article you read yesterday.

9. Relax!

Your child is a wonderful gift, but don't feel the need to maximize his potential at every moment. As a side benefit, just relaxing about his genius may in fact increase it. Our own family found that some of our best test scores came after a year off of most formal schooling. Not what we would have planned, but a very valuable insight. Living life also equals learning, so maximize that!

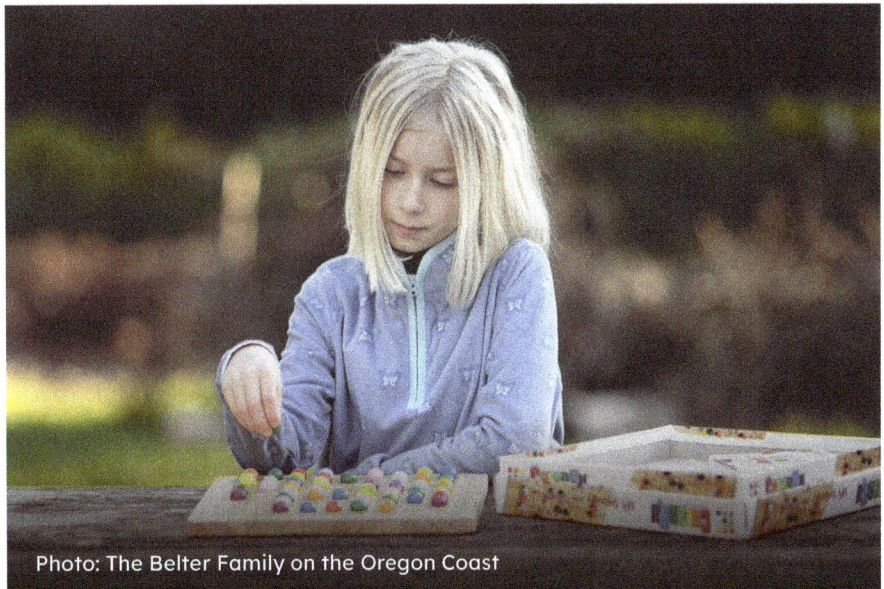

Photo: The Belter Family on the Oregon Coast

11 Thoughts for Homeschooling Struggling Children

From a Family Who Knows This Journey Too!

If you were to call me up and ask for help with a struggling child, these are some of the questions I might toss your way as our conversation got underway.

What Do You Mean by "Struggling"?

If you tell me that your child stomps his foot and walks away when you mention it's almost school time, I will have a different answer than I will for the child who cries because his math is too complex or the 10-year-old who cannot seem to grasp phonics. Each child is struggling, but the answers must vary! So as you go through my questions here, please disregard any that don't apply and always feel free to reach out to us with a more specific question.

1. Investigate Root Issues

Is every visual task a challenge? Consider a thorough eye and tracking exam. Perhaps phonics are a struggle. How's his hearing? We've had sad, grumpy children respond to addressing underlying health issues like undiagnosed stomach pain, untreated sleep challenges, or vitamin deficiencies. (Don't worry. We aren't about to start preaching certain supplements—but if the idea to consider things like this has never occurred to you, our story may be helpful!) We've also had children whose anxiety or ADHD made it incredibly hard to focus. Knowing *why* something is a struggle may open up new ideas for solving the problem.

2. Embrace Repetition

Does doing more reps solve the problem? If your child finds that a single page of math isn't enough to cement the concept, what if you assign 2 pages? Or if reading is the issue, could you go back to square one with a different program and get a different result?

3. Check His Memory

If you ask him to repeat back random letters or digits, how many can he accurately imitate (e.g., "7, A, Y, 2")? Do this orally to check auditory memory / processing and visually to assess his visual processing / memory.

You generally want to see 7 digits or more in ages 7+. Any less than that and you may have found a huge clue to what skill to work on!

4. Back Up

While you could continue with math work that is on-grade and explain each component over and over, it is highly likely that your student will advance much faster if he starts over with the basics and races through. And he'll do that with less strain on your relationship and less stress for either of you. The same applies to many subjects, particularly if you were not the one who was teaching him when he was at a previous level or if you now know that the old program wasn't using the approach best suited for him.

5. Check Engagement

Is it possible that this is a motivational issue? Even if that is not the primary issue, motivation may help. We have some children who struggle academically due to early life trauma. Rather than throwing up our hands, it has been very helpful to realize that yes, he will work harder at this than his peers might, so he may also need a bigger carrot than his peers. If you pull out all the stops for a week, does that help at all?

6. Really Invest in His Learning Style

How does your child learn best? If he needs auditory repetition, can you record the lesson for him to play back or choose an audio-based course? Or if he's hands-on, make sure you pull out the manipulatives every time for now. Not sure? Take some time to study the skills he has mastered and how he learned them.

7. Make Accommodations

Just as you might do for your gifted child, you want to be careful that a weakness in one area doesn't impede his progress in other ways. For instance, a child may struggle with writing because his brain works much faster than his hands. While we still encourage such a child to work on handwriting skills, we will probably also get him started on typing (TTRS can be very helpful!) and allow him to complete writing assignments on the computer. This lets him continue to build his writing skills instead of holding him back because of his lack of handwriting speed.

For your ADHD child, this may look like installing a trampoline in your dining room and encouraging short breaks to calm his system. What might make this better for him? How do you get there?

8. Timers

We are an ADHD-type household, and one huge impact this has is in time management. Rather than stress over lost time, a visual timer has helped us all. Your student can race

the timer, enjoy a special privilege if he beats the timer, or receive practice work if he is opting to daydream instead of working.

9. Emphasize Humility and Service

Just like your gifted child, your struggling child will be much healthier (and happier!) if he realizes these 3 things:
- His identity is *never* found in his brainpower.
- He is indeed gifted in some areas. (Help him find these!)
- His gifts are not for himself alone but for serving others, and he is excellent at that.

Encourage his learning, but don't forget to cultivate his character. In 10 years, his response to rebuke will be much more telling than his test score this year, so don't put an inordinate amount of stress on intellectual pursuits.

10. Tutors

You aren't abdicating your role as a teacher if you realize that separating parenting from math would be helpful for your teen right now!

11. Relax!

When your child is an adult out in the real world, it really won't matter if he learned to read at age 2 or 12. Yes, you want to make progress toward your academic goals, but there is no time limit here!

Living life also equals learning, so engage him in farming, volunteering, swim class, or whatever doors are open, knowing that these are not lesser activities but part of the real work of education. As mentioned elsewhere, our own family found that some of our best test scores came after a year off of most formal schooling. Not what we would have planned, but a very valuable insight.

Convergent & Divergent Thinking

What These Skills Are and Why They Matter

Have you considered the necessity of incorporating both convergent and divergent thinking into your learning time? Experts recognize these as the 2 major types of brain challenges every human encounters.

Does that just sound like a whole bunch of big words? No worries—let's break it down. Your child needs to be able to find the right answer when needed (math, medicine dosage) and also needs to be able to come up with a creative, unscripted answer when the situation warrants (art, architecture).

A child who can only find the "right" answer will be a rigid thinker who can't problem-solve well or think outside the box.

A child who only thinks creatively will not be able to follow procedures or do anything that involves math.

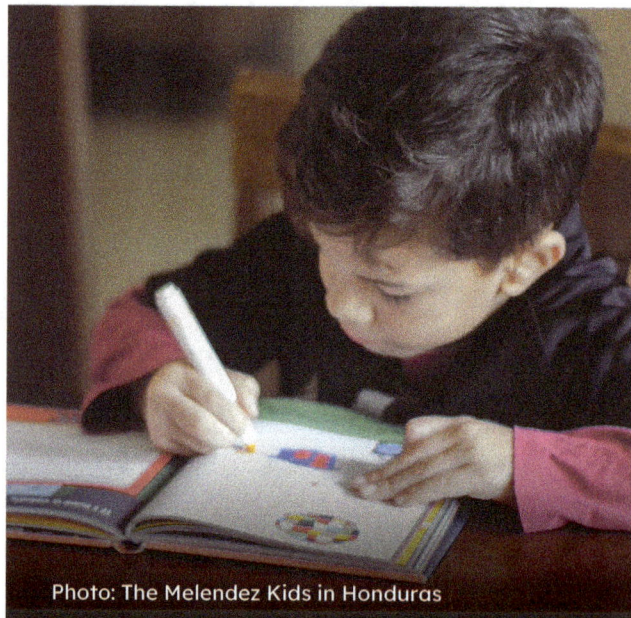

Photo: The Melendez Kids in Honduras

What Is Convergent Thinking?

Convergent thinking generally involves finding a single best answer and is important in the study of math and science. Convergent thinking is the backbone of the majority of curricula and is crucial for future engineers, doctors, and even parents. Much of daily life is a series of determining right and wrong answers, and standardized tests favor the convergent thinker. But when we pursue only convergent-rich curricula, we miss the equally vital arena of divergent thinking.

Is Divergent Thinking Different?

Yes! Divergent thinking encourages your child's mind to explore many possible solutions—maybe even ideas that aren't necessarily apparent at first. It is in use when he discovers that there is more than one way to build a bridge with blocks, to animate a movie, or even to complete a doodle. Radically different from read-and-regurgitate textbooks, not only are divergent activities intellectually stimulating, but kids love them too.

Make a Conscious Effort to Include Both in Your Curriculum

Admittedly, because most textbooks and even puzzles are designed for convergent thinking, you will need to make a conscious effort to expose your children to multiple opportunities for divergent thinking. This is imperative because both divergent and convergent thinking are necessary for critical thinking to be effective.

Why Doctors Need Both Skills

As an example, let's look at a medical doctor. A physician needs to be extraordinarily skilled at convergent thinking to dose medications correctly, diagnose life-threatening emergencies, and follow safety procedures to avoid infection.

However, the first person to wash his hands before surgery or to find a treatment for Ebola used divergent thinking. They were thinking outside of the usual box to solve the problem.

Some of the best doctors today are those who employ powerful convergent skills to accurately diagnose, paired with curiosity and divergent thinking to find the most effective or previously undiscovered treatment plans.

Convergent in Fourth Grade

From reading to math, the backbone of your curriculum this year is convergent. This makes sense because so much of learning at this level is marveling at facts. Sometimes there really is a right answer!

What Is Divergent in Fourth Grade?

If you think about it, these are the same skills a lawyer uses to find legal precedents for her case, a teacher uses to engage her classroom, or an airline pilot uses in the case of emergency.

These tools all include strong divergent aspects to help your child become a well-rounded thinker:

- *My Crazy Inventions*
- ROBOTIS OLLO Spark
- Quixo
- Tropical Forest 3D Painting
- Have I Got a Story for You!

Crazy Inventions Sketchbook is solidly in the divergent camp. Your child is coming up with their own invention to solve a challenge. ROBOTIS OLLO Spark works your child's convergent and divergent skills. As he recreates the exact models shown, he's working on convergent skills (and so much more!). But when he revises that model or builds his own designs, that's capitalizing on divergent learning.

Similarly, games like Quixo also include both elements. The fixed rules are the convergent portion, while the way in which you choose to play the game (which pieces you put where, and at which point in the game) is uniquely divergent.

In fact, you could also add Studiostone Alabaster Polar Bear carving kit and Tropical Forest 3D Painting to this list. There is structure to each, but no single right answer to the outcome. It is up to your student!

How Do I Fit This Much Reading into My Day?

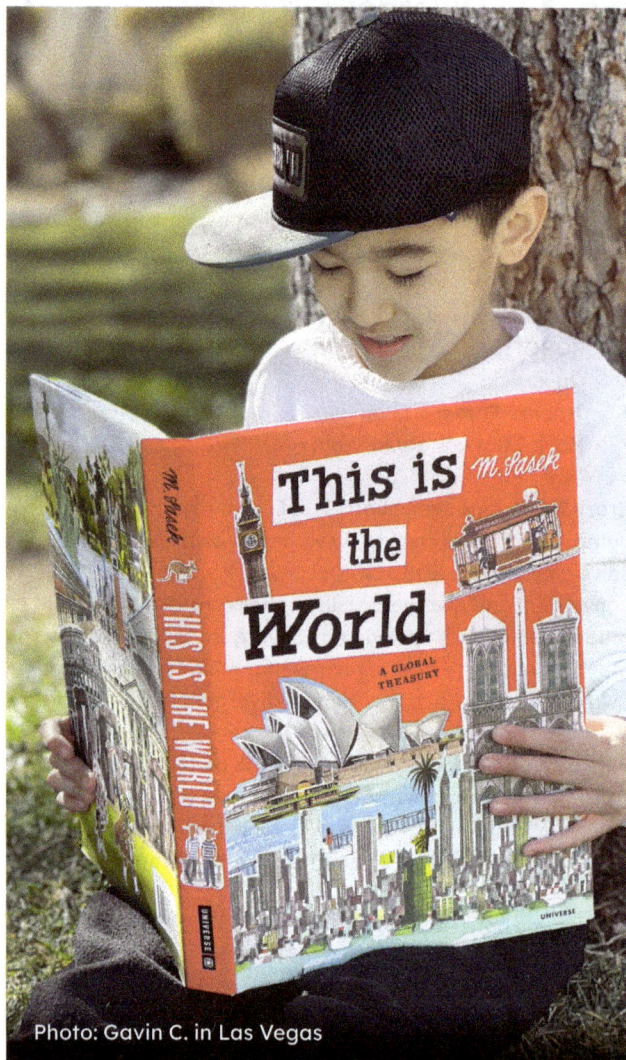

Photo: Gavin C. in Las Vegas

Here are 9 ideas to incorporate more reading into your family's busy schedule and unique schooling style:

1. Use Books of Various Lengths

A longer book than you'd usually pick may be perfect as an audiobook. On the flip side, if your child will be reading to a younger sibling or you are picking a new read-aloud for the whole gang, feel free to gear the book toward the younger participants, particularly if you're short on time.

2. Assign Independent Reading

This can be done in conjunction with quiet time or throughout the day. Our household often uses it as a strategy to calm the hyper and soothe the sad: I need you to go and snuggle into your favorite blanket and read one book and then come back ,and we'll try again. (Of course, your child does not need to be a competent reader yet to employ this strategy. Pictures may also be "read"!)

3. Quiet Time!

Does your family implement a quiet time already? Reading is a natural perk for that time. Quiet time can be as simple as setting a timer for 30 minutes (or more) and having your child relax with his favorite blanket or weighted lap pad and, of course, his book.

If it's possible for you to grab a book that you've been wanting to read and embrace the same plan, you'll be modeling what an ageless wonder reading can be. Of course, if your household is filled with little ones, it may be more practical for you to use this time for feeding babies or fixing dinner, and there's no shame in that, but consider your options as you plan your year.

4. Sneak Reading into Your Existing Routines

What routines are already going well for you? Could you incorporate a reading time into your existing bedtime routine, family devotions, car time, snack time, or other routine?

5. Audiobooks

Incorporate audiobooks and save the designated reader some time and energy. This is a particularly spectacular move for car time, art time, or puzzle time or even to smooth over particularly grumpy and hectic mealtimes.

6. Put the Busy Ones to Work

Encourage quiet activities such as puzzles, this year's STEM kit, or coloring while you read aloud or play the audiobook. It can be legitimately impossible for your kinesthetic learner to sit perfectly still and listen angelically, but break out the listening-time-only tools, and suddenly everyone looks forward to reading!

7. Brothers and Sisters

You don't have to be the only one reading to your child. Have your big kid read to a younger sibling as part of his school lessons. The older sibling will gain fluency as your younger one soaks up the one-on-one time. (No siblings in your home? How about cousins, playmates, grandparents, or even the family pet?)

8. Grandpa, Grandma, Aunties, Oh My!

Perhaps an auntie would welcome the opportunity to have Friday evenings be read-aloud time, complete with hot cocoa and scones. Or Grandma might love the idea of hosting all of her grandchildren once a month for a giant book party —each child could bring his favorite book to share. Too far away? Grandpa could record his favorite book (any audio recording app should work), then send the book to your child so that he can read along with Grandpa.

9. Get a Library Routine Going

Our family has loved reading since our toddler days, but we didn't use the library well until we settled into a simple routine. For us, that involves a central location for all library books and switching to a library branch with a slightly longer drive but more accessible hours. Those simple steps have quickly borne fruit with many more hours spent reading new books!

Help! My Book Says "Common Core"!

The Truth about Whether Your Timberdoodle Curriculum Kit Is Aligned with Common Core

Photo: The Glasman Family in Montana

There's been a lot of buzz, discussion, and anxiety in the homeschool community for more than a decade about the Common Core State Standards. Many of you have asked us what our stance is on the standards and whether our curriculum is designed to comply with them.

What Is the Common Core?

According to the CCSS website, "The Common Core State Standards Initiative is a state-led effort that established a single set of clear educational standards for kindergarten through 12th grade in English language arts and mathematics that states voluntarily adopt."

But Isn't That a Good Idea?

Growing up as an Air Force "brat," Deb, Timberdoodle's founder, attended many different schools throughout her educational career. She can tell you just how much easier it would have been for her if all of the schools had covered the same materials in the same order. Then she could have transferred effortlessly between them instead of missing critical information because the new school had already covered something her old school hadn't addressed yet. So yes, the concept may be brilliant, but there are some very valid concerns.

Why Homeschoolers Are Concerned

There is some real concern in the homeschooling community about what the Common Core Standards Initiative will mean to our families.

In an early article posted by the Homeschool Legal Defense Association, HSLDA Director of Federal Relations William Estrada wrote, "The CCSS specifically do not apply to private or homeschools….However, HSLDA has serious concerns with the rush to adopt the CCSS. HSLDA has fought national education standards for the past two decades. Why? National standards lead to national curriculum and national tests, and subsequent pressure on homeschool students to be taught from the same curricula."

Declining Quality?

Some in the homeschooling community have also expressed concern that as curriculum publishers endeavor to align with the CCSS, the educational quality in those texts will actually decrease rather than improve. Others are disenchanted with the atypical teaching methods employed by the CCSS, among other concerns.

What We Are Doing

At Timberdoodle, our approach is simple. We are ignoring the CCSS and continuing to search out crazy-smart curricula—exactly what we've been doing since 1985. Our specialty has always been hand-picking the best products in every subject area and offering the families who trust us the same products we have used or would happily use ourselves. And we have no plans to change the way we carefully review every resource we sell.

Some Products Do Say "Common Core"

Some of the items in almost every kit do, in fact, align with the CCSS. Not because we've sought that out but because the quality resources we've chosen for our curriculum are already up to that standard or beyond. It is no surprise to us that the excellent tools we are excited about are also good enough to exceed the qualifications for the CCSS.

This Has Never Changed and Will Not Change Now

At Timberdoodle, we work with trusted publishers and products we review carefully—not just in math and language arts but in all subject areas—so that we feel confident we are providing some of the best resources available for your children. Every time an item we've loved is revised (or stamped "Common Core"), we make sure that it has not been watered down or made confusing. Our goal is to exceed educational requirements, not by aligning our curriculum with any government standard but by continuing to find products that work well and meet the high standards we hold for our families and yours.

I Need a Homeschool Group, Right?

Community vs. Co-ops and More

No doubt you're familiar with some homeschool curricula that demand that their families form a group, take turns teaching, and meet weekly to press forward together. You may even wonder why you don't see pop-up Timberdoodle groups across the country/world.

This is a great question! The answer is very simple. You don't need one. Timberdoodle kits stand alone and are not teacher-intensive, meaning you can do it yourself and likely will!

Setting Your Own Pace—The Good

If you customized your kit at all, or if you have adjusted your schedule to your own life, it will make sense to you that your child does not need to be bound to any other child's progress. This is a huge goal of homeschooling: untether your child to proceed at precisely his own pace.

Setting Your Own Pace—The Bad

However, completely isolating yourself from other homeschoolers is far from ideal as well. You may not realize that the attention-span issues you are experiencing are completely age-appropriate or that it is atypical for your first-grader to be unable to follow a story without a lot of help.

Perhaps more importantly, there is a bit of good peer pressure for you in the form of community. If you are a relaxed "we'll do that next week" kind of person, it may be extremely helpful to have a friend asking you if you ever did get around to it and how it went.

Setting Your Own Pace—The Ugly

We are designed for community, and without it, the ugly side shows. From families who seem to care only about themselves to children who don't know how to interact with others, isolation is challenging on many fronts. COVID has certainly highlighted that for all of us!

We need each other, and we need to be deeply in each other's lives in order to flourish.

So Should I Start a Homeschool Group?

You could. And it could be lovely! But first take a look at your goals. Here are some that might apply:

- spend time with people I respect
- invest in others (Kids in your community? Parents who could use a mentor?)
- engage my kids with people who are different from them
- learn some skills
- have friends in real life, not just on social media
- team up for the parts of homeschooling I find stressful
- be encouraged to read widely
- get outside more

So many more ideas could be added! What things do you hope for this year, outside of finishing the materials in your kit? Once you know your goals, pick a format that works well for you and get the ball rolling.

Community Starters

- Start a group that meets at a different local park every Tuesday at noon. Pack lunch and enjoy some time with local moms and kids. Make a group text or other low-key way to make sure everyone knows they are welcome and knows which weeks are where.
- Join a local Facebook group that hosts several kid-friendly hikes a month. Participate those you can.
- Capitalize on P.E. and set aside time and money for ballet class, karate, or swim lessons this year.
- Find your local therapeutic riding / hippotherapy program and see if your horse-crazy teens could volunteer as sidewalkers.
- Google your child's interests. Is there a cooking class you could take together? Perhaps a theater club is starting, or a robotics camp?
- Don't despair if you, like us, find yourself limited by the ages or special needs of your children. A Zoom book study scheduled for after the children are in bed might be just the community you need.
- Buddy up! Look for opportunities for your children to serve. Can they help first-graders practice reading? Assist in after-school programming down the street? Take art or cookies to the local nursing home or shut-in every week? Assist a widow with yard work on Friday afternoons? Your opportunities will vary widely based on your children's ages and abilities, along with local needs. But this is well worth thinking through!
- If you've been involved with the foster care system, you know how critical and yet how draining it can be. Can you team up with a local family to bring lunch once a week and hang out with the kids for a few hours? Or could your teens go help teach younger children a skill? We had a teen come over each week to teach our little girls ballet. Not only is her relationship a huge investment in the girls' lives, but the fact that she comes here is a tremendous blessing as we juggle our erratic schedules and more medically complex little ones.
- Or, if you are that foster family, could you invite a local lonely grandmother-type to join you right in the crazy mess every Monday afternoon for art or reading time?
- Feel like you really need some accountability this year? Ask a friend if she'd be willing to go through your weekly checklists with you each Saturday morning and help you grow in your teaching skills / consistency.
- Make Thursday your Friends & Soup Night and have a standing invitation for friends to join you when possible.

Principles to Keep in Mind

If you're going to set a goal (e.g., get outside more with others), make a specific plan for doing that. (We will take a walk every morning at 9:00, and we will invite families A, B, and C to join us and invite their friends whenever they can.)

You aren't looking for perfection. You won't be able to meet every single week or complete every project you start. Don't panic if you're missing your walk this week because the baby has a doctor appointment or if you woke up with a cold and need to cancel swimming today. But if you make that your exception rather than your norm, you will see tremendous growth this year!

We all need community, but what it "should" look like in each family is something for you to decide, not us. Choose your adventure and get started. We suspect you'll find it is an amazing part of your routine!

Item-Specific Helps

Mosdos Ruby Weekly Assignments

A Sample Detailed Schedule

Here's one way to break down the Mosdos Ruby assignments to fit a 36-week schedule. The page numbers refer to the current student reader as of this writing.

You'll notice that some weeks have more titles assigned than others. We've taken into account the number of corresponding workbook pages and the length of the readings to come up with this schedule, but you should always feel free to rearrange in whatever fashion works for you. The surrounding content (e.g., introductory matter or sidebars) varies too, and your bright student will quickly notice that no two weeks have identical page counts. Remind him that this is a good time to be flexible and persistent. After all, he may even find that the longer stories end up being his favorites!

Please note that you need to complete only as many of the corresponding activity pages and assignments as you determine to be appropriate for your reader. Our family would have chosen to answer the Studying the Selection questions in the readers orally rather than in writing. We would also likely skip the writing assignments since you'll be covering writing systematically with *Daily 6-Trait Writing*.

Unit 1: The Things That Matter

Week 1
Lesson in Literature...What Is a Story? — page 2
Leah's Pony — page 4
The Way — page 16
Jill's Journal: On Assignment from the Dirty Thirties — page 18
Activity pages and assignments

Week 2
Lesson in Literature...What Is Plot? — page 22
Supergrandpa — page 24
If You Think You Are Beaten — page 36
Activity pages and assignments

Week 3
Lesson in Literature...Characters — page 38
Two Big Bears — page 40
March Bear — page 51
Jill's Journal: On Assignment in China — page 53
Activity pages and assignments

Week 4
Lesson in Literature...What Is Setting? — page 56
Mom's Best Friend — page 58
Activity pages and assignments

Week 5
Lesson in Literature...What Is Theme? — page 70
The Tiger, the Persimmon, and the Rabbit's Tail — page 72
Here She Is — page 84
Unit 1 Wrap-Up — page 86
Activity pages and assignment

Unit 2: Clarity

Week 6
Lesson in Literature...What Is Internal Conflict? — page 92
Sato and the Elephants — page 94
Purple Snake — page 108
Activity pages and assignment

Week 7
Lesson in Literature...What Is External Conflict? — page 110
Amelia's Road — page 112
Since Hanna Moved Away — page 122
Jill's Journal: On Assignment in the Supermarket and
   the Field — page 124
Activity pages and assignment

Week 8
Lesson in Literature...What Is Sequence? — page 128
The Hatmaker's Sign — page 130
Activity pages and assignment

Week 9
Lesson in Literature...What Is Foreshadowing? — page 144
Dad, Jackie, and Me — page 146
Analysis of Baseball — page 158
Activity pages and assignment

Week 10
Lesson in Literature...What Is a Main Idea? — page 160
And Now the Good News — page 162
Hurt No Living Thing — page 173
Jill's Journal: "They Loaded Up Their Trunks and They Moved
   to Tennessee" — page 175

Unit 2 Wrap-Up — page 180
Activity pages and assignment

Unit 3: Head, Hands, Heart

Week 11
Lesson in Literature...Characters — page 186
Eddie, Incorporated — page 188
Jill's Journal: On Assignment at the Town Dump — page 209
Activity pages and assignment

Week 12
Lesson in Literature...Major and Minor Characters — page 212
Heatwave! — page 214
Be Glad Your Nose Is on Your Face — page 228
Activity pages and assignment

Week 13
Lesson in Literature...What Is Dialogue? — page 230
The Wright Brothers — page 232
The Inventor Thinks Up Helicopters — page 244
Jill's Journal: On Assignment in Dayton, Ohio — page 246
Activity pages and assignment

Week 14
Lesson in Literature...What Is Internal Dialogue? — page 250
The Imperfect/Perfect Book Report — page 252
You and I — page 264
Activity pages and assignment

Week 15
Lesson in Literature...Point of View — page 266
Justin Lebo — page 268

Holding Up the Sky: A Tale from China — page 278
Unit 3 Wrap-Up — page 280
Activity pages and assignment

Poetry

These weeks have no workbook pages. Enjoy the break!

Week 16
Bird's Square Dance — page 288
Thistles — page 289
Whirligig Beetles — page 290
This Is the Key — page 291
Any assignment

Week 17
A Bridge Engineer — page 294
A Bugler Named Dougal MacDougal — page 294
A Funny Young Fellow Named Perkins — page 295
A Native of Chalamazug — page 295
A Gullible Rancher Named Clyde — page 295
Any assignment

Week 18
Seasons Haiku — page 298
A Seeing Poem — page 302
Popsicle — page 303
Any assignment

Week 19
The Shark — page 306
Dust of Snow — page 307
Any assignment

Week 20
Some Opposites — page 310
Tortillas Like Africa — page 311
Any assignment

Week 21
Good Hotdogs — page 314
Jackrabbit — page 316
Any assignment

Unit 4: Caring

Week 22
Lesson in Literature...Creating a Setting — page 324
Earthquake Terror — page 326
Michael Is Afraid of the Storm — page 343
Jill's Journal: On Assignment in New Madrid — page 345
Activity pages and assignment

Week 23
Lesson in Literature...What Is Imagery? — page 348
The Gift — page 350
For You — page 364
Activity pages and assignment

Week 24
Lesson in Literature...Comparing Settings — page 366
Toto — page 368
In This Jungle — page 382
Activity pages and assignment

Week 25
Lesson in Literature...What Is Mood? — page 384
Owl Moon — page 386
Activity pages and assignment

Week 26
Lesson in Literature...What Is Biography? — page 398
Homeward the Arrow's Flight — page 400
Jill's Journal: On Assignment in Britain to Speak with the
    Lady with the Lamp — page 415
Unit 4 Wrap-Up — page 420
Activity pages and assignment

Unit 5: Determination

Week 27
Lesson in Literature...Author's Purpose — page 426
Underwater Rescue — page 428
Today the Dolphins Came to Play — page 442
Jill's Journal: On Assignment Exploring the Mesoamerican
    Reef — page 444
Activity pages and assignment

Week 28
Lesson in Literature...What Is Stated Theme? — page 446
The Seven Children — page 448
Activity pages and assignment

Week 29
Lesson in Literature...What Is Implied Theme? — page 460
The Garden of Happiness — page 462
Johnny Appleseed — page 475

Jill's Journal: On Assignment in Crista's Garden — page 477
Activity pages and assignment

Week 30
Lesson in Literature...Drawing Conclusions — page 480
One Grain of Rice — page 482
Activity pages and assignment

Week 31
Lesson in Literature...Compare and Contrast — page 498
Maria's House — page 500
City I Love — page 518
Unit 5 Wrap-Up — page 520
Activity pages and assignment

Unit 6: The Grand Finalé

Week 32
Lesson in Literature...Elements of Fiction — page 526
The Bridge Dancers — page 528
Activity pages and assignment

Week 33
Lesson in Literature...Elements of Nonfiction — page 542
Dancing Bees — page 544
Activity pages and assignment

Week 34
Lesson in Literature...Elements of Drama — page 550
Name This American — page 552
Activity pages and assignment

Week 35
Lesson in Literature...Fictionalized Biography — page 568
Boss of the Plains — page 571
Activity pages and assignment

Week 36
Lesson in Literature...Pulling It All Together — page 584

Stone Fox — page 586
Unit 6 Wrap-Up — page 602
Activity pages and assignment

Now celebrate! You've made your way through a very rich study of literature!

Photo: The Whitaker Family in Unalaska, Alaska

The Reading Challenge

Reading Challenge Questions & Answers

Practical Details to Set Up a Productive Routine

So you love the idea of the reading challenge, but you'd like a boost to get you started? You've come to the right place!

Customize This!

You'll find a few ideas here for each challenge, but don't forget that you're not bound to our list. There are literally hundreds more options that may be even better for your family. Use these pages as starter ideas, not as your final list.

Will I See the Same Books Over and Over?

You might see some books repeated, but not too often. Each grade has its own set of books to read, so most books won't show up in multiple places, though about 25% might appear in more than one grade. This happens if a book fits really well in different challenges.

However, many books within your grade could fit into more than one category, but we only list them in one place within your challenges to make it easier for you. So if you want to read more than one book from a certain challenge, you'll probably find another challenge that fits the book if you skim through the list.

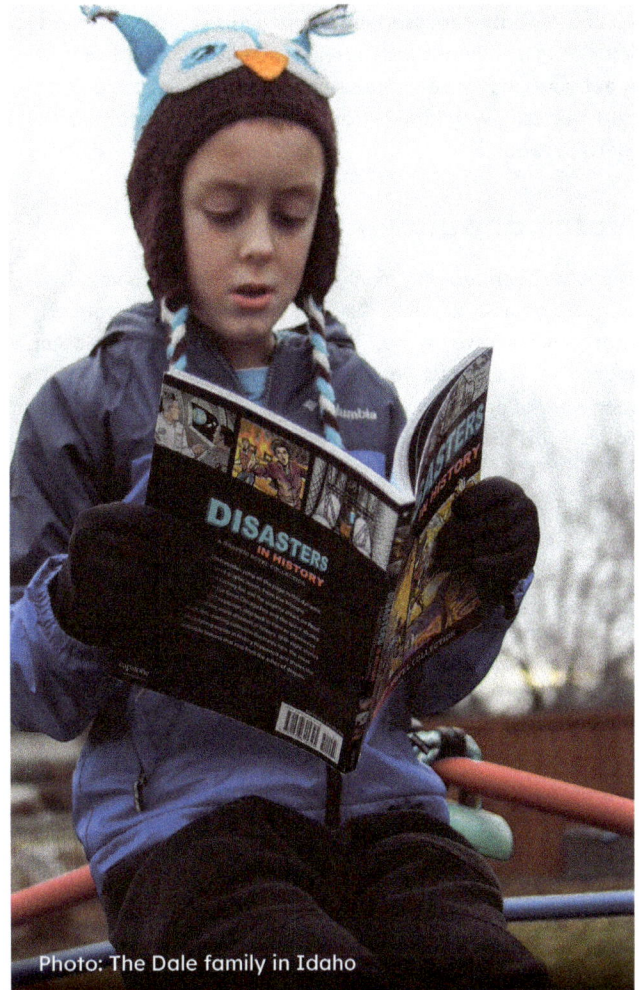

Photo: The Dale family in Idaho

A Variety of Reading Levels

As you probably guessed, these are a mix of books to read to your child and books that he will read himself. Read-alouds meet your child's tremendous need for literacy, language, and stories, giving him a strong sense of why he wants to learn to read.

Notes about Our Book Ideas

If you've been reading to your child long (or if you've perused your local public library), you've probably noticed that families have very different standards for their reading materials. The books we've listed here are ones that members of our team have read, have added to their "I want to read this" list, or have had recommended to them.

Even among our team there is a wide range in what titles our families would find acceptable. Some of us find fantasy objectionable but will gladly read a scarier adventure story than other families would be comfortable with. Others of us consider those fantasy titles to be an interesting addition and worthy of much discussion!

Similarly, some of us prefer to avoid titles with troublesome language, bad attitudes, or other concerns, while others prefer to read and discuss them. We've opted to include titles with abandon, knowing that you can flip through them at the library to determine if they are a good fit for your family.

This is not a "Timberdoodle would sell these books if we could" list. We can't vouch for each of the titles, and we certainly can't know which ones are a good fit for your particular family. We even include titles with things we don't like, knowing that what is a "burn the book" moment for one family is a discussion starter for others. And if ever there was a time for deep discussion around many topics, this is that time!

We also are not above editing on the fly. If a book will be helpful for our kids except for a particular line, we'll often edit that line out as we read aloud. This would likely be a poor solution for permanent bookshelf residents, but it's perfect for library books!

Mostly we're providing this list to give you some ideas, just in case you're drawing a blank in thinking of books for a particular topic. Use these ideas as the jumping-off point for which they are intended, and, as always, we highly recommend previewing the books yourself.

Use Your Library

We can't overemphasize how useful your local library will be to you this year. Now that most libraries allow you to place books on hold online, you'll find that you can use any spare hour in your day to request books for the next challenges, and then whoever is in town next can swing by the library and pick them up. If you've not yet become a dedicated library user, start now!

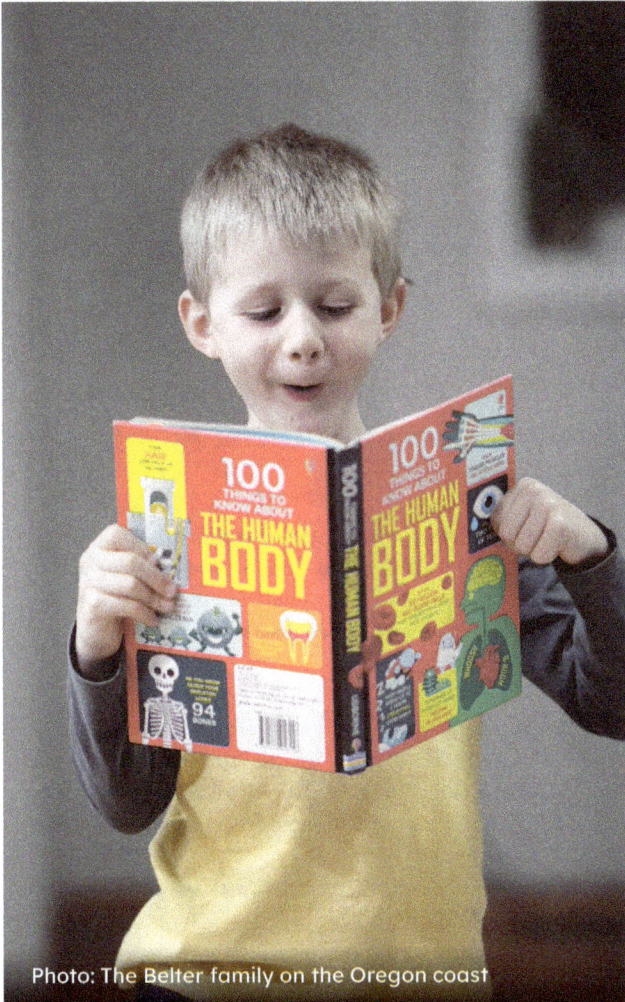

Photo: The Belter family on the Oregon coast

When we checked, roughly half of these books were available in some format from our local library. Since each library's selection varies, we've opted to keep them all listed here knowing that your selection will be different from ours.

If you have Kindle Unlimited or Everand, you will have still another library to choose from.

Reading and Talking

If you're newer to reading together, our biggest tips for you are these. First, just read together. Whether you read through one book a month or several a day, you are making memories and enjoying stories together.

Second, make sure you're discussing what you're reading. This doesn't need to be a formal book report on every book you encounter (please no!) or a tedious question-and-answer session every evening. Instead, talk as you go about the character qualities you see displayed, the kindnesses done (and undone), and the problems being solved. What does your child like about the book? What would he change if he could? If he was a character, which one would he be?

Simple questions build connection, emotional intelligence, worldview, logic, observational skills, and so much more.

Photo: The Foy Family

Reading and Racism

It is worth noting that many of the books we grew up on have terrible racist undertones (e.g., the neighbor in *Little House on the Prairie* who announces that "the only good Indian is a dead Indian" or those Tintin titles which portray people of color in negative ways). We have kept some of these titles on our reading list because racism is a crucial issue to discuss thoughtfully with your child, rather than just pretending it doesn't exist.

What Can You Do: Teaching Your Family To Be Anti-Racist by Tasha

Being anti-racist requires intentional and continuous action on your part as a mom. You set the tone for your home. Your children see what you truly value and believe. Waiting for "the right time" or when your child is "old enough" will be too late.

1. Point out racism in movies and literature. Classics especially. Think Little House on the Prairie *for a minute. Dr. Seuss. To Kill a Mockingbird. Adventures of Huckleberry Finn. I am not saying don't have these books on your shelves, but I am saying read them with your child and discuss why the author depicted the People of Color in those negative or rude ways.*

2. *Discuss hard stuff. You should always be explicit with children, of all ages, that racism is very hurtful and always wrong. Teach your child to be an ally. Teach them to speak up when they hear someone saying racist comments or jokes. Teach them to be a friend to the refugees, the low-income kids, the disabled kids, the Hispanic kids, etc., etc.*

3. *Diversify your shelves. Find books and movies about People of Color, preferably where the storyline isn't about diversity. Continuously expose your child to the beauty and richness of the world—the peoples, cultures, religions, buildings, fashions, and foods. Watch the hard things. Read hard books. Don't shy away from the hard conversations.*

4. *Don't make racist jokes. Period. Racist jokes are so hurtful because they are basically saying, "You are so far beneath me, I can both conceal and express my prejudice and you can't do anything about it because it's socially acceptable—it's 'only' a joke."*

We've quoted Tasha (previously a Timberdoodle blogger) here with her permission. Thank you, Tasha!

Reading and Gender Bias

Have you ever reflected that girls are commonly expected to enjoy books with both male and female protagonists, while boys are told that books featuring girls are "girl books" and unworthy of their attention? (Want to read up on this? See the thought-provoking book *A Place to Belong* by Amber O'Neal Johnston.)

I'm not talking about following interests here. By all means your dragon lover should enjoy books on dragons and your artsy person will appreciate books detailing technique. (And in our household it is a girl who loves the dragon books and a boy who is a particularly gifted artist.)

So what do I mean? Don't relegate books with female heroes to the girls' shelves. Just as girls enjoy books with male heroes, boys can and should enjoy books featuring female heroines. Enjoy each book for its content and teach your boys that yes, girls (and their stories) matter and are worthy of their time and attention.

Make This List Even Better

We love your book recommendations and feedback! Did you find a book you loved this year? We'd love to add your recommendations! Just shoot us a note at books@timberdoodle.com and let us know. Or were you perhaps disenchanted with one of our suggestions? Please let us know!

At the end of the year, fill out the Book Awards page near the end of this handbook and submit that. We'll be thrilled to credit you 50 Doodle Dollar reward points (worth $2.50 off your next order) as our thank-you for taking the time to share.

Tracking Your Reading Challenge

Can You Completely Fill This In?

If you're doing the topics out of order, check off completed topics as you go, and you'll be able to tell at a glance which topics are left. Across the page, color in one book after completing each week's reading to see your progress through the challenge at a glance. You can also record your book choices using the chart on each topic's page. If you prefer a printable version of the progress tracker please visit your Timberdoodle.com account for your printable download. You can even print it poster-sized! (Didn't order directly from Timberdoodle.com? Contact us with your order number, and we'll get you set up!)

Reading Challenge Topics

United Kingdom	☐	China	☐
Indian Subcontinent	☐	Late 1800s in the U.S.	☐
Eastern Asia	☐	Early 1900s in the U.S.	☐
Middle East	☐	Central America	☐
Southern Europe	☐	World War I	☐
American Civil War	☐	Fantasy / Sci-Fi	☐
Canada	☐	The Great Depression	☐
Western Europe	☐	Northern Europe	☐
Eastern Europe	☐	Nazi Invasion / Holocaust	☐
Western Africa	☐	World War II	☐
Northern Africa	☐	The Cold War	☐
Oceania	☐	Space Exploration	☐
Central Africa	☐	Civil Rights Movement	☐
Eastern Africa	☐	Health	☐
Southern Africa	☐	1970s-1990s in the U.S.	☐
South America	☐	21st Century in the U.S.	☐
Southeast Asia	☐	Caribbean Islands	☐
United States	☐	Travel/Transportation	☐

timberdoodle
2024-2025
READING CHALLENGE

United Kingdom

Challenge 1

Anno's Britain by Mitsumasa Anno

Celtic Tales: Fairy Tales and Stories of Enchantment from Ireland, Scotland, Brittany, and Wales by Kate Forrester

Kings & Queens of Great Britain: A Very Peculiar History by Antony Mason

Meet Our New Student from Great Britain by Tamra Orr

Susan by Kate Klimo (Dog Diaries)

This Is Britain by M. Sasek

United Kingdom by Madeline Donaldson (Country Explorers)

United Kingdom by Sarah Tieck (Explore the Countries)

Victoria: May Blossom of Britannia, England, 1829 by Anna Kirwan (The Royal Diaries)

Who Was Queen Elizabeth II? by Megan Stine (Who HQ)

Who Was Queen Victoria? by Jim Gigliotti (Who HQ)

Who Was Winston Churchill? by Ellen Labrecque(Who HQ)

England

The 101 Dalmatians by Dodie Smith

The Adventures of Robin Hood by Marcia Williams

Air Raid Search and Rescue by Marcus Sutter (Soldier Dogs)

Archie's War by Marcia Williams

Bard of Avon by Diane Stanley

Basil and the Royal Dare by Cathy Hapka (The Great Mouse Detective)

Basil of Baker Street by Eve Titus (The Great Mouse Detective)

A Bear Called Paddington by Michael Bond

Big Ben by Kristine Spanier (Whole Wide World)

The Big London Treasure Hunt by Jennifer Gray (The Travels of Ermine)

B Is for Big Ben: An England Alphabet by Pamela Duncan Edwards

The Bluebeard Room by Carolyn Keene (Nancy Drew)

The Boy, the Bear, the Baron, the Bard by Gregory Rogers

Brick City: London by Warren Elsmore

Burn: Michael Faraday's Candle by Darcy Pattison (Moments in Science)

The Castle Crime by Ron Roy (A to Z Mysteries)

Charles Dickens: The Man Who Had Great Expectations by Diane Stanley

Charlotte in London by Joan MacPhail Knight

The Cheshire Cheese Cat: A Dickens of a Tale by Carmen Agra Deedy

Clue in the Castle Tower by Sarah Masters Buckey (American Girl)

Dangerous Plays by Carolyn Keene (Nancy Drew Girl Detective)

The Dangerous Transmission by Franklin W. Dixon (Hardy Boys)

Don't Know Much about the Kings and Queens of England by Kenneth C. Davis

The Door in the Wall by Marguerite de Angeli

Elizabeth I: Red Rose of the House of Tudor by Kathryn Lasky (The Royal Diaries)

England by Jean F. Blashfield (Enchantment of the World)

England by Jessica Dean (All Around the World)

England by Anita Ganeri (Benjamin Blog and His Inquisitive Dog)

England by Elma Schemenauer (Countries: Faces and Places)

England by Walter Simmons (Exploring Countries)

The Family from One End Street by Eve Garnett

Goldwhiskers by Heather Vogel Frederick (Spy Mice)

Good Masters! Sweet Ladies! by Laura Amy Schlitz

Good Queen Bess: The Story of Elizabeth I of England by Diane Stanley

Hettie and the London Blitz: A World War II Survival Story by Jenni L. Walsh (Girls Survive)

In Search of the Black Rose by Carolyn Keene (Nancy Drew)

Isabel: Taking Wing by Annie Dalton (Girls of Many Lands)

A Kid's Guide to England by Jack L. Roberts

Let's Visit London! by Lisa Manzione (The Adventures of Bella and Harry)

The London Deception by Franklin W. Dixon (Hardy Boys)

Mac Undercover by Mac Barnett (Mac B., Kid Spy)

Magical Mission by Geronimo Stilton

May Goes to England by Bonnie Bryant (Pony Tails)

The Mystery at Big Ben by Carole Marsh (Around the World Iin 80 Mysteries)

Mystery at Moorsea Manor by Carolyn Keene (Nancy Drew)

The Mystery of the Queen's Jewels by Gertrude Chandler Warner (The Boxcar Children)

Paddington Here and Now by Michael Bond

Patsy Goes to England: An American Girl's Adventures in 1950s Britain by Patricia Daoust

Peggy's Letters by Jacqueline Halsey (Orca Young Readers)

Peter Pan by J.M. Barrie

A Place to Hang the Moon by Kate Albus

Pup at the Palace by Ben M. Baglio (Animal Ark)

Rags and Riches by Mary Pope Osborne (Magic Tree House Fact Tracker)

The Railway Children by E. Nesbit

Rip to the Rescue by Miriam Halahmy

The Secret Garden by Frances Hodgson Burnett

Sherlock Holmes and the Disappearing Diamond by Sam Hearn (Baker Street Academy)

Stage Fright on a Summer Night by Mary Pope Osborne (Magic Tree House)

The Story of London by Richard Brassey

Terror in the Tower of London by W. N. Brown (Great Escapes)

Thea Stilton and the Phantom of the Orchestra by Thea Stilton

This Is London by M. Sasek

Welcome to England by Elma Schemenauer

Where Is Stonehenge? by True Kelley (Who HQ)

Where Is the Tower of London? by Janet B. Pascal (Who HQ)

Who Was A.A. Milne? by Sarah Fabiny (Who HQ)

Who Was Beatrix Potter? by Sarah Fabiny (Who HQ)

Who Was Henry VIII? by Ellen Labrecque (Who HQ)

Who Was Jane Austen? by Sarah Fabiny (Who HQ)

Who Was J.R.R. Tolkien? by Pam Pollack (Who HQ)

Who Was Lewis Carroll? by Pam Pollack (Who HQ)

Who Was Queen Elizabeth? by June Eding (Who HQ)

Who Was William Shakespeare? by Celeste Davidson Mannis (Who HQ)

Will's Words by Jane Sutcliffe

The Wind in the Willows by Kenneth Grahame

Wishes and Wellingtons by Julie Berry

You Wouldn't Want to Be a Medieval Knight! by Fiona Macdonald

You Wouldn't Want to Be a Shakespearean Actor! by Jacqueline Morley

You Wouldn't Want to Be a Victorian Miner! by John Malam

You Wouldn't Want to Be a Victorian Schoolchild! by John Malam

You Wouldn't Want to Be a Victorian Servant! by Fiona Macdonald

You Wouldn't Want to Be Ill in Tudor Times! by Kathryn Senior

England, continued

You Wouldn't Want to Be in a Medieval Dungeon! by Fiona Macdonald

You Wouldn't Want to Be in the Great Fire of London! by Jim Pipe

You Wouldn't Want to Be Married to Henry VIII! by Fiona Macdonald

You Wouldn't Want to Live in a Medieval Castle! by Jacqueline Morley

You Wouldn't Want to Work in a Victorian Mill! by John Malam

Scotland

Beyond the Heather Hills by Melissa Wiley (Little House: The Martha Years)

B Is for Bagpipes: A Scotland Alphabet by Eve Begley Kiehm

A Clash of Swords in Scotland by Karyn Collett

The Clue of the Whistling Bagpipes by Carolyn Keene (Nancy Drew)

Down to the Bonny Glen by Melissa Wiley (Little House: The Martha Years)

The Far Side of the Loch by Melissa Wiley (Little House: The Martha Years)

Let's Visit Edinburgh! by Lisa Manzione (The Adventures of Bella and Harry)

Little House in the Highlands by Melissa Wiley (Little House: The Martha Years)

Rollo in Scotland by Jacob Abbott

The Secret of the Cave by Arthur S. Maxwell

The Scotch Twins by Lucy Fitch Perkins

Scotland by Janeen R. Adil (A Question and Answer Book)

Scotland by Anita Ganeri (Benjamin Blog and His Inquisitive Dog)

Scotland by Marycate O'Sullivan (Countries: Faces and Places)

Scotland by Kristine Spanier (All Around the World)

Scotland by Melanie Waldron (Countries Around the World)

Scotland by Nel Yomtov (Enchantment of the World)

Scotland by Derek Zobel (Exploring Countries)

Scottish Fairy Tales by Donald A. Mackenzie (Dover Children's Thrift Classics)

Sputnik's Guide to Life on Earth by Frank Cottrell Boyce

Thea Stilton and the Secret of the Old Castle by Thea Stilton

This Is Edinburgh by M. Sasek

The Water Horse by Dick King-Smith

You Wouldn't Want to Be Mary, Queen of Scots! by Fiona Macdonald

Wales

Elen's Island by Eloise Williams

Lily by Whitney Sanderson (Horse Diaries)

A String in the Harp by Nancy Bond

Sweet Pizza by G.R. Gemin

Wales by Liz Sonneborn (Enchantment of the World)

The Welsh Fairy Book by W. Jenkyn Thomas

Welsh Fairytales by Philip Wilson

Who Was Princess Diana? by Ellen Labrecque (Who HQ)

	The Book You Chose	Date Completed
1.1 *Light Reader*		
1.2 *Interested Reader*		
1.3 *Avid Reader*		
1.4 *Committed Reader*		
1.5 *Enthralled Reader*		

Indian Subcontinent

Challenge 2

Bangladesh

Bangladesh by Heather Adamson (Blastoff Readers: Exploring Countries)

Bangladesh by Sweetie Peason (Countries We Come From)

Bangladesh by Tamra B. Orr (Enchantment of the World)

Country Jumper in Bangladesh by Claudia Dobson-Largie

Iqbal and His Ingenious Idea: How a Science Project Helps One Family and the Planet by Elizabeth Suneby

Rickshaw Girl by Matali Perkins

Twenty-Two Cents: Muhammad Yunus and the Village Bank by Paula Yoo

India

All My Noble Dreams and Then What Happens by Gloria Whelan

Balarama: A Royal Elephant by Ted and Betsy Lewin (Adventures Around the World)

Basil and the Cave of Cats by Eve Titus (The Great Mouse Detective)

Bollywood Burglary by Geronimo Stilton

Book Uncle and Me by Uma Krishnaswami

Boys without Names by Kashmire Sheth

The Cherry Tree by Ruskin Bond

A Children's History of India by Subhadra Sen Gupta

Country Jumper in India by Claudia Dobson-Largie

A Crazy Day with Cobras by Mary Pope Osborne (Magic Tree House)

Cultural Traditions in India by Molly Aloian

Daughter of the Mountains by Louise A. Rankin

The Diaries of Robin's Travels: Agra by Ken and Angie Lake

The Elephant's Friend and Other Tales from Ancient India retold by Marcia Williams

The Elephant Doctor of India by Janie Chodosh

Finders Keepers? A Bus Trip in India by Robert Arnett

Follow Me around India by Wiley Blevins

Gandhi (DK Eyewitness)

Immigrants from India and Southeast Asia by Nel Yomtov (Fact Finders: Immigration Today)

In Andal's House by Gloria Whelan (Tales of the World)

India by Sunita Apte (A True Book)

India by Jim Bartell (Blastoff Readers: Exploring Countries)

India by Anita Ganeri (Benjamin Blog and His Inquisitive Dog)

India by Lisa Harkrader (Top Ten Countries of Recent Immigrants)

India by Joyce Markovics (Countries We Come From)

India by Joanne Mattern (All Around the World)

India by Julie Murray (Explore the Countries)

India by Don Nardo (Enchantment of the World)

India by Anna Obiols (On the Way to School)

India by Lucia Raatma (Social Studies Explorers: It's Cool to Learn about Countries)

India by Patrick Ryan (Countries: Faces and Places)

India by Tom Streissguth (Country Explorers)

India by Lisa Zamosky (Social Studies Readers)

Indian Children's Favorite Stories: Fables, Myths and Fairy Tales by Rosemarie Somaiah

Indian Culture by Anita Ganeri (Global Cultures)

In the Heart of the Village: The World of the Indian Banyan Tree by Barbara Bash

Jahanara: Princess of Princesses, India, 1627 by Kathryn Lasky (The Royal Diaries)

The Jungle Book by Rudyard Kipling

Just So Stories by Rudyard Kipling

A Kid's Guide to India by Jack L. Roberts

Manjhi Moves a Mountain by Nancy Churnin

My Life in India by Patience Coster (A Child's Day In…)

The Mystery of the Suspicious Spices by Harper Paris (Greetings from Somewhere)

The Mystery of the Taj Mahal by Carole Marsh (Around the World in 80 Mysteries)

Neela: Victory Song by Chitra Banerjee Divakaruni (Girls of Many Lands)

Nur Juhan of India by Shirin Yim Bridges (The Thinking Girl's Treasury of Real Princesses)

Prita Goes to India by Prodeepta Das (Children Return to Their Roots)

The Rajah's Rice: A Mathematical Folktale from India by David Barry

Rickshaw Girl by Mitali Perkins

The Secret Kingdom: Nek Chand, a Changing India, and a Hidden World of Art by Barb Rosenstock

T Is for Taj Mahal: An India Alphabet by Varsha Bajaj

Taj Mahal: A Story of Love and Empire by Elizabeth Mann (Wonders of the World)

Tales from India retold by J. E. B. Gray

Tales of India: Folk Tales from Bengal, Punjab, and Tamil Nadu illustrated by Svabhu Kohli and Viplov Singh

Thea Stilton and the Prince's Emerald by Thea Stilton

Tiger Boy by Mitali Perkins

Tigers in Terai by Amanda Lumry and Laura Hurwitz (Adventures of Riley)

Travel to India by Matt Doeden (Searchlight Books: World Traveler)

Welcome to India by Patrick Ryan

Where Is the Taj Mahal? by Dorothy and Thomas Hoobler (Who HQ)

Who Was Gandhi? by Dana Meachen Rau (Who HQ)

The Wolf Girls by Jane Yolen and Heidi E. Y. Stemple (An Unsolved Mystery from History)

Nepal

The Breathtaking Mystery on Mt. Everest: The Top of the World by Carole Marsh (Around the World in 80 Mysteries)

Chandra's Magic Light: A Story in Nepal by Theresa Heine

A Dog Named Haku: A Holiday Story from Nepal by Margarita Engle

I, Doko: The Tale of a Basket by Ed Young

Kami and the Yaks by Andrea Stenn Stryer

Mountain Mission by Kristin Earhart (Race the Wild)

Nepal by Chaya Glaser (Countries We Come From)

Nepal by Lisa Owings (Blastoff Readers: Exploring Countries)

Nepali Heritage by Tamra Orr

Pakistan

For the Right to Learn: Malala Yousafzai's Story by Rebecca Langston-George

Iqbal by Francesca D'Adamo

Let's Visit Pakistan by John C. Caldwell

Malala: My Story of Standing Up for Girls' Rights by Malala Yousafzai and Sarah J. Robbins

Pakistan by Madeline Donaldson (Country Explorers

Pakistan by Ann Heinrichs (Enchantment of the World)

Pakistan by Ellen Labrecque (Social Studies Explorers: It's Cool to Learn about Countries)

Pakistan, continued

Pakistan by Julie Murray (Explore the Countries)
Pakistan by Gillia M. Olson (A Question and Answer Book)
Pakistan by Sharon Sharth (Countries: Faces and Places)
Pakistan by Kate Shroup (Exploring World Cultures)
Pakistan by Walter Simmons (Exploring Countries)
She Dared: Malala Yousafzai by Jenni L. Walsh
A Thousand Questions by Saadia Faruqi
We Visit Pakistan by Bonnie Hinman
Who Is Malala Yousafzai? by Dinah Brown (Who HQ)

Sri Lanka

Cultural Traditions in Sri Lanka by Cynthia O'Brien
Sri Lanka by Laura L. Sullivan (Exploring World Cultures)
Your Passport to Sri Lanka by Nancy Dickmann

	The Book You Chose	Date Completed
2.1 *Light Reader*		
2.2 *Interested Reader*		
2.3 *Avid Reader*		
2.4 *Committed Reader*		
2.5 *Enthralled Reader*		

Eastern Asia

Challenge 3

Japan

All About Japan: Stories, Songs, Crafts and Games for Kids by Willamarie Moore

The Battle of Iwo Jima: Turning the Tide of War in the Pacific by Steven Otfinoski (Tangled History)

The Big Wave by Pearl S. Buck

The Boy Who Drew Cats and Other Japanese Fairy Tales by Lafcadio Hearn (Dover Children's Thrift Classics)

The Cat Who Went to Heaven by Elizabeth Coatsworth

Chibi: A True Story from Japan by Barbara Brenner

Country Jumper in Japan by Claudia Dobson-Largie

Cultural Traditions in Japan by Lynn Peppas

Dragon of the Red Dawn by Mary Pope Osborne (Magic Tree House)

The Dropping of the Atomic Bombs by Roberta Baxter (Perspectives Library)

The Fox's Kettle by Laura Langston

The Ghost in the Takaido Inn by Dorothy Hoobler

Hachiko Waits by Leslea Newman

Heart of a Samurai by Margi Preus

Hiroshima and Nagasaki: The Atomic Bombings That Shook the World by Michael Burgan (Tangled History)

I Survived the Japanese Tsunami 2011 by Lauren Tarshis

Japan by Ruth Bjorkland (Enchantment of the World)

Japan by Michael Burgan (A Question and Answer Book)

Japan by Jessica Dean (All Around the World)

Japan by Julie Murray (Explore the Countries)

Japan by Anita Ganeri (Benjamin Blog and His Inquisitive Dog)

Japan by Elma Schemenauer (Countries: Faces and Places

Japan by Colleen Sexton (Blastoff Readers: Exploring Countries)

Japan by Barbara A. Somervill (Social Studies Explorers: It's Cool to Learn about Countries)

Japan by Thomas Streissguth (Country Explorers)

Japanese Culture by Teresa Heapy (Global Cultures)

The Japanese Ninja Surprise by Jeff Brown (Flat Stanley's Worldwide Adventures)

Kazunomiya: Prisoner of Heaven, Japan, 1858 by Kathryn Lasky (The Royal Diaries)

A Kid's Guide to Japan by Jack L. Roberts

Lost in the Wilderness of Japan by Anna Hagele (Where's Eli Moore?)

Mac Cracks the Code by Mac Barnett (Mac B., Kid Spy)

Manjiro: The Boy Who Risked His Life for Two Countries by Emily Arnold McCully

Mieko and the Fifth Treasure by Eleanor Coerr

My Awesome Japan Adventure: A Diary about the Best 4 Months Ever! by Rebecca Otowas

The Mystery at Mt. Fuji by Carole Marsh (Around the World in 80 Mysteries)

Night of the Ninjas by Mary Pope Osborne (Magic Tree House)

Sadako and the Thousand Paper Cranes by Eleanor Coerr

A Samurai Castle by Fiona MacDonald

Shipwrecked! The True Adventures of a Japanese Boy by Rhoda Blumberg

Spotlight on Japan by Bobbie Kalman

Swept Away: The Story of the 2011 Japanese Tsunami by Rebecca Rissman (Tangled History)

Sword of the Samurai: Adventure Stories from Japan by Eric A. Kimmel

Japan, continued

Tales from Japan retold by Helen and William McAlpine

Tales of Japan: Traditional Stories of Monsters and Magic by Kotaro Chiba

Thea Stilton and the Cherry Blossom Adventure by Thea Stilton

The Thirteenth Pearl by Carolyn Keene (Nancy Drew)

Tokyo City Trails by Anna Claybourne (Lonely Planet Kids)

Travel to Japan by Matt Doeden (Searchlight Books: World Traveler)

The Way of the Samurai by Geronimo Stilton

What Was the Bombing of Hiroshima? by Jess Brallier (Who HQ)

Yuki and the One Thousand Carriers by Gloria Whelan (Tales of the World)

Korea

All About Korea: Stories, Songs, Crafts and More by Ann Martin Bowler

Brother's Keeper by Julie Lee

Country Jumper in North Korea by Claudia Dobson-Largie

Country Jumper in South Korea by Claudia Dobson-Largie

I Escaped North Korea by Ellie Crowe and Scott Peters

In the Shadow of the Sun by Anne Sibley O'Brien

The Kite Fighters by Linda Sue Park

Korean Celebrations: Festivals, Holidays and Traditions by Tina Cho

Korean Children's Favorite Stories: Fables, Myths, and Fairy Tales by Kim So-Un

Korean Heritage by Tamra Orr

The Korean War by Joe Giorello (Great Battles for Boys)

The Korean War by Gary Jeffrey (Graphic Modern History: Cold War Conflicts)

The Korean War: An Interactive Modern History Adventure by Michael Burgan (You Choose: Modern History)

The Legend of Hong Kil Dong: The Robin Hood of Korea by Anne Sibley O'Brien

North Korea by Patricia J. Kummer (Enchantment of the World)

North Korea by Susan E. Haberle (A Question and Answer Book)

North Korea by Julie Murray (Explore the Countries)

Pigling: A Cinderella Story by Dan Jolley (Graphic Myths and Legends)

Seesaw Girl by Linda Sue Park

Sergeant Reckless Braves the Battlefield: Heroic Korean War Horse by Bruce Berlund (Graphic Library)

Sgt. Reckless the War Horse by Melissa Higgins (Animal Heroes)

A Single Shard by Linda Sue Park

Sondok: Princess of the Moon and Stars, Korea, 595 A.D. by Sheri Holman (Royal Diaries)

South Korea by Susan E. Haberle (A Question and Answer Book)

South Korea by Lisa Harkrader (Top Ten Countries of Recent Immigrants)

South Korea by Joanne Mattern (All Around the World)

South Korea by Jennifer A. Miller (Country Explorers)

South Korea by Julie Murray (Explore the Countries)

South Korea by Barbara Somervill (Enchantment of the World)

South Korea by Derek Zobel (Blastoff Readers: Exploring Countries)

Spotlight on South Korea by Bobbie Kalman

Tales of a Korean Grandmother: 32 Traditional Tales from Korea by Frances Carpenter
Welcome to South Korea by Patrick Ryan
We Visit South Korea by Amie Leavitt
Your Passport to South Korea by Nancy Dickmann (World Passport)

Mongolia

Ghengis Khan and the Mongol Horde by Harold Lamb (Landmark)
The Gobi Desert by Molly Aloian (Deserts Around the World)
The Great Bear Rescue: Saving the Gobi Bears by Sandra Markle
Horse Song: The Naadam of Mongolia by Ted Lewin (Adventures Around the World)
The Khan's Daughter: A Mongolian Folktale by Laurence Yep
Mongolia by Ruth Bjorklund (Enchantment of the World)
Mongolia by Jan Reynolds (Vanishing Cultures)
Mongolian Empire (DinoBibi: History for Kids)
Mongolian Wild Horse by Susan H. Gray (Road to Recovery)

The Moose of Ewenki by Gerelchimeg Blackcrane
Saving the Ghost of the Mountain by Sy Montgomery (Scientists in the Field)
Sorghaghtani of Mongolia by Shirin Yim Bridges (The Thinking Girl's Treasure of Real Princesses)
Valley of the Giant Skeletons by Geronimo Stilton
Where the Winds Meet by Mi-hwa Joo (Global Kids Storybooks)
Who Was Genghis Khan? by Nico Medina (Who HQ)

Taiwan

Evie and Andrew's Asian Adventures in Taiwan by Katie Do Guthrie
Taiwan by Lisa Owings (Exploring Countries)
Taiwan: Just in Time by Crameye Junker (The Adventurous Mailbox)
Typhoon Holidays by Yi Ling Hsu (Global Kids Storybooks)
Welcome to Taiwan by Vanessa Wan (Welcome to My Country)

	The Book You Chose	**Date Completed**
3.1 *Light Reader*		
3.2 *Interested Reader*		
3.3 *Avid Reader*		
3.4 *Committed Reader*		
3.5 *Enthralled Reader*		

Middle East

Challenge 4

Afghanistan

Afghan Dreams: Young Voices of Afghanistan by Tony O'Brien

Afghanistan by Ariel Factor Birdoff (Countries We Come From)

Afghanistan by Ruth Bjorkland (Enchantment of the World

Afghanistan by Julie Murray (Explore the Countries)

Afghanistan by Kathryn Stevens (Countries: Faces and Places)

Afghanistan by Gillia M. Olson (A Question and Answer Book

Afghanistan by Lisa Owings (Blastoff Readers: Exploring Countries)

Afghanistan by Peggy Parks (Nations in Conflict)

Ali's Story: A Real-Life Account of His Journey from Afghanistan by Andy Glynne (Seeking Refuge)

Brave with Beauty: A Story of Afghanistan by Maxine Rose Schur

Caesar the War Dog by Stephen Dando-Collins

Country Jumper in Afghanistan by Claudia Dobson-Largie

Extra Credit by Andrew Clements

I See the Sun in Afghanistan by Dedie King

Immigrants from Afghanistan and the Middle East by Nel Yomtov (Immigration Today)

The Library Bus by Bahram Rahman (Global Kids Storybooks)

Nasreen's Secret School: A True Story from Afghanistan by Jeanette Winter

Razia's Ray of Hope: One Girl's Dream of an Education by Elizabeth Suneby (CitizenKid)

A Refugee's Journey from Afghanistan by Helen Mason (Leaving My Homeland)

Returning to Afghanistan by Linda Barghoorn (Leaving My Homeland)

Ryan Pitts: Afghanistan: A Firefight in the Mountains of Wanat by Michael P. Spradlin (Medal of Honor)

Saving Kabul Corner by N. H. Senzai

Semper Fido by C. Alexander London (Dog Tags)

Shooting Kabul by N. H. Senzai

The Soviet War in Afghanistan by Gary Spender Jeffrey (Graphic Modern History: Cold War Conflicts)

Waiting for the Owl's Call by Gloria Whelan (Tales of the World)

War in Afghanistan: An Interactive Modern History Adventure by Matt Doeden and Blake Hoena (You Choose: Modern History)

Armenia

Armenia by Sakina Dhilawala (Cultures of the World)

Armenia by Martin Hintz (Enchantment of the World)

Country Jumper in Armenia by Claudia Dobson-Largie

Azerbaijan

Country Jumper in Azerbaijan by Claudia Dobson-Largie

Bahrain

Bahrain by Robert Cooper and Jo-Ann Spilling (Cultures of the World)

Bahrain by Mary Virginia Fox (Enchantment of the World)

Bahrain by Kristine Spanier (All Around the World)

Country Jumper in Bahrain by Claudia Dobson-Largie

Iran

Ali Baba: Fooling the Forty Thieves by Marie P. Croall (Graphic Myths and Legends)

The Girl with a Brave Heart: A Tale from Tehran by Rita Jahanfouz

The Green Musician by Mahvash Shaheg

Iran by Brandy Bauer (A Question and Answer Book)

Iran by Madeline Donaldson (Country Explorers)

Iran by Julie Murray (Explore the Countries)

Iran by G.S. Prentzas (Social Studies Explorers: It's Cool to Learn about Countries)

Iran by Elma Schemenauer (Countries: Faces and Places)

Iran by Walter Simmons (Blastoff Readers: Exploring Countries)

Iran by Barbara A. Somervill (Enchantment of the World)

Iran by Kristine Spanier (All Around the World)

The Knight, the Princess, and the Magic Rock: A Classic Persian Tale by Sara Azizi

My New Home after Iran by Heather C. Hudak (Leaving My Homeland)

Navid's Story: A Real-Life Account of His Journey from Iran by Andy Glynne (Seeking Refuge)

Qutlugh Terkan Khatun of Kirman by Shirin Yim Bridges (The Thinking Girl's Treasury of Real Princesses)

Soldier Bear by Bibi Dumon Tak

Welcome to Iran by Elma Schemenauer

We Visit Iran by Pete DiPrimio

Your Passport to Iran by Sara Petersohn (World Passport)

Iraq

Alia's Mission: Saving the Books of Iraq by Mark Alan Stamaty

Country Jumper in Iraq by Claudia Dobson-Largie

Iraq by Joanne Mattern (All Around the World)

Iraq by Julie Murray (Explore the Countries)

Iraq by Lisa Owings (Blastoff Readers: Exploring Countries)

Iraq by Kremena Spengler (A Question and Answer Book)

Iraq by Nel Yomtov (Enchantment of the World)

Iraq in Pictures by Stacy Taus-Bolstad (Visual Geography)

The Librarian of Basra by Jeanette Winter

My New Home after Iraq by Ellen Rodger (Leaving My Homeland)

A Refugee's Journey from Iraq by Ellen Rodger (Leaving My Homeland)

Silent Music: A Story of Baghdad by James Rumford

Sinbad: Sailing into Peril by Marie P. Croall (Graphic Myths and Legends)

War Heroes: Voices from Iraq by Allan Zullo (10 True Tales)

Welcome to Iraq by Kathryn Stevens

We Visit Iraq by Claire O'Neal

The World Is Not a Rectangle: A Portrait of Architect Zaha Madid by Jeanette Winter

Israel

Bible Lands (DK Eyewitness)

Cultural Traditions in Israel by Molly Aloian

Israel by Marcia Gresko (Country Explorers)

Israel by Julie Murray (Explore the Countries)

Israel by Lisa Owings (Countries of the World)

Israel by Thomas Persano (Countries We Come From)

Israel by Walter Simmons (Blastoff Readers: Exploring Countries)

Israel by Kristine Spanier (All Around the World)

Israel by Kremena Spengler (A Question and Answer Book)

Israel by Nel Yomtov (Enchantment of the World)

Jewish Fairy Tales by Gerald Friedlander (Dover Children's Thrift Classics)

Let's Visit Jerusalem! by Lisa Manzione (The Adventures of Bella and Harry)

Travel to Israel by Matt Doeden (Searchlight Books: World Traveler)

Welcome to Israel by Elma Schemenauer

We Visit Israel by Laya Saul

Jordan

Country Jumper in Jordan by Claudia Dobson-Largie
The Double Helix by Trudi Trueit (Explorer Academy)
Jordan by Amy Rechner (Country Profiles)
Jordan by Liz Sonneborn (Enchantment of the World)
Petra by Kristine Spanier (Whole Wide World)
Welcome to Jordan by Grace Pundyk

Kuwait

Country Jumper in Kuwait by Claudia Dobson-Largie
Kuwait by Kristine Spanier (All Around the World)
Kuwait by Terri Willis (Enchantment of the World)
We Visit Kuwait by Kathleen Tracy

Lebanon

Lebanon by Mary L. Englar (A Question and Answer Book)
Lebanon by Lisa Owings (Blastoff Readers: Exploring Countries)
Lebanon by Thomas Persano (Countries We Come From)
Sami and the Time of the Troubles by Florence Parry Heide

Oman

Oman by David C. King (Cultures of the World)
Oman by Leila Merrell Foster (Enchantment of the World)
The Turtle of Oman by Naomi Shihab Nye
We Visit Oman by Khadija Ejaz (Your Land and My Land)

Palestine

A Queen to the Rescue: The Story of Henrietta Szold, Founder of Hadassah by Nancy Churnin
Sitti and the Cats: A Tale of Friendship by Sally Bahous Allen
Sitti's Secrets by Naomi Shihab Nye
The Sound of Freedom by Kathy Kacer (The Heroes Quartet)

Saudi Arabia

Saudi Arabia by Abby Anderson (Country Explorers)
Saudi Arabia by Kathleen W. Deady (A Question and Answer Book)
Saudi Arabia by Lisa Owings (Blastoff Readers: Exploring Countries)
Saudi Arabia by Bob Temple (Countries: Faces and Places)
Saudi Arabia by Nel Yomtov (Enchantment of the World)
Tales from the Arabian Nights by Donna Jo Napoli
Usborne Illustrated Arabian Nights by Anna Milbourne
Welcome to Saudi Arabia by Bob Temple
We Visit Saudi Arabia by Kathleen Tracy
Yatimah by Catherine Hapka (Horse Diaries)

Syria

The Cat Man of Aleppo by Karim Shamsi-Basha
My New Home after Syria by Linda Barghoorn (Leaving My Homeland)
A Refugee's Journey from Syria by Helen Mason (Leaving My Homeland)
Syria by Mary L. Englar (A Question and Answer Book)
Syria by Dale Eva Gelfand (Countries of the World)
Syria by Julie Murray (Explore the Countries)
Syria by Nel Yomtov (Enchantment of the World)

Turkey

Artemisa of Caria by Shirin Yim Bridges (The Thinking Girl's Treasury of Real Princesses)
The Donkey Who Carried the Wounded by Jackie French
The Diaries of Robin's Travels: Istanbul by Ken and Angie Lake
Kitu and the Architecture Adventures in Istanbul by Julia-Su Gursu
Let's Visit Istanbul! by Lisa Manzione (The Adventures of Bella and Harry)

Turkey, continued

Leyla: The Black Tulip by Alev Lytle Croutier (Girls of Many Lands)

The Mysterious Mannequin by Carolyn Keene (Nancy Drew)

The Star Dunes by Trudi Trueit (Explorer Academy)

Thea Stilton and the Riddle of the Ruins by Thea Stilton

Turkey by Madeline Donaldson (Country Explorers)

Turkey by Mary L. Englar (A Question and Answer Book)

Turkey by Vicky Franchino (Social Studies Explorers: It's Cool to Learn about Countries)

Turkey by Julie Murray (Explore the Countries)

Turkey by Tamra B. Orr (Enchantment of the World)

Turkey by Lisa Owings (Blastoff Readers: Exploring Countries)

We Visit Turkey by Amelia Laroche (Your Land and My Land)

Your Passport to Turkey by Nancy Dickmann (World Passport)

United Arab Emirates

Ali's Amazing Adventures in Dubai by Janeen Tedford

The Diaries of Robin's Travels: Dubai by Ken and Angie Lake

United Arab Emirates by David C. King (Cultures of the World)

United Arab Emirates by Barbara A. Somervill (Enchantment of the World)

United Arab Emirates by Kristine Spanier (All Around the World)

Yemen

My New Home after Yemen by Heather C. Hudak (Leaving My Homeland)

A Refugee's Journey from Yemen by Heather Hudak (Leaving My Homeland)

We Visit Yemen by Claire O'Neal (Your Land and My Land)

Yemen by Jean F. Blashfield (Countries Around the World)

Yemen by Liz Sonneborn (Enchantment of the World)

	The Book You Chose	Date Completed
4.1 *Light Reader*		
4.2 *Interested Reader*		
4.3 *Avid Reader*		
4.4 *Committed Reader*		
4.5 *Enthralled Reader*		

Southern Europe

Challenge 5

Albania

Albania by Corey Anderson (Countries We Come From)
Albania by Wil Mara (Enchantment of the World)
Country Jumper in Albania by Claudia Dobson-Largie

Bosnia and Herzegovina

Bosnia and Herzegovina by Kevin Blake (Countries We Come From)
Bosnia and Herzegovina by JoAnn Milovojevic (Enchantment of the World)
Country Jumper in Bosnia–Herzegovina by Claudia Dobson-Largie
Flowers for Sarajevo by John McCutcheon
World In Between by Kenan Trebincevic and Susan Shapiro

Bulgaria

Bulgaria by Meish Goldish (Countries We Come From)
Bulgaria by Kirilka Stavreva (Cultures of the World)
Country Jumper in Bulgaria by Claudia Dobson-Largie
Folk Tales and Fables from Bulgaria translated by Diana Nikolova
Looking at Bulgaria by Bronja Prazdny
Myths and Legends from Bulgaria translated by Diana Nikolova

Croatia

Country Jumper in Croatia by Claudia Dobson-Largie
Croatia by Martin Hintz (Enchantment of the World)
Croatia by Emily Rose Oachs (Exploring Countries)
The Traveling Circus by Marie-Louise Gay and David Homel
Who Was Nikola Tesla? by Jim Gigliotti (Who HQ)

Greece

Ancient Greece (DK Eyewitness)
Ancient Greece by Linda Bailey (Good Times Travel Agency)
Ancient Greece by Sandra Newman (A True Book)
Ancient Greece and the Olympics by Mary Pope Osborne (Magic Tree House Fact Tracker)
Ancient Greece for Kids by Catherine Fet
Ancient Greeks by Stephanie Turnbull
Country Jumper in Greece by Claudia Dobson-Largie
Cultural Traditions in Greece by Lynn Peppas
The Curse of the Acropolis: Athens, Greece by Carole Marsh (Around the World in 80 Mysteries)
D'Aulaires Book of Greek Myths by Ingri and Edgar Parin d'Aulaire
Greece by Jim Bartell (Exploring Countries)
Greece by Madeline Donaldson (Country Explorers)
Greece by Ann Heinrichs (Enchantment of the World)
Greece by Julie Murray (Explore the Countries)
Greece by Patrick Ryan (Countries: Faces and Places)
Greece by Kristine Spanier (All Around the World)
Greece by Kremena Spengler (A Question and Answer Book)
Greece by Lisa Zamosky (Primary Source Readers)
Greece: Why Ask Why by Crameye Junker (The Adventurous Mailbox)
Growing Up in Ancient Greece by Chris Chelepi
Hour of the Olympics by Mary Pope Osborne (Magic Tree House)
Let's Visit Athens! by Lisa Manzione (The Adventures of Bella and Harry)
The Mystery of the Secret Society by Harper Paris (Greetings from Somewhere)
Parthenon by Kristine Spanier (Whole Wide World)

Greece, continued

The Parthenon: The Height of Greek Civilization by Elizabeth Mann (Wonders of the World)

The Shattered Helmet by Franklin W. Dixon (Hardy Boys)

Thea Stilton and the Missing Myth by Thea Stilton

This Is Greece by M. Sasek

Tools of the Ancient Greeks by Kris Bordessa

What Are the Summer Olympics? by Gail Herman (Who HQ)

What's Your Angle, Pythagoras? by Julie Ellis

Where Is the Parthenon? by Roberta Edwards (Who HQ)

You Wouldn't Want to Be a Greek Athlete! by Michael Ford

You Wouldn't Want to Be a Slave in Ancient Greece! by Fiona MacDonald

You Wouldn't Want to Be in the Ancient Greek Olympics! by Michael Ford

Z Is for Zeus: A Greek Mythology Alphabet by Helen L. Wilbur

Italy

The Adventures of Seymour and Hau: Italy by Melanie Morse and Thomas McDade

All the Way to America by Dan Yaccarino

Beppo by Emma Brock

Biancabella and Other Italian Fairy Tales by Anne Macdonell

Blockhead: The Life of Fibonacci by Joseph D'Agnese

Colosseum by Kristine Spanier (Whole Wide World)

Country Jumper in Italy by Claudia Dobson-Largie

Cultural Traditions in Italy by Adrianna Morganelli

Detectives in Togas by Henry Winterfeld

The Diaries of Robin's Travels: Venice by Ken and Angie Lake

Folk Tales from Italy translated by Diana Nikolova

Follow Me around Italy by Wiley Blevins

The Happy Hollisters and the Punch and Judy Mystery by Jerry West

Italy by Mary Berendes (Countries: Faces and Places)

Italy by Jessica Dean (All Around the World)

Italy by Madeline Donaldson (Country Explorers)

Italy by Anita Ganeri (Benjamin Blog and His Inquisitive Dog)

Italy by Walter Simmons (Exploring Countries)

Italy by Sarah Tieck (Explore the Countries)

Jack Montgomery, World War II: Gallantry at Anzio by Michael P. Spradlin

Leonardo: Beautiful Dreamer by Robert Byrd

Leonardo da Vinci by Diane Stanley

Leonardo's Horse by Jean Fritz

Let's Visit Florence! by Lisa Manzione (The Adventures of Bella and Harry)

Let's Visit Rome! by Lisa Manzione (The Adventures of Bella and Harry)

Let's Visit Venice! by Lisa Manzione (The Adventures of Bella and Harry)

The Lure of the Italian Treasure by Franklin W. Dixon (Hardy Boys)

Maria and the Plague: A Black Death Survival Story by Natasha Deen (Girls Survive)

Michelangelo by Diane Stanley

Michelangelo for Kids by Simonetta Carr

Miranda the Great by Eleanor Estes

The Mystery at the Roman Colosseum by Carole Marsh (Around the World in 80 Mysteries)

The Mystery in Venice by Geronimo Stilton

The Mystery of the Mosaic by Harper Paris (Greetings from Somewhere)

Mystery of the Roman Ransom by Henry Winterfeld
Operation Secret Recipe by Geronimo Stilton
The Phantom of Venice by Carolyn Keene (Nancy Drew)
Pippo the Fool by Tracey E. Fern
Pompeii–Buried Alive! by Edith Kudhardt
Red Sails to Capri by Ann Weil
The Roman Colosseum: The Story of the World's Most Famous Stadium and Its Deadly Games by Elizabeth Mann (Wonders of the World)
A Roman Holiday by Thea Stilton
Rome City Trails by Moira Butterfield (Lonely Planet Kids)
The Sound of Danger by Mac Barnett (Mac B., Kid Spy)
Starry Messenger by Peter Sis
Thea Stilton and the Dancing Shadows by Thea Stilton
Thea Stilton and the Venice Masquerade by Thea Stilton
This Is Rome by M. Sasek
This Is Venice by M. Sasek
Travel to Italy by Matt Doeden (Searchlight Books: World Traveler)
Vacation under the Volcano by Mary Pope Osborne (Magic Tree House)
Vivaldi and the Invisible Orchestra by Stephen Costanza
Welcome to Italy by Mary Berendes
Where Is the Colosseum? by Jim O'Connor (Who HQ)
Your Passport to Italy by Nancy Dickmann
You Wouldn't Want to Be a Roman Gladiator! by John Malam
You Wouldn't Want to Be a Roman Soldier! by David Stewart
You Wouldn't Want to Live in Pompeii! by Johm Malam

Portugal

A Children's History of Portugal by Sergio Luis De Carvalho
Mouse Overboard! by Geronimo Stilton
Portugal by Ettagale Blauer (Enchantment of the World)
Portugal by Kari Schuetz (Exploring Countries)
The Secret of the Soldiers Gold by Franklin W. Dixon (Hardy Boys)
Who Was Ferdinand Magellan? by Sydelle Kramer (Who HQ)
Who Was Leonardo da Vinci? by Roberta Edwards (Who HQ)

Spain

Anno's Spain by Mitsumasa Anno
Barcelona City Trails by Moira Butterfield
Calvino by Whitney Sanderson (Horse Diaries)
The Diaries of Robin's Travels: Barcelona by Ken and Angie Lake
Favorite Fairy Tales Told in Spain by Virginia Haviland
Isabel: Jewel of Castilla, Spain, 1466 by Carolyn Meyer (The Royal Diaries)
Isabella of Castile by Shirin Yim Bridges (The Thinking Girl's Treasury of Real Princesses)
Let's Visit Barcelona! by Lisa Manzione (The Adventures of Bella and Harry)
Spain by Marcia Amidon Lusted (Countries of the World)
Spain by William Anthony (Welcome to My World)
Spain by Mary Berendes (Countries: Faces and Places)
Spain by Madeline Donaldson (Country Explorers)
Spain by Anita Ganeri (Benjamin Blog and His Inquisitive Dog)

Spain by Rachel Grack (Exploring Countries)
Spain by Amy Rechner (Country Profiles)
Spain by Barbara A. Somervill (Enchantment of the World)
Spain by Kristine Spanier (All Around the World)
Spain by Kremena Spengler (A Question and Answer Book)
Spain by Sarah Tieck (Explore the Countries)
Thea Stilton and the Spanish Dance Mission by Thea Stilton

Welcome to Spain by Mary Berendes
Who Was Pablo Picasso? by True Kelley (Who HQ)
Your Passport to Spain by Douglas Hustad
You Wouldn't Want to Be a Pirate's Prisoner! by John Malam
You Wouldn't Want to Sail in the Spanish Armada! by Johm Malam

	The Book You Chose	**Date Completed**
5.1 Light Reader		
5.2 Interested Reader		
5.3 Avid Reader		
5.4 Committed Reader		
5.5 Enthralled Reader		

American Civil War

Challenge 6

Amelina Carrett: Bayou Grand Coeur, Louisiana, 1863 by Kathleen Duey (American Diaries)

At Battle in the Civil War: An Interactive Battlefield Adventure by Allison Lassieur (You Choose: Battlefields)

At the Battle of Antietam: An Interactive Battlefield Adventure by Matt Doeden (You Choose: American Battles)

At the Battle of Bull Run: An Interactive Battlefield Adventure by Eric Braun (You Choose: American Battles)

At the Battle of the Ironclads: An Interactive Battlefield Adventure by Matt Doeden (You Choose: American Battles)

The Battle of Bull Run by Martin Gitlin (Perspectives Library)

The Battle of Bunker Hill: An Interactive History Adventure by Michael Burgan (You Choose: History)

The Battle of Gettysburg by Roberta Baxter (Perspectives Library)

Ben and the Emancipation Proclamation by Pat Sherman

Big Bad Ironclad! by Nathan Hale (Hazardous Tales)

B Is for Battle Cry: A Civil War Alphabet by Patricia Bauer

Black Civil War Soldiers: The 54th Massachusetts Regiment by Susan K. Baumann (Jr. Graphic African American History)

Boys of Wartime: Will at the Battle of Gettysburg, 1863 by Laurie Calkhoven

Bull Run by Paul Fleischman

Chance of a Lifetime by Deborah Kent (Saddles, Stars, and Stripes)

Charlotte Spies for Justice: A Civil War Survival Story by Nikki Shannon Smith (Girls Survive)

Civil War (DK Eyewitness)

The Civil War by Bentley Boyd (Chester the Crab Comix with Content)

The Civil War by Joe Giorello (Great Battles for Boys)

The Civil War: An Interactive History Adventure by Matt Doeden (You Choose: History)

Civil War Battleship: The Monitor by Gare Thompson

Civil War Breakout by W. N. Brown (Great Escapes)

The Civil War: Confederate Leaders by Bentley Boyd (Chester the Crab Comix with Content)

The Civil War: Early Battles by Jim Ollhoff

The Civil War Experience: An Interactive History Adventure by Matt Doeden (You Choose: History)

The Civil War for Kids: A History with 21 Activities by Janis Herbert

The Civil War: Leaders and Generals by Jim Ollhoff

The Civil War: Spies, Secret Missions, and Hidden Facts by Stephanie Bearce

Civil War Sub by Kate Boehm Jerome

The Civil War: The Final Years by Jim Ollhoff

The Civil War through Photography by Darlene R. Stille (Documenting U.S. History)

The Civil War: Turning Points by Jim Ollhoff

Civil War Witness: Mathew Brady's Photos Reveal the Horrors of War by Don Nardo

Diary of Carrie Berry: A Confederate Girl by Carrie Berry

Divided We Fall by C. Alexander London (Dog Tags)

Escape by Night by Laurie Myers

The Gettysburg Address: A Graphic Adaptation by Jonathan Hennessey

Gettysburg by MacKinlay Kantor

I Survived the Battle of Gettysburg by Lauren Tarshis

John Brown's Raid on Harpers Ferry by Jason Glaser (Graphic Library)

John Greenwood's Journey to Bunker Hill by Mary Rhodes Figley

John Lincoln Clem: Civil War Drummer Boy by E. F. Abbott
The Journal of Rufus Rowe: A Witness to the Battle of Fredericksburg by Sid Hite
The Last Brother: A Civil War Tale by Trinka Hakes Noble
A Light in the Storm by Karen Hesse (Dear America)
Maddie Retta Lauren: Georgia, 1864 by Kathleen Duey (American Diaries)
The Mystery at Fort Sumter by Carole Marsh (Real Kids, Real Places)
On Enemy Soil by Jim Murphy
The Perilous Road by William O. Steele
A Savage Thunder: Antietam and the Bloody Road to Freedom by Jim Murphy
Silent Thunder: A Civil War Story by Andrea Davis Pinkney
The Songs of Stones River: A Civil War Novel by Jessica Gunderson
Spies of the Civil War: An Interactive Espionage Adventure by Michael Burgan (You Choose: Spies)
True Stories of the Civil War by Nel Yomtov
Turn Homeward, Hannalee by Patricia Beatty

United No More! Stories of the Civil War by Doreen Rappaport and Joan Verniero
Virginia's Civil War Diary series by Mary Pope Osborne (My America)
We Were There at the Battle of Gettysburg by Alida Sims Malkus
We Were There When Grant Met Lee at Appomattox by Earl Schenck Miers
When Were the First Slaves Set Free during the Civil War? And Other Questions about the Emancipation Proclamation by Shannon Knudsen
When Will This Cruel War Be Over? by Barry Deneberg (Dear America)
Willie McLean and the Civil War Surrender by Candice Ransom
Yankee Blue or Rebel Gray? A Family Divided by the Civil War by Kate Connell
You Wouldn't Want to Be a Civil War Soldier! by Thomas Ratliff

The Book You Chose		**Date Completed**
6.1 Light Reader		
6.2 Interested Reader		
6.3 Avid Reader		
6.4 Committed Reader		
6.5 Enthralled Reader		

Canada

Challenge 7

A Is for Algonquin: An Ontario Alphabet by Lovenia Gorman

The Adventures of Sajo and Her Beaver People by Grey Owl

After Peaches by Michelle Mulder

Amelia and Me by Heather Stemp

Anne of Green Gables by L.M. Montgomery

B Is for Bluenose: A Nova Scotia Alphabet by Susan Tooke

Belle of Batoche by Jacqueline Guest (Orca Young Readers)

The Big Book of Canada: Exploring the Provinces and Territories by Christopher Moore

The Big Snapper by Katherine Holubitsky (Orca Young Readers)

Birdie for Now by Jean Little (Orca Young Readers)

The Broken Blade by William Durbin

C Is for Chinook: An Alberta Alphabet by Dawn Welykochy

Call of the Klondike: A True Gold Rush Adventure by David Meissner and Kim Richardson

Canada by Jessica Dean (All Around the World)

Canada by Anita Ganeri (Benjamin Blog and His Inquisitive Dog)

Canada by Karen Latchana Kenney (Countries of the World)

Canada by Julie Murray (Explore the Countries)

Canada by Nathan Olson (A Question and Answer Book)

Canada by Elma Schemenauer (Countries: Faces and Places)

Canada by Colleen Sexton (Exploring Countries)

Canada by Liz Sonneborn (Enchantment of the World)

Canadian Summer by Hilda van Stockum

Catching Spring by Sylvia Olsen (Orca Young Readers)

Country Jumper in Canada by Claudia Dobson-Largie

The Creature in Ogopogo Lake by Gertrude Chandler Warner (The Boxcar Children)

Crossing Niagara: The Death–Defying Tightrope Adventures of the Great Blondin by Matt Tavares

Discovering Emily by Jacqueline Pearce (Orca Young Readers)

Elijah of Buxton by Christopher Paul Curtis

Ellie's New Home by Becky Citra (Orca Young Readers)

Emily of New Moon by L.M. Montgomery

Emily's Dream by Jacqueleine Pearce (Orca Young Readers)

F Is for Fiddlehead: A New Brunswick Alphabet by Marilyn Lohnes

F Is for French: A Quebec Alphabet by Elaine Arsenault

Far North by Will Hobbs

Field Trip to Niagara Falls by Geronimo Stilton

Five Stars for Emily by Kathleen Cook Waldron (Orca Young Readers)

Flight from Bear Canyon by Anita Daher (Orca Young Readers)

Flight from Big Tangle by Anita Daher (Orca Young Readers)

G Is for Golden Boy: A Manitoba Alphabet by Larry Verstraete

The Gift of the Inuksuk by Michael Ulmer (Tales of the World)

Going Places by Fran Hurcomb (Orca Young Readers)

Great Bear Rainforest by Patti Wheeler and Keith Hemstreet (Travels with Gannon and Wyatt)

Grizzly Peak by Jonathan London (Aaron's Wilderness)

Growing Up in Wild Horse Canyon by Karen Autio

The Happy Hollisters and the Ice Carnival Mystery by Jerry West

The Happy Hollisters at Snowflake Camp by Jerry West

Helen Thayer's Arctic Adventure: A Woman and a Dog Walk to the North Pole by Sally Isaacs

Hidden Mountain by Franklin W. Dixon (Hardy Boys)

I Is for Island: A Prince Edward Island Alphabet by Hugh MacDonald

The Intrepid Canadian Expedition by Jeff Brown (Flat Stanley's Worldwide Adventures)

The Island Horse by Susan Hughes

Jake Reynolds: Chicken or Eagle? by Sara Leach (Orca Young Readers)

Jo's Journey by Nikki Tate (Orca Young Readers)

The Kids Book of Aboriginal Peoples in Canada by Diane Silvey

The Kids Book of Canada by Barbara Greenwood

The Kids Book of Canadian History by Carlotta Hacker

L Is for Land of Living Skies: A Saskatchewan Alphabet by Linda Aksomitis

The Last Loon by Rebecca Upjohn (Orca Young Readers)

Let's Visit Vancouver! by Lisa Manzione (The Adventures of Bella and Harry)

Loonies and Toonies: A Canadian Number Book by Michael Ulmer

Lucky's Mountain by Dianne Maycock (Orca Young Readers)

M Is for Maple: A Canadian Alphabet by Michael Ulmer

M Is for Mountie: A Royal Canadian Mounted Police Alphabet by Polly Harvath

Mighty Muskrats Mystery series by Michael Hutchinson

Milligan Creek series by Kevin Miller

Murphy and Mousetrap by Sylvia Olsen (Orca Young Readers)

The Mystery of the Calgary Stampede by Gertrude Chandler Warner (The Boxcar Children)

The Mystery of the Northern Lights by Carol Marsh (Around the World in 80 Mysteries)

The Niagara Falls Mystery by Gertrude Chandler Warner (The Boxcar Children)

No Way Out by Franklin W. Dixon (Hardy Boys)

On the Trail of the Bushman by Anita Daher (Orca Young Readers)

Owls in the Family by Farley Mowat

P Is for Puffin: A Newfoundland and Labrador Alphabet by Janet Skirving

Paddle-to-the-Sea by Holling Clancy Holling

Pat of Silver Bush by L.M. Montgomery

Poachers in the Pingos by Anita Daher (Orca Young Readers)

Polar Bear Puzzle by Amanda Lumry (Adventures of Riley)

Racing for Diamonds by Anita Daher (Orca Young Readers)

Rainbow Valley by L.M. Montgomery

The Reunion by Jacqueline Pearce (Orca Young Readers)

Road Block by Yolanda Ridge (Orca Young Readers)

S Is for Spirit Bear: A British Columbia Alphabet by G. Gregory Roberts

Saara's Passage by Karen Autio

Second Watch by Karen Autio

The Secret of Devil Lake by Robert Sutherland

Secret of the Night Ponies by Joan Hiatt Harlow

Secret Signs by Jacqueline Guest (Orca Young Readers)

The Snake Scientist by Sy Montgomery (Scientists in the Field)

Somebody's Girl by Maggie De Vries (Orca Young Readers)

Spotlight on Canada by Bobbie Kalman

The St. Lawrence: River Route to the Great Lakes by Lynn Peppas (Rivers Around the World)

Star in the Storm by Joan Hiatt Harlow)

Stealing Home by J. Torres and David Namisato

The Story Girl by L.M. Montgomery

A Stranger at Home by Christy Jordan-Fenton and Margaret Pokiak-Fenton

Strawberry Moon by Becky Citra (Orca Young Readers)
Summer in the City by Marie-Louise Gay and David Homel
Survival in the Wilderness by Steven Otfinoski (Great Escapes)
T Is for Territories: A Yukon, Northwest Territories, and Nunavut Alphabet by Michael Kusugak
Thea Stilton and the Niagara Splash by Thea Stilton
Thunder from the Sea by Joan Hiatt Harlow
Trouble at Lachine Mill by Bill Freeman

Under a Living Sky by Joseph Simons (Orca Young Readers)
Underground to Canada by Barbara Smucker
The Viking Symbol Mystery by Franklin W. Dixon (Hardy Boys)
Weird but True! Canada: 300 Outrageous Facts about the True North by Chelsea Lin (National Geographic Kids)
Whiteout by Becky Citra (Orca Young Readers)
The Wreck of the Ethie by Hilary Hyland
Yossi's Goal by Ellen Schwartz (Orca Young Readers)

	The Book You Chose	**Date Completed**
7.1 Light Reader		
7.2 Interested Reader		
7.3 Avid Reader		
7.4 Committed Reader		
7.5 Enthralled Reader		

Western Europe

Challenge 8

Austria

Austria by Lisa Owings (Exploring Countries)

Austria by Kristine Spanier (All Around the World)

Beethoven Lives Upstairs by Barbara Nichol

The Big Chunk of Ice: The Last Known Adventure of the Mad Scientists' Club by Bertrand R. Brinley

Captive Witness by Carolyn Keene (Nancy Drew)

Country Jumper in Austria by Claudia Dobson-Largie

The Devil in Vienna by Doris Orgel

Elisabeth: The Princess Bride, Austria–Hungary, 1853 by Barry Denenberg (The Royal Diaries)

Faraway Home by Marilyn Taylor

Maestoso Petra by Jane Kendall (Horse Diaries)

Moonlight on the Magic Flute by Mary Pope Osborne (Magic Tree House)

Mozart Finds a Melody by Stephen Costanza

Mystery at the Christmas Market by Janelle Diller (Pack-n-Go Girls)

Mystery of the Ballerina Ghost by Janelle Diller (Pack-n-Go Girls)

Mystery of the Secret Room by Janelle Diller (Pack-n-Go Girls)

The Night Crossing by Karen Ackerman

One Eye Laughing, the Other Weeping: The Diary of Julie Weiss, Vienna, Austria to New York, 1938 by Barry Denenberg (Dear America)

One False Note by Gordon Korman (The 39 Clues)

The Star of Kazan by Eva Ibbotson

White Stallion of Lipizza by Marguerite Henry

Who Was Wolfgang Amadeus Mozart? by Yona Zeldis McDonough (Who HQ)

Belgium

Belgium by Michael Burgan (Enchantment of the World)

Belgium by Lisa Owings (Exploring Countries)

Country Jumper in Belgium by Claudia Dobson-Largie

France

Anni's Diary of France by Anni Axworthy

Basil and the Big Cheese Cookoff by Eve Titus (The Great Mouse Detective)

Black Radishes by Susan Lynn Meyer

Brick City: Paris by Warren Elsmore (Lonely Planet Kids)

The Boy Who Wanted to Cook by Gloria Whelan (Tales of the World)

The Butterfly by Patricia Polacco

The Castle Conundrum by Franklin W. Dixon (Hardy Boys)

Catherine's War by Julia Billet

Cecile: Gates of Gold by Mary Casanova (Girls of Many Lands)

Charlotte in Giverny by Joan MacPhail Knight

Charlotte in Paris by Joan MacPhail Knight

The Christmas Donkey by Alta Halverson Seymour

City Spies by James Ponti

Clang! Ernst Chladni's Sound Experiments by Darcy Pattison (Moments in Science)

Country Jumper in France by Claudia Dobson-Largie

Cultural Traditions in France by Lynn Peppas

Danger in Paris: A Samantha Mystery by Sarah Masters Buckey (American Girl)

Eiffel Tower by Kristine Spanier (Whole Wide World)

Eleanor: Crown Jewel of Aquitaine, France, 1136 by Kristiana Gregory (The Royal Diaries)

The Family Under the Bridge by Natalie Savage Carlson

Family Sabbatical by Carol Ryrie Brink

Framed in France by Jeff Brown (Flat Stanley's Worldwide Adventures)

France by Jessica Dean (All Around the World)

France by Anita Ganeri (Benjamin Blog and His Inquisitive Dog)

France by Rachel Grack (Exploring Countries)

France by Liz Sonneborn (Enchantment of the World)

France by Kremena T. Spengler (A Question and Answer Book)

France by Kathryn Stevens (Countries: Faces and Places)

France by Tom Streissguth (Country Explorers)

France by Sarah Tieck (Explore the Countries)

Genevieve's War by Patricia Reilly Giff

Grace series by Mary Casanova (American Girl)

Gustave Eiffel's Spectacular Idea: The Eiffel Tower by Sharon Katz Cooper

The Invention of Hugo Cabret by Brian Selznik

I Survived the Battle of D-Day, 1944 by Lauren Tarshis

Joan of Arc by Demi

Joan of Arc by Diane Stanley

The Journey That Saved Curious George: The True Wartime Escape of Margret and H.A. Rey by Louise Borden

A Kid's Guide to France by Jack L. Roberts

Let's Visit Paris! by Lisa Manzione (The Adventures of Bella and Harry)

Mac Cracks the Code by Mac Barnett (Mac B., Kid Spy)

Marguerite Makes a Book by Bruce Robertson

Marie Antoinette: Princess of Versailles, Austria-France, 1769 by Kathryn Lasky (The Royal Diaries)

Masters of Silence by Kathy Kacer (The Heroes Quartet)

Michael at the Invasion of France, 1943 by Laurie Calkhoven (Boys of Wartime)

My Life in France by Patience Coster (A Child's Day In…)

The Mystery at the Eiffel Tower by Carole Marsh (Around the World in 80 Mysteries)

The Mystery of the 99 Steps by Carolyn Keene (Nancy Drew)

The Mystery of the Stolen Painting by Harper Paris (Greetings from Somewhere)

No Strings Attached by Carolyn Keene (Nancy Drew)

On the Road Again: More Travels with My Family by Marie-Louise Gay and David Homel

Paris City Trails by Helen Greathead (Lonely Planet Kids)

Passport to Danger by Franklin W. Dixon (Hardy Boys)

Rags: Hero Dog of WWI by Margot Theis Raven

Rescue by Jennifer A. Nielsen

Rollo in Paris by Jacob Abbott

Shooting at the Stars: The Christmas Truce of 1914 by John Hendrix

Something Out of Nothing: Marie Curie and Radium by Carla Killough McClafferty

Sophie Takes to the Sky by Katherine Woodfine

Spotlight on France by Bobbie Kalman

Tales from a Not-So-Posh Paris Adventure by Rachel Renee Russell (Dork Diaries)

Thea Stilton and the Mystery in Paris by Thea Stilton

This Is Paris by M. Sasek

Twenty and Ten by Claire Hutchet Bishop

Victory at Normandy by Marcus Sutter (Soldier Dogs)

The Way to the Orsay Museum by Hyo-mi Park (Global Kids Storybooks)

A Whale in Paris by Daniel Presley and Claire Polders

What Was D-Day? by Patricia Brennan Demuth (Who HQ)

Where Is the Eiffel Tower? by Dina Anastasio (Who HQ)

France, continued

Who Was Claude Monet? by Ann Waldron (Who HQ)

Who Was Jacques Cousteau? by Nico Medina (Who HQ)

Who Was Joan of Arc? by Pam Pollack (Who HQ)

Who Was Jules Verne? by James Buckley (Who HQ)

Who Was Marie Antoinette? by Dana Meachen Rau (Who HQ)

Who Was Napoleon? by Jim Gigliotti (Who HQ)

Your Passport to France by Charly Haley

You Wouldn't Want to Be Joan of Arc! by Fiona Macdonald

Germany

After the Train by Gloria Whelan

The Ark by Margot Benary-Isbert

Battle of the Bulge by Marcus Sutter (Soldier Dogs)

The Battle of the Bulge: Nazi Germany's Final Attack on the Western Front by Michael Burgan (Tangled History)

Bedlam in Berlin by Alba Arango (JJ Bennett: Junior Spy)

Benno and the Night of Broken Glass by Meg Wiviott

The Berlin Wall: An Interactive Modern History Adventure by Matt Doeden (You Choose: Modern History)

Candy Bomber by Michael O. Tunnell

Country Jumper in Germany by Claudia Dobson-Largie

Cultural Traditions in Germany by Lynn Peppas

German Hero-Sagas and Folk-Tales by Barbara Leonie Picard

Germany by Mary Berendes (Countries: Faces and Places)

Germany by Jean F. Blashfield (Enchantment of the World)

Germany by Jessica Dean (All Around the World)

Germany by Vicky Franchino (Social Studies Explorers: It's Cool to Learn about Countries)

Germany by Anita Ganeri (Benjamin Blog and His Inquisitive Dog)

Germany by Kremena Spengler (A Question and Answer Book)

Germany by Sarah Tieck (Explore the Countries)

The Happy Hollisters and the Cuckoo Clock Mystery by Jerry West

Henry's Red Sea by Barbara Smucker

Johann Sebastian Bach: The Story of the Boy Who Sang in the Streets by Thomas Tapper

Let's Visit Berlin! by Lisa Manzione (The Adventures of Bella and Harry)

Mac Saves the World by Mac Barnett (Mac B., Kid Spy)

Mercedes and the Chocolate Pilot by Margot Theis Raven

The Mystery at the Crystal Castle: Bavaria, Germany by Carole Marsh (Real Kids, Real Places)

Nazi Prison Camp Escape by Michael Burgan (Great Escapes)

One Thousand Tracings: Healing the Wounds of World War II by Lita Judge

The Pied Piper of Hamelin by Robert Browning

Rowan Farm by Margo Benary-Isbert

Ruth and the Night of Broken Glass: A World War II Survival Story by Emma Carlson Berne (Girls Survive)

Sebastian: A Book about Bach by Jeanette Winter

Thea Stilton and the Black Forest Burglary by Thea Stilton

This Is Munich by M. Sasek

Travel to Germany by Christine Layton (Searchlight Books: World Traveler)

The Watcher by Joan Hiatt Harlow

What Was the Berlin Wall? by Nico Medina (Who HQ)

Who Were the Brothers Grimm? by Avery Reed (Who HQ)

Ireland

The Adventures of Seymour and Hau: Ireland by Melanie Morse and Thomas McDade

Ballywhinney Girl by Eve Bunting

Bike Tour Mystery by Carolyn Keene (Nancy Drew)

The Cottage at Bantry Bay by Hilda van Stockum (Bantry Bay)

Country Jumper in Ireland by Claudia Dobson-Largie

Danger in Dublin by Alba Arango (JJ Bennett, Junior Spy)

Darcy by Whitney Sanderson (Horse Diaries)

Favorite Fairy Tales Told in Ireland by Virginia Haviland

Francie on the Run by Hilda van Stockum (Bantry Bay)

The Impossible Crime by Mac Barnett (Mac B., Kid Spy)

Ireland by Jean F. Blashfield (Enchantment of the World)

Ireland by Jessica Dean (All Around the World)

Ireland by Julie Murray (Explore the Countries)

Ireland by Amy Rechner (Country Profiles)

Ireland by Patrick Ryan (Countries: Faces and Places)

Ireland by Colleen Sexton (Exploring Countries)

Ireland by Mary Dodson Wade (A Question and Answer Book)

Ireland by Patti Wheeler and Keith Hemstreet (Travels with Gannon and Wyatt)

Irish Fairy Tales edited by Philip Smith (Dover Children's Thrift Classics)

The Island of Horses by Eilis Dillon

Kathleen: The Celtic Knot by Siobhan Parkinson (Girls of Many Lands)

The King of Ireland's Son by Padraic Colum

The Legend of the Irish Castle by Gertrude Chandler Warner (The Boxcar Children)

Leprechauns and Irish Folklore by Mary Pope Osborne (Magic Tree House Fact Tracker)

Leprechaun in Late Winter by Mary Pope Osborne (Magic Tree House)

Let's Visit Dublin! by Lisa Manzione (The Adventures of Bella and Harry)

The Lost Island by Eilis Dillon

Megan's Year: An Irish Traveler's Story by Gloria Whelan (Tales of the World)

Nory Ryan's Song by Patricia Reilly Giff

Ireland, continued

Pegeen by Hilda van Stockum (Bantry Bay)

Ponies at the Point by Ben M. Baglio (Animal Ark)

Red Hugh, Prince of Donegal by Robert T. Reilly

Republic of Ireland by Anita Ganeri (Benjamin Blog and His Inquisitive Dog)

Sean and Sheela by Marian King

S Is for Shamrock: An Ireland Alphabet by Eve Bunting

Small Beauties: The Journey of Darcy Heart O'Hara by Elvira Woodruff

Tales from Old Ireland by Malachy Doyle

This Is Ireland by M. Sasek

Netherlands

The Christmas Compass by Alta Halverson Seymour

Dutch Fairy Tales for Young Folks by William Elliot Griffis

The Dutch Twins by Lucy Fitch Perkins

The Fantastic Journey of Pieter Bruegel by Anders C. Shafer

The Greatest Skating Race by Louise Borden

Hans Brinker and the Silver Skates by Mary Mapes Dodge

Hiding from the Nazis by David A. Adler

Hunger Winter: A World War II Novel by Rob Currie

The Little Riders by Margaretha Shemin

Luna by Catherine Hapka (Horse Diaries)

Miep and the Most Famous Diary: The Woman Who Rescued Anne Frank's Diary by Meeg Pincus

The Netherlands by Martin Hintz (Enchantment of the World)

Netherlands by Julie Murray (Explore the Countries)

The Netherlands by Lisa Owings (Exploring Countries)

Rollo in Holland by Jacob Abbott

Storm Horse by Nick Garlick

Thea Stilton and the Great Tulip Heist by Thea Stilton

When the Dikes Broke by Alta Halverson Seymour

When We Were Shadows by Janet Wees

Who Was Anne Frank? by Ann Abramson (Who HQ)

The Wheel on the School by Meindert DeJong

Windmill De Kat by Hyo-mi Park

The Winged Watchman by Hilda Van Stockum

Switzerland

The Apple and the Arrow by Mary and Conrad Buff

Angelo Goes to Switzerland by Earle Goodenow

Barry by Kate Klimo (Dog Diaries)

Basil and the Lost Colony by Eve Titus (The Great Mouse Detective)

Bloomability by Sharon Creech

The Christmas Stove by Alta Halverson Seymour

Cuckoo Clock Secrets in Switzerland by Karyn Collett

Dogs in the Dead of Night by Mary Pope Osborne (Magic Tree House)

The Happy Hollisters and the Swiss Echo Mystery by Jerry West

Heidi by Joanna Spyri

High in the Mountains: Robi and Hanni in the Swiss Alps by Emma Brock

Jeopardy in Geneva by Alba Arango (JJ Bennett: Junior Spy)

Rollo in Switzerland by Jacob Abbott

The Swiss Twins by Lucy Fitch Perkins

Switzerland by Lyn Larson (Country Explorers)

Switzerland by Derek Zobel (Exploring Countries)

Switzerland by Julie Murray (Explore the Countries)

Switzerland by Lura Rogers Seavey (Enchantment of the World)

Switzerland by Kristine Spanier (All Around the World)

Ticking Along with Swiss Kids by by Dianne Dicks and Katalin Fekete

Welcome to Switzerland by Pamela K. Harris and Brad Clemmons

William Tell: One against an Empire by Paul D. Storrie (Graphic Myths and Legends)

	The Book You Chose	**Date Completed**
8.1 Light Reader		
8.2 Interested Reader		
8.3 Avid Reader		
8.4 Committed Reader		
8.5 Enthralled Reader		

Eastern Europe

Challenge 9

Czech Republic

A Boy of Old Prague by Sulamith Ish-Kishor (Dover Children's Classics)

Country Jumper in the Czech Republic by Claudia Dobson-Largie)

Czech Republic by Charlotte Guillain (Countries Around the World)

Czech Republic by Lura Rogers Seavey (Enchantment of the World)

The Czech Republic by Walter Simmons (Blastoff Readers: Exploring Countries)

Czech Republic by Efstathia Sioras (Cultures of the World)

Favorite Fairy Tales Told in Czechoslovakia by Virginia Holland

Hana's Suitcase: The Quest to Solve a Holocaust Mystery by Karen Levine

Let's Visit Prague! by Lisa Manzione (The Adventures of Bella and Harry)

Looking at the Czech Republic by Jan Willem Bultje

Nicky and Vera: A Quiet Hero of the Holocaust and the Children He Rescued by Peter Sis

Philomena by Kate Seredy

Problems in Prague by Alba Arango (JJ Bennett: Junior Spy)

Rivka's Way by Teri Kanefield

The Three Golden Keys by Peter Sis

The Wall: Growing Up Behind the Iron Curtain by Peter Sis

Estonia

Estonia by Emily Anderson (Cultures of the World)

Estonia by Richard Spilbury (Countries Around the World)

Looking at Estonia by Piret Hiisjarv and Ene Hiiepuu

Hungary

The Chestry Oak by Kate Seredy

Country Jumper in Hungary by Claudia Dobson-Largie

The Good Master by Kate Seredy

Hanna's Cold Winter by Trish Marx

Hungary by Ruth Bjorkland (Enchantment of the World)

Hungary by Charlotte Guillain (Countries Around the World)

Hungary by Lisa Owings (Blastoff Readers: Exploring Countries)

Hungary by Kristine Spanier (All Around the World)

The Singing Tree by Kate Seredy

The White Stag by Kate Seredy

Lithuania

Eli Remembers by Ruth Vander Zee

Lithuania by Sakina Kagda (Cultures of the World)

Lithuania by Melanie Waldron (Countries Around the World)

Looking at Lithuania by Jan Willem Bultje

Passage to Freedom: The Sugihara Story by Ken Mochizuki

Words on Fire by Jennifer Nielson

Poland

Best of Polish Fairy Tales by Sergiej Nowikow

The Cats in Kraskinski Square by Karen Hesse

The Champion of Children: The Story of Janusz Korczak by Tomek Bogacki

Cultural Traditions in Poland by Linda Barghoorn

A Gift for Mama by Esther Hautzig

The Glass Mountain: Tales from Poland by David Walser

A Hero and the Holocaust: The Story of Janusz Korczak

and His Children by David A. Adler
I Survived the Nazi Invasion, 1944 by Lauren Tarshis
Jacob's Rescue by Malka Drucker
Jars of Hope: How One Woman Helped Save 2,500 Children During the Holocaust by Jennifer Roy
Let's Visit Poland by Susie Brooks
Looking at Poland by Jan Kadziolka and Tadeusz Wojciechowski
Marie Curie for Kids: Her Life and Scientific Discoveries by Amy M. O'Quinn
Poland by Teresa Fisher (Letters from Around the World)
Poland by Sean McCollom (Country Explorers)
Poland by Julie Murray (Explore the Countries)
Poland by Walter Simmons (Exploring Countries)
Poland by Wil Mara (Enchantment of the World)
A Ticket to Poland by Sean McCollom
Welcome to Poland by Patrick Ryan
The Wren and the Sparrow by J. Patrick Lewis

Romania
Looking at Romania by Jan Willem Bos
The Mystery at Dracula's Castle: Transylvania, Romania by Carole Marsh (Around the World in 80 Mysteries)
Nadia: The Girl Who Couldn't Sit Still by Karlin Gray
Romania by Laura L. Sullivan (Exploring World Cultures)
Romania by Terrie Willis (Enchantment of the World)
The Story That Cannot Be Told by J. Kasper Kramer

Russia
Anastasia: The Last Grand Duchess by Carolyn Meyer (The Royal Diaries)

Breaking Stalin's Nose by Eugene Yelchin
Catherine: The Great Journey by Kristiana Gregory (The Royal Diaries)
The Diaries of Robin's Travels: St. Petersburg by Ken and Angie Lake
The Disastroud Wrangel Island Expedition by Katrina M. Phillips (Graphic Library)
The Endless Steppe by Esther Hautzig
Favorite Fairy Tales Told in Russia by Virginia Haviland
Favorite Russian Fairy Tales by Arthur Ransome (Dover Children's Thrift Classics)
The House on Walenska Street by Charlotte Herman
Journey through Russia by Anita Ganeri (Benjamin Blog and His Inquisitive Dog)
Koshka's Tales by James Mayhew
Let's Visit Saint Petersburg! by Lisa Manzione (The Adventures of Bella and Harry)
Luba and the Wren by Patricia Polacco
Masha and the Bear by Lari Don (Stories from Around the World)
The Miracle of Saint Nicholas by Gloria Whelan
Mussorgsky's Pictures at an Exhibition by Anna Harwell Celenza
The Mystery of the Onion Domes by Carole Marsh (Around the World in 80 Mysteries)
The Night Journey by Kathryn Lasky
Peril at the Top of the World by James Patterson (Treasure Hunters)
Peter the Great by Diane Stanley
Russia by Jim Bartell (Exploring Countries)
Russia by Jessica Dean (All Around the World)

Russia, continued

Russia by Anita Ganeri (Benjamin Blog and His Inquisitive Dog)

Russia by Jilly Hunt (Countries Around the World)

Russia by Katie Marscio (Social Studies Explorers: It's Cool to Learn about Countries)

Russia by Kathleen Berton Murrell (Eyewitness)

Russia by Julie Murray (Explore the Countries)

Russia by Andrea Pelleschi (Countries of the World)

Russia by Amy Rechner (Country Profiles)

Russia by Kremena Spengler (A Question and Answer Book)

Russia by Tom Streissguth (Country Explorers)

Russia by Nel Yomtov (Enchantment of the World)

Russian Tales: Traditional Stories of Quests and Enchantments by Dinara Mirtalipova

Sasha's Matrioshka Dolls by Jana Dillon

The Sea King's Daughter by Aaron Shepard

Spotlight on Russia by Bobbie Kalman

The Tale of the Firebird by Gennady Spirin

Thea Stilton and the Lost Letters by Thea Stilton

Travel to Russia by Christine Layton (Searchlight Books: World Traveler)

Welcome to Russia by Elma Schemenauer

Where Is the Kremlin? by Deborah Hopkinson (Who HQ)

Who Was Catherine the Great? by Pam Pollack (Who HQ)

Your Passport to Russia by Douglas Hustad

Slovakia

Looking at Slovakia by Daniel Kollar

The Night Spies by Kathy Kacer

The Secret of Gabi's Dresser by Kathy Kacer

Slovakia by Ted Gottfried and Debbie Nevins (Cultures of the World)

Ukraine

The Adventures of Hershel of Ostropol by Eric A. Kimmel

Don't Tell the Nazis by Marsha Forchuk Skrypuch (Ukraine)

Louder Than Words by Kathy Kacer (The Heroes Quartet)

Radiant Girl by Andrea White

A Refugee's Journey from Ukraine by Ellen Rodger (Leaving My Homeland)

Secret of the Glass Mountain and Other Folktales from Ukraine by Maria Zemko Tetro

Trapped in Hitler's Web by Marsha Forchuk Skrypuch

Ukraine by Megan Borgert-Spaniol (Exploring Countries)

Ukraine by Deborah Kent (Enchantment of the World)

Ukraine by Julie Murray (Explore the Countries)

Ukraine by Anastasiya Vasilyeva and Karla Ruiz (Countries We Come From)

Welcome to Ukraine by Katharine Elizabeth Brown (Welcome to My Country)

The Book You Chose	Date Completed
9.1 *Light Reader*	
9.2 *Interested Reader*	
9.3 *Avid Reader*	
9.4 *Committed Reader*	
9.5 *Enthralled Reader*	

West Africa

Challenge 10

Benin

The Adventures of Obi and Titi: The Great Walls of Benin by O.T. Begho

Benin by Martha Kneib (Cultures of the World)

Country Jumper in Benin by Claudia Dobson-Largie

Explore! Benin by Izzi Howell

The Genius of the Benin Kingdom by Sonya Newland

The Great Benin Empire by John Adoga (Nigeria Heritage Series)

Idia of the Benin Kingdom by Ekiuwa Aire (Our Ancestories)

Queen Idia of Benin by John Adoga (Nigeria Heritage Series)

Burkina Faso

Country Jumper in Burkina Faso by Claudia Dobson-Largie

The Red Bicycle by Jude Isabella (CitizenKid)

Ghana

Country Jumper in Ghana by Claudia Dobson-Largie

Cultural Traditions in Ghana by Joan Marie Galat

Ghana by Ettagale Blauer (Enchantment of the World)

Ghana by Lyn Larson (Country Explorers)

Ghana by Thomas Persano (Countries We Come From)

Ghana by Barbara Aoki Poisson (The Evolution of Africa's Major Nations)

Grace Goes to Ghana by M. Mimi Sutton

One Hen: How One Small Loan Made a Big Difference by Katie Smith Milway (CitizenKid)

Sosu's Call by Mashack Asare

The Spider Weaver: A Legend of Kente Cloth by Margaret Musgrove

We Visit Ghana by John Bankston (Your Land and My Land)

Ivory Coast

Akissi: Tales of Mischief by Marguerite Abouet

Cote d'Ivoire by Ruth Bjorklund (Enchantment of the World)

Country Jumper in Cote d'Ivoire by Claudia Dobson-Largie

Ivory Coast by William Mark Habeeb (The Evolution of Africa's Major Nations)

Liberia

Liberia by Brian Baughan (The Evolution of Africa's Major Nations)

Liberia by Ruth Bjorklund (Enchantment of the World)

Liberia by Robin Doak (Countries Around the World)

Liberia by Muriel L. Dubois (A Question and Answer Book)

Why Leopard Has Spots: Dan Stories from Liberia by Won-Ldy Paye

Mali

Jaja: King of Opobo by John Adoga (Nigeria Heritage Series)

Mansa Musa: The Lion of Mali by Khephra Burns

Meet Our New Student from Mali by Oludamini Ogunnaike

Never Forgotten by Patricia C. McKissack

Sunjata of the Mande Empire by Ekiuwa Aire (Our Ancestries)

Sunjata: Warrior King of Mali by Justine Fontes (Graphic Myths and Legends)

Yatandou by Gloria Whelan (Tales of the World)

Nigeria

Beat the Story Drum, Pum-Pum by Ashley Bryan

Funmilayo Ransome-Kuti by John Adoga (Nigeria Heritage Series)

Hajiya Gambo Sawaba by John Adoga (Nigeria Heritage Series)

Hoping for a Home after Nigeria by Heather C. Hudak (Leaving My Homeland)

Ladi Kwali: The Pottery Queen by John Adoga (Nigeria Heritage Series)

Lost in the African Forest of Zuki by Onyeka Opara

Margaret Ekpo: A Woman of the People by John Adoga (Nigeria Heritage Series)

Mary Mitchell Slessor by John Adoga (Nigeria Heritage Series)

Meet Our New Student from Nigeria by Anna M. Ogunnike

Nigeria by Lisa Owings (Exploring Countries)

Nigeria by Lura Rogers Seavey (Enchantment of the World)

Nigeria by Kristine Spanier (All Around the World)

Nigeria by Kristin Thoennes Keller (Countries of the World)

Nigeria by Ida Walker (The Evolution of Africa's Major Nations)

The No. 1 Car Spotter by Atinuke

Olaudah Equiano: A Voice for Africa by John Adoga (Nigeria Heritage Series)

A Refugee's Journey from Nigeria by Ellen Rodger (Leaving My Homeland)

Samuel Ajayi Crowther: From Slave Boy to Bishop by John Adoga (Nigeria Heritage Series)

Travel to Nigeria by Matt Doeden (Searchlight Books: World Traveler)

Senegal

Senegal by Ruth Bjorklund (Enchantment of the World)

Senegal by Tanya Mulroy (The Evolution of Africa's Major Nations)

Senegal by Debbie Nevins and Elizabeth Berg (Cultures of the World)

Senegal by Anna Obiols (On the Way to School)

Sierra Leone

Sierra Leone by Judy Hasday (The Evolution of Africa's Major Nations)

Sierra Leone by Suzanne Levert (Cultures of the World)

Tamba and the Chief: A Temne Tale by Melinda Lilly

	The Book You Chose	**Date Completed**
10.1 Light Reader		
10.2 Interested Reader		
10.3 Avid Reader		
10.4 Committed Reader		
10.5 Enthralled Reader		

North Africa

Challenge 11

Algeria

Algeria by Daniel E. Harmon (The Evolution of Africa's Major Nations)

Algeria by Martin Hintz (Enchantment of the World)

Algeria by Kristine Spanier (All Around the World)

Country Jumper in Algeria by Claudia Dobson-Largie

Egypt

1,000 Facts about Ancient Egypt by Nancy Honovich (National Geographic Kids)

The 5,000-Year-Old Puzzle: Solving a Mystery of Ancient Egypt by Claudia Logan

The Adventurers and the Temple of Treasure by Jemma Hatt

Adventures in Ancient Egypt by Linda Bailey (Good Times Travel Agency)

Ancient Egypt: An Interactive History Adventure by Heather Adamson (You Choose: Historical Eras)

Ancient Egypt (DK Eyewitness)

Awesome Egyptians by Terry Deary and Peter Hepplewhite (Horrible Histories)

Awful Egyptians by Terry Deary (Horrible Histories)

Cinderella of the Nile by Beverly Naidoo

Cleopatra and Ancient Egypt for Kids: Her Life and World with 21 Activities by Simonetta Carr

Cleopatra VII: Daughter of the Nile, Egypt, 57 B.C. by Kristiana Gregory (The Royal Diaries)

Country Jumper in Egypt by Claudia Dobson-Largie

Cultural Traditions in Egypt by Lynn Peppas

The Curse of the Cairo Cat by Dan Metcalf (A Lottie Lipton Adventure)

The Curse of the Cheese Pyramid by Geronimo Stilton

Danger down the Nile by James Patterson (Treasure Hunters)

Egypt by Jessica Dean (All Around the World)

Egypt by Anita Ganeri (Benjamin Blog and His Inquisitive Dog)

Egypt by William Mark Habeeb (The Evolution of Africa's Major Nations)

Egypt by Ann Heinrichs (Enchantment of the World)

Egypt by Shirley Jordan (Primary Source Readers)

Egypt by Katie Marsico (Social Studies Explorers: It's Cool to Learn about Countries)

Egypt by Julie Murray (Explore the Countries)

Egypt by Patrick Ryan (Countries: Faces and Places)

Egypt by Walter Simmons (Blastoff Readers: Exploring Countries)

Egypt by Christine Webster (A Question and Answer Book)

Egypt by Patti Wheeler and Keith Hemstreet (Travels with Gannon and Wyatt)

The Egyptian Enchantment by Dan Metcalf (A Lottie Lipton Adventure)

Everything Ancient Egypt by Crispin Boyer (National Geographic Kids)

Follow Me around Egypt by Wiley Blevins

Gods and Goddesses of Ancient Egypt: Egyptian Mythology for Kids by Morgan E. Moroney

The Great Egyptian Grave Robbery by Jeff Brown (Flat Stanley's Worldwide Adventures)

The Great Pyramid: The Story of the Farmers, the God-King, and the Most Astounding Structure Ever Built by Elizabeth Mann (Wonders of the World)

Hatshepsut of Egypt by Shirin Yim Bridges (The Thinking Girl's Treasury of Real Princesses)

High Time for Heroes by Mary Pope Osborne (Magic Tree House)

Hot on the Trail in Ancient Egypt by Linda Bailey (The Time Travel Guides)

Kid Detective Zet series by Scott Peters

A Kid's Life in Ancient Egypt by Sara Machajewski

Mummies and Pyramids by Mary Pope Osborne (Magic Tree House Fact Trackers)

Mummies in the Morning by Mary Pope Osborne (Magic Tree House)

Mummy (DK Eyewitness)

The Mummy's Curse by Franklin W. Dixon (Hardy Boys Undercover Brothers)

The Mystery of the Ancient Pyramid: Cairo, Egypt by Carole Marsh (Around the World in 80 Mysteries)

The Pharaohs of Ancient Egypt by Elizabeth Payne (Landmark)

The Secret of the Sphinx by Geronimo Stilton

Secrets according to Humphrey by Betty G. Birney

Spotlight on Egypt by Bobbie Kalman

Thea Stilton and the Blue Scarab Hunt by Thea Stilton

Treasury of Egyptian Mythology by Donna Jo Napoli (National Geographic Kids)

Where Are the Great Pyramids? by Dorothy and Thomas Hoobler (Who HQ)

Who Was King Tut? by Roberta Edwards (Who HQ)

You Wouldn't Want to Be an Egyptian Mummy! Digusting Things You'd Rather Not Know by David Stewart

You Wouldn't Want to Be a Pyramid Builder! A Hazardous Job You'd Rather Not Have by Jacqueline Morley

You Wouldn't Want to Be Cleopatra! An Egyptian Ruler You'd Rather Not Be by Jim Pipe

You Wouldn't Want to Be Tutankhamen! A Mummy Who Really Got Meddled With by David Stewart

Libya

Across the Minefields by Pamela D. Toler (Great Escapes)

Libya by Judy Hasday (The Evolution of Africa's Major Nations)

Libya by Peter Malcolm (Cultures of the World)

Libya by Terri Willis (Enchantment of the World)

We Visit Libya by Claire O'Neal (Your Land and My Land)

Morocco

The Adventures of Seymour and Hau: Morocco by Melanie Morse and Thomas McDade

Morocco by Ettagale Blauer and Jason Laure (Enchantment of the World)

Morocco by Dorothy Kavanaugh (The Evolution of Africa's Major Nations)

Morocco by Joyce Markovics (Countries We Come From)

Morocco by Patrick Merrick (Countries: Faces and Places)

Morocco by Robin Nelson (Country Explorers)

Morocco by Walter Simmons (Exploring Countries)

Morocco by Kristine Spanier (All Around the World)

Travel to Morocco by Matt Doeden (Searchlight Books: World Traveler)

Sudan

Brothers in Hope: The Story of the Lost Boys of Sudan by Mary Williams

My Great-Grandmother's Gourd by Cristina Kessler

My Name Is Sangoel by Karen Lynn Williams and Khadra Mohammed

Sudan, continued

The Red Pencil by Andrea Davis Pinkney

A Refugee's Journey from South Sudan by Ellen Rodger
(Leaving My Homeland)

South Sudan by Lisa Owings (Exploring Countries)

Sudan and Southern Sudan by Dorothy Kavanaugh (The
Evolution of Africa's Major Nations)

	The Book You Chose	**Date Completed**
11.1 Light Reader		
11.2 Interested Reader		
11.3 Avid Reader		
11.4 Committed Reader		
11.5 Enthralled Reader		

Oceania

Challenge 12

Australia

The Alice Stories: Our Australian Girl by Davina Bell

Australia by Anita Ganeri (Benjamin Blog and His Inquisitive Dog)

Australia by Jean F. Blashfield (Enchantment of the World)

Australia by Jessica Dean (All Around the World)

Australia by Sean McCollom (Country Explorers)

Australia by Nathan Olson (A Question and Answer Book)

Australia by Colleen Sexton (Exploring Countries)

Australia by Sarah Tieck (Explore the Countries)

Australia Outback by Patti Wheeler and Keith Hemstreet (Travels with Gannon and Wyatt)

The Australian Boomerang Bonanza by Jeff Brown (Flat Stanley's Worldwide Adventures)

Australia's Pink Lakes by Patricia Hutchison (Nature's Mysteries)

Claws of the Crocodile by Bear Grylls (Mission: Survival)

Country Jumper in Australia by Claudia Dobson-Largie

Cultural Traditions in Australia by Molly Aloian

Dingoes at Dinnertime by Mary Pope Osborne (Magic Tree House)

Down and Out Down Under by Geronimo Stilton

Down Under by Jan Reynolds (Vanishing Cultures)

Escape to Australia by James Patterson (Middle School)

The Firebird Rocket by Franklin W. Dixon (Hardy Boys)

Fly on the Wall by Remy Lai

Great Reef Games by Kristin Earhart (Race the Wild)

The Great Victoria Desert by Lynn Peppas (Deserts Around the World)

The Horse Who Bit a Bushranger by Jackie French

Indigenous Australian Cultures by Mary Colson (Global Cultures)

Jodie's Journey by Colin Thiele

Kira's Animal Rescue by Erin Teagan (American Girl)

Kira Down Under by Erin Teagan (American Girl)

The Letty Books: Our Australian Girl by Alison Lloyd

Meet Our New Student from Australia by Ann Weil

The Mystery on the Great Barrier Reef by Carole Marsh (Around the World in 80 Mysteries)

Outback All-Stars by Kristin Earhart (Race the Wild)

Sand Swimmers: The Secret Life of Australia's Desert Wilderness by Narelle Oliver

Saving the Tasmanian Devil: How Science Is Helping the World's Largest Marsupial Carnivore Survive by Dorothy Hinshaw Patent (Scientists in the Field)

The Secret World of Wombats by Jackie French

Seven Little Australians by Ethel Turner

Sun on the Stubble by Colin Thiele

The Switherby Pilgrims by Eleanor Spence

Sydney City Trails by Helen Greathead (Lonely Planet Kids)

Tasmanian Devils by Sandra Markle (Animal Scavengers)

Thea Stilton and the Mountain of Fire by Thea Stilton

Top to Bottom Down Under by Ted and Betsy Lewin (Adventures Around the World)

Travel to Australia by Matt Doeden (Searchlight Books: World Traveler)

Welcome to Australia by Mary Berendes (Welcome to the World)

Welcome, Wombat by Kama Einhorn (True Tales of Rescue)

Where Is the Great Barrier Reef? by Nico Medina (Who HQ)

Whitewater Courage by Jake Maddox

Who Was Steve Irwin? by Dina Anastasio (Who HQ)

You Wouldn't Want to Be a Convict Sent to Australia! by Meredith Costain

Easter Island

Let's Visit Easter Island! by Lisa Manzione (The Adventures of Bella and Harry)

Mysteries of Easter Island by Laura Hamilton Waxman

Ruin Hunters and the Easter Island Egg Hunt by Rob Beare

The Treasure of Easter Island by Geronimo Stilton

Where Is Easter Island? by Megan Stine (Who HQ)

Fiji

Country Jumper in Fiji by Claudia Dobson-Largie

Danger on the Reef by Jake Maddox

Fiji by Debbie Nevins and Roseline Ngcheong-Lum (Cultures of the World)

Fiji by Kathryn Stevens (Countries: Faces and Places)

Guam

Guam Adventures: Mystery of the Cave by Lynda W. McCroskery and Terry W. Heintz

Secret Mission: Guam by Marcus Sutter (Soldier Dogs)

Moorea

Dolphins in Danger by Amanda Lumry and Laura Hurwitz (Adventures of Riley)

Kupe and the Corals by Jacqueline L. Padilla-Gamino

The Octopus Scientists by Sy Montgomery (Scientists in the Field)

New Zealand

Little House in the Bush: Growing Up in New Zealand by Wendy Hamilton

Meet Our New Student from New Zealand by Ann Weil

New Zealand by Ellen Frazel (Exploring Countries)

New Zealand by Rebecca Hersch (Countries of the World)

New Zealand by Alicia Z. Klepeis (Country Profiles)

New Zealand by Lyn Larson (Country Explorers)

New Zealand by Julie Murray (Explore the Countries)

New Zealand by Donna Walsh Shepherd (Enchantment of the World)

New Zealand by Pat Ryan (Countries: Faces and Places)

New Zealand by Kristine Spanier (All Around the World)

Showtym Adventures series by Kelly Wilson

The Thunderbolt Pony by Stacy Gregg

Welcome to New Zealand by Patrick Ryan

Papua New Guinea

James Chalmers: The Rainmaker's Friend by Irene Howat (Torchbearers)

Papua New Guinea by Ingrid Gascoigne (Cultures of the World)

The Quest for the Tree Kangaroo by Sy Montgomery (Scientists in the Field)

Samoa

Fetu and Afu's Wintry Samoa Adventude by Gerald Aflague

	The Book You Chose	**Date Completed**
12.1 *Light Reader*		
12.2 *Interested Reader*		
12.3 *Avid Reader*		
12.4 *Committed Reader*		
12.5 *Enthralled Reader*		

Central Africa

Challenge 13

Angola

Angola by Bethany Bryan and Sean Sheehan (Cultures of the World)

Angola by Rob Staeger (The Evolution of Africa's Major Nations)

Country Jumper in Angola by Claudia Dobson-Largie

Njinga of Ndongo and Matamba by Ekiuwa Aire (Our Ancestries)

Nzinga: The Great Warrior of Angola by Desree Crooks

Nzinga: Warrior Queen of Matamba, Angola, Africa, 1595 by Patricia McKissack (Royal Diaries)

Cameroon

Cameroon by Diane Cook (The Evolution of Africa's Major Nations)

Cameroon by Patricia K. Kummer (Enchantment of the World)

Cameroon by Sean Sheehan (Cultures of the World)

Country Jumper in Cameroon by Claudia Dobson-Largie

I Am Farmer: Growing an Environmental Movement in Cameroon by Baptiste and Miranda Paul

Sense Pass King: A Story from Cameroon by Katrin Hyman Tchana

The Village of Round and Square Houses by Ann Grifalconi

Central African Republic

Central African Republic in Pictures by Matt Doeden (Visual Geography)

Country Jumper in Central African Republic by Claudia Dobson-Largie

Chad

Chad by Martha Kneib (Cultures of the World)

Country Jumper in Chad by Claudia Dobson-Largie

Rain School by James Rumford

Democratic Republic of the Congo

Country Jumper in the Democratic Republic of the Congo by Claudia Dobson-Largie

Democratic Republic of the Congo by G. Scott Prentzas (Social Studies Explorers: It's Cool to Learn about Countries)

Democratic Republic of the Congo by Jay Heale (Cultures of the World)

Democratic Republic of the Congo by Rita Milios (The Evolution of Africa's Major Nations)

Monkey Sunday: A Story from a Congolese Village by Sanna Stanley

My New Home after the Democratic Republic of Congo by Ellen Rodger (Leaving My Homeland)

A Refugee's Journey from the Democratic Republic of the Congo by Ellen Rodger (Leaving My Homeland)

Welcome to the Democratic Republic of the Congo by Jo Wynaden and Nina Kushner

Where Is the Congo? by Megan Stine

Gabon

Country Jumper in Gabon by Claudia Dobson-Largie

	The Book You Chose	Date Completed
13.1 *Light Reader*		
13.2 *Interested Reader*		
13.3 *Avid Reader*		
13.4 *Committed Reader*		
13.5 *Enthralled Reader*		

East Africa

Challenge 14

Tales of East Africa by Jamill Okubo

Burundi

Burundi by Kristine Brennan (The Evolution of Africa's Major Nations)

Burundi by Marian Frances Wolbers (Places and Peoples of the World)

Country Jumper in Burundi by Claudia Dobson-Largie

Eritrea

Country Jumper in Eritrea by Claudia Dobson-Largie

Eritrea by Roseline NgCheong-Lum (Cultures of the World)

Hamid's Story: A Real–Life Account of His Journey from Eritrea by Andy Glynne (Seeking Refuge)

The Mangrove Tree: Planting Trees to Feed Families by Susan L. Roth and Cindy Trumbore

A Refugee's Journey from Eritrea by Linda Barghoorn (Leaving My Homeland)

Ethiopia

Andromeda, Princess of Ethiopia by Worku Mulat, Ellenore and Leyla Angelidis

The Best Beekeeper of Lalibela: A Tale from Africa by Cristina Kesller

Country Jumper in Ethiopia by Claudia Dobson-Largie

Ethiopia by Spencer Brinker (Countries We Come From)

Ethiopia by Jim Corrigan (The Evolution of Africa's Major Nations)

Ethiopia by Mary L. Englar (A Question and Answer Book)

Ethiopia by Ellen Frazel (Exploring Countries)

Ethiopia by Elma Schemenauer (Countries: Faces and Places)

Ethiopia by Lura Rogers Seavey (Enchantment of the World

Ethiopia by by Barbara A. Somervill (Social Studies Explorers: It's Cool to Learn about Countries)

Ethiopian Voices: Tsion's Life by Stacy Bellward

Faraway Home by Jane Kurtz

Fire on the Mountain by Jane Kurtz

Looking at Ethiopia by Kathleen Pohl (Looking at Countries)

Only a Pigeon by Jane Kurtz

Saba: Under the Hyena's Foot by Jane Kurtz (Girls of Many Lands)

A Thirst for Home: A Story of Water across the World by Christine Ieronimo

Welcome to Ethiopia by N. Macknish and E. Berg (Welcome to My Country)

We Visit Ethiopia by John Bankston

Wherever I Go by Mary Wagley Copp

Your Passport to Ethiopia by Ryan Gale (World Passport)

Kenya

14 Cows for America by Carmen Agra Deedy

The African Safari Discovery by Jeff Brown (Flat Stanley's Worldwide Adventures)

Beatrice's Dream: A Story of Kibera Slum by Karen Williams

Country Jumper in Kenya by Claudia Dobson-Largie

Cultural Traditions in Kenya by Kylie Burns

The Hyena Scientist by Sy Montgomery (Scientists in the Field)

Kenya by Jessica Dean (All Around the World)

Kenya by Jim Bartell (Exploring Countries)

Kenya by Michael Burgan (Enchantment of the World)

Kenya by Jim Corrigan (The Evolution of Africa's Major Nations)

Kenya by Justine and Ron Fontes (A-Z)

Kenya by Sara Louise Kras (A Question and Answer Book)

Kenya by Julie Murray (Explore the Countries)

A Kid's Guide to Kenya by Jack L. Roberts

Mimi's Village and How Basic Health Care Transformed It by Katie Smith Milway (CitizenKid)

Moto and Me: My Year as a Wildcat's Foster Mom by Suzi Eszterhas

My Brother Is a Runner by Jin-Ha Gong (Global Kids Storybooks)

My Life in Kenya by Patience Coster (A Child's Day In…)

My Name Is Blessing by Eric Walters

The Mystery of the Black Rhino by Franklin W. Dixon (Hardy Boys)

The Mystery of the Lion's Tail by Harper Paris (Greetings from Somewhere)

The Paper House by Lois Peterson (Orca Young Readers)

Race Forever by R. A. Montgomery (Choose Your Own Adventure)

Seeds of Change: Wangari's Gift to the World by Jen Cullerton Johnson

The Spider Sapphire Mystery by Carolyn Keene (Nancy Drew)

Spotlight on Kenya by Bobbie Kalman

Thea Stilton and the Journey to the Lion's Den by Thea Stilton

A Ticket to Kenya by Sean McCollom

Travel to Kenya by Matt Doeden (Searchlight Books: World Traveler)

Welcome to Kenya by Patrick Ryan

Your Passport to Kenya by Kaitlyn Duling (World Passport)

Madagascar

Animals of Madagascar by Paula Steen

In Search of Lemurs by Joyce Ann Powzyk

Into Wild Madagascar by Elaine Pascoe (The Jeff Corwin Experience)

Madagascar by Ellen Frazel (Blastoff Readers: Exploring Countries)

Madagascar by Mary Oluonye (Country Explorers)

Madagascar by Tamra B. Orr (Enchantment of the World)

Madagascar by Kristine Spanier (All Around the World)

Mission to Madagascar by Amanda Lumry (Adventures of Riley)

The New King by Doreen Rappaport

Pollen: Darwin's 130-Year Prediction by Darcy Pattison (Moments in Science)

Thank You, Baobab Tree! by Mi-hwa Joo (Global Kids Storybooks)

Thea Stilton and the Madagascar Madness by Thea Stilton

Torina's World: A Child's Life in Madagascar by Joni Kabana

Malawi

The Boy Who Harnessed the Wind: Young Readers Edition by William Kamkwamba and Bryan Mealer

Mozambique

A Girl Named Disaster by Nancy Farmer

Mozambique by David C. King (Cultures of the World)

Mozambique by Tanya Mulroy (The Evolution of Africa's Major Nations)

Rwanda

Gorilla Doctors: Saving Endangered Great Apes by Pamela S. Turner (Scientists in the Field)

Her Own Two Feet: A Rwandan Girl's Brave Fight to Walk by Meredith Davis and Rebeka Uwitonze

Rwanda by Kathleen W. Deady (A Question and Answer Book)

Rwanda by Andy Koopmans (The Evolution of Africa's Major Nations)

We Visit Rwanda by John Bankston (Your Land and My Land)

Somalia

Immigrants from Somalia and Other African Countries by Jessica Gunderson (Fact Finders: Immigration Today)

My New Home after Somalia by Heather C. Hudak (Leaving My Homeland)

A Refugee's Journey from Somalia by Linda Barhoorn (Leaving My Homeland)

Somali Heritage by Tamra Orr (21st Century Junior Library)

Somalia by Lisa Owings (Exploring Countries)

Somalia by Elma Schemenauer (Countries: Faces and Places)

Somalia by Kristine Spanier (All Around the World)

Welcome to Somalia by Elma Schemenauer (Welcome to the World)

Tanzania

The Banana-Leaf Ball: How Play Can Change the World by Katie Smith Milway (CitizenKid)

Is It Far to Zanzibar? Poems about Tanzania by Nikki Grimes

Meet Our New Student from Tanzania by Ann Weil

Mighty Mount Kilimanjaro by Geronimo Stilton

Tanzania: A Scream in the Night by Crameye Junker (The Adventurous Mailbox)

Tanzania by Anna Cavallo (Country Explorers)

Tanzania by Joan Vos MacDonald (The Evolution of Africa's Major Nations)

Tanzania by Emily Rose Oachs (Blastoff Readers: Exploring Countries)

Under the Same Sun by Sharon Robinson

Untamed: The Wild Life of Jane Goodall by Anita Silvey (National Geographic Kids)

Where Is the Serengeti? by Nico Medina (Who HQ)

Who Is Jane Goodall? by Roberta Edwards (Who HQ)

Uganda

Breakfast in the Rainforest: A Visit with Mountain Gorillas by Richard Sobol

Gorilla Walk by Ted and Betsy Lewin

Orange for the Sunsets by Tina Athaide

Ryan and Jimmy and the Well in Africa That Brought Them Together by Herb Shoveller (CitizenKid)

Search for the Mountain Gorillas by Jim Wallace (Choose Your Own Adventure)

Uganda by Ettagale Blauer (Enchantment of the World)

Uganda by Lauri Kubuitsile (The Evolution of Africa's Major Nations)

When Water Makes Mud: A Story of Refugee Children by Janie Reinart

Zambia

Bulu: African Wonder Dog by Dick Houston

The Elephant Keeper: Caring for Orphaned Elephants in Zambia by Margriet Ruurs (CitizenKid)

The Girl Who Buried Her Dreams in a Can: A True Story by Tererai Trent

Meet Our New Student from Zambia by John A. Torres

Zimbabwe

Juliane's Story: A Real-Life Account of Her Journey from Zimbabwe by Andy Glynne (Seeking Refuge)

The Last Leopard by Lauren St. John (Legend of the Animal Healer)

Zimbabwe by Michael Baughan (The Evolution of Africa's Major Nations)

Zimbabwe by Sean Sheehan and Michael Spilling (Cultures of the World)

Zimbabwe by Kristine Spanier (All Around the World)

	The Book You Chose	Date Completed
14.1 Light Reader		
14.2 Interested Reader		
14.3 Avid Reader		
14.4 Committed Reader		
14.5 Enthralled Reader		

South Africa

Challenge 15

Botswana

Botswana by Kelly Wittman (The Evolution of Africa's Major Nations)

Botswana by Patti Wheeler and Keith Hemstreet (Travels with Gannon and Wyatt)

Botswana by Sara Louise Kras (Enchantment of the World)

Country Jumper in Botswana by Claudia Dobson-Largie

Desert Danger by J. Burchett and S. Vogler (Wild Rescue)

The Great Cake Mystery by Alexander McCall Smith (Precious Ramotswe)

The Kalahari Desert by Molly Aloian (Deserts Around the World)

The Mystery at Meerkat Hill by Alexander McCall Smith (Precious Ramotswe)

Precious and the Monkeys by Alexander McCall Smith (Precious Ramotswe)

This Is Botswana by Peter Joyce

Namibia

Follow Those Zebras: Solving a Migration Mystery by Sandra Markle

Sand and Fog: Adventures in Southern Africa by Jim Brandenburg

This Is Namibia by Peter Joyce

South Africa

Books and Bricks: How a School Rebuilt the Community by Sindiwe Magona

Cultural Traditions in South Africa by Molly Aloian

Goal! by Mina Javaherbin

The Great Penguin Rescue: Saving the African Penguins by Sandra Markle

Hector: A Boy, a Protest, and the Photograph that Changed Apartheid by Adrienne Wright

The Herd Boy by Niki Daly

Journey to Jo'Burg by Beverley Naidoo

Mama Africa! How Miriam Makeba Spread Hope with Her Song by Kathryn Erskine

Mandela: The Hero Who Led His Nation to Freedom by Ann Kramer (National Geographic Kids)

Meet Our New Student from South Africa by Melissa Koosmann

Nelson Mandela by Kadir Nelson

Rage of the Rhino by Bear Grylls (Mission: Survival)

The Rip-Roaring Mystery on the African Safari by Carole Marsh (Around the World in 80 Mysteries)

Safari in South Africa by Amanda Lumry and Laura Hurwitz (Adventures of Riley)

Shaka: King of the Zulus by Diane Stanley

South Africa by Ettagale Blauer and Jason Lauer (Enchantment of the World)

South Africa by Mary N. Oluonye (Country Explorers)

South Africa by Anita Ganeri (Benjamin Blog and His Inquisitive Dog)

South Africa by Sheila Smith Noonan (The Evolution of Africa's Major Countries)

South Africa by Lisa Owings (Blastoff Readers: Exploring Countries)

South Africa by Kremena Spengler (A Question and Answer Book)

Spotlight on South Africa by Bobbie Kalman

Welcome to South Africa by Patrick Ryan

We Visit South Africa by Tammy Gagne

The White Giraffe by Lauren St. John (Legend of the Animal Healer)

Who Was Nelson Mandela? by Pam Pollack and Meg Belviso (Who HQ)

	The Book You Chose	Date Completed
15.1 *Light Reader*		
15.2 *Interested Reader*		
15.3 *Avid Reader*		
15.4 *Committed Reader*		
15.5 *Enthralled Reader*		

South America

Challenge 16

Argentina

Argentina by Jean F. Blashfield (Enchantment of the World)

Argentina by Suzanne Paul Dell'Oro (Country Explorers)

Argentina by Mary L. Englar (A Question and Answer Book)

Argentina by Joanne Mattern (Exploring World Cultrues)

Argentina by Julie Murray (Explore the Countries)

Argentina by Kari Schuetz (Exploring Countries)

Argentina by Kristine Spanier (All Around the World)

Argentina by Kathryn Stevens (Countries: Faces and Places)

Chucaro: Wild Pony of the Pampa by Francis Kalnay

Country Jumper in Argentina by Claudia Dobson-Largie

Cultural Traditions in Argentina by Adrianna Morganelli

The Khipu and the Final Key by Gertrude Chandler Warner (The Boxcar Children)

On the Pampas by Maria Cristina Brusca

Spotlight on Argentina by Bobbie Kalman

Your Passport to Argentina by Nancy Dickmann

Bolivia

Bolivia by Lisa Owings (Exploring Countries)

Bolivia by Nel Yomtov (Enchantment of the World)

Country Jumper in Bolivia by Claudia Dobson-Largie

Brazil

Afternoon on the Amazon by Mary Pope Osborne (Magic Tree House)

Amazon Adventure: How Tiny Fish Are Saving the World's Largest Rainforest by Sy Montgomery (Scientists in the Field)

The Amazon (DK Eyewitness)

Brazil by Brandy Bauer (A Question and Answer Book)

Brazil by Susie Brooks (The Land and the People)

Brazill by Kate A. Conley (Countries)

Brazil by Anita Ganeri (Benjamin Blog and His Inquisitive Dog)

Brazil by Ann Heinrichs (Enchantment of the World)

Brazil by Joanne Mattern (All Around the World)

Brazil by Elma Schemenauer (Countries: Faces and Places)

Brazil by Colleen Sexton (Exploring Countries)

Brazil by Sarah Tieck (Explore the Countries)

Brazil by Daniel Turner (Simple Geography)

Brazil by Elizabeth Weitzman (Country Explorers)

Brazil: Devil in a Twister by Crameye Junker (The Adventurous Mailbox)

Country Jumper in Brazil by Claudia Dobson-Largie

The Diaries of Robin's Travels: Rio de Janeiro by Ken and Angie Lake

Discovering the Legend of the Amazon by Anna Hagele (Where's Eli Moore?)

The Doomed Search for the Lost City of Z by Cindy L. Rodriguez (Graphic Library)

I Escaped Amazon River Pirates by Ellie Crowe and Scott Peters

The Great Monkey Rescue: Saving the Golden Lion Tamarins by Sandra Markle

Lea Dives In by Lisa Yee (American Girl)

Lea Leads the Way by Lisa Yee (American Girl)

Let's Visit Rio de Janeiro! by Lisa Manzione (The Adventures of Bella and Harry)

The Masked Monkey by Franklin W. Dixon (Hardy Boys)

My Life in Brazil by Patience Coster (A Child's Day In...)

The Mystery in the Amazon Rainforest by Carole Marsh (Around the World in 80 Mysteries)

Mystery of the Lazy Loggerhead by Lisa Travis (Pack-n-Go Girls)

Mystery of the Troubled Toucan by Lisa Travis (Pack-n-Go Girls)

The Quest for Z: The True Story of Explorer Percy Fawcett and a Lost City in the Amazon by Greg Pizzoli

Rain Forest Relay by Kristin Earhart (Race the Wild)

Rumble in the Jungle by Geronimo Stilton

Spotlight on Brazil by Bobbie Kalman

The Tapir Scientist by Sy Montgomery (Scientists in the Field)

Travel to Brazil by Christine Layton (Searchlight Books: World Traveler)

Thea Stilton and the Race for Gold by Thea Stilton

We Visit Brazil by Kathleen Tracy

Where Is the Amazon? by Sarah Fabiny (Who HQ)

The Woolly Monkey Mysteries: The Quest to Save a Rain Forest Species by Sandra Markle

The Worst Case Scenario: Amazon by Hena Khan and David Borgenicht

Chile

The Atacama Desert by Lynn Peppas (Deserts Around the World)

Chile by Michael Burgan (Enchantment of the World)

Chile by Jennifer A. Miller (Country Explorers)

Chile by Lisa Owings (Exploring Countries)

Chile by Kristine Spanier (All Around the World)

Chile by Kremena Spengler (A Question and Answer Book)

Country Jumper in Chile by Claudia Dobson-Largie

Folk Tales from Chile by Brenda Hughes

Lucia's Travel Bus by Nam-joong Kim (Global Kids Storybooks)

Trapped: How the World Rescued 33 Miners... by Marc Aronson

We Visit Chile by Tamra Orr (Your Land and My Land)

Colombia

Biblioburro: A True Story from Colombia by Jeanette Winter

Colombia by Cheryl Blackford (Country Explorers)

Colombia by Carol Hand (Countries of the World)

Colombia by Joyce Markovics (Countries We Come From)

Colombia by Julie Murray (Explore the Countries)

Colombia by Caleb Owens (Countries: Faces and Places)

Colombia by Walter Simmons (Exploring Countries)

Colombia by Kremena Spengler (A Question and Answer Book)

Colombia by Nel Yomtov (Enchantment of the World)

Colombia Treasure Quest by Steven Wolfe Pereira and Susie Jaramillo

Country Jumper in Colombia by Claudia Dobson-Largie

Gold of the Gods by Bear Grylls (Mission: Survival)

Meet Our New Student from Colombia by Rebecca Thatcher Murcia

A Refugee's Journey from Colombia by Linda Barghoorn (Leaving My Homeland)

Returning to Colombia by Linda Barghoorn (Leaving My Homeland)

The Walls of Cartagena by Julia Durango

We Visit Colombia by Rebecca Thatcher Murcia

Ecuador

Country Jumper in Ecuador by Claudia Dobson-Largie
Ecuador by Joanne Mattern (All Around the World)
Ecuador by JoAnn Milivojevic (Enchantment of the World)
Ecuador by Lisa Owings (Exploring Countries)
Escape Galapagos by Ellen Prager (The Wonder List Adventures)
Expedition to the Galapagos Islands by Grayson Rigby
Galapagos Island by Clive Gifford (In Focus)
The Search for Olinguito: Discovering a New Species by Sandra Markle
Thea Stilton and the Chocolate Sabotage by Thea Stilton
Tuki and Moka: A Tale of Two Tamarins by Judy Young (Tales of the World)
Where Are the Galapagos Islands? by Megan Stine (Who HQ)
Your Passport to Ecuador by Sarah Cords

Guyana

Country Jumper in Guyana by Claudia Dobson-Largie
The Granny JJ Adventures series by Joshua Cartwright
Guyana by Lisa Ally (Countries We Come From)
Guyana by Marion Morrison (Enchantment of the World)
New Shoes by Sara Varon
The Rice Bag Hammock by Shaeeza Haniff

Paraguay

Country Jumper in Paraguay by Claudia Dobson-Largie

Peru

The Clue in the Crossword Cipher by Carolyn Keene (Nancy Drew)
Country Jumper in Peru by Claudia Dobson-Largie
Festival of the Sun by Jong-soon Jo (Global Kids Storybooks)
Late Lunch with Llamas by Mary Pope Osborne (Magic Tree House)
Let's Visit Machu Picchu! by Lisa Manzione (The Adventures of Bella and Harry)
Lola Levine and the Vacation Dream by Monica Brown
Lost City: The Discovery of Machu Picchu by Ted Lewin
Lost in the Amazon: A Battle for Survival in the Heart of the Amazon by Tod Olson
Machu Picchu by Kristine Spanier (Whole Wide World)
Machu Picchu: The Lost Civilization by Christina Leaf (Abandoned Places)
Machu Picchu: The Story of the Amazing Inkas and Their City in the Cloud by Elizabeth Mann (Wonders of the World)
The Mystery across the Secret Bridge by Harper Paris (Greetings from Somewhere)
The Mystery at Machu Picchu, Lost City of the Incas by Carole Marsh (Around the World in 80 Mysteries)
Peru by Michael Burgan (Enchantment of the World)

Peru by Anna Cavallo (Country Explorers)
Peru by Muriel L. Dubois (A Question and Answer Book)
Peru by Marycate O'Sullivan (Countries: Faces and Places)
Peru by Lisa Owings (Exploring Countries)
Peru: Questions and Answers by Crameye Junker (The Adventurous Mailbox)
Quest for the City of Gold by James Patterson
Secret of the Andes by Ann Nolan Clark
Secrets of the Machu Picchu by Suzanne Garbe (Archaeological Mysteries)
Sharuko: Peruvian Archaeologist by Monica Brown
Spotlight on Peru by Bobbie Kalman
Thea Stilton and the Secret City by Thea Stilton
We Visit Peru by Bonnie Hinman (Your Land and My Land)
Where Is Machu Picchu? by Megan Stine   (Who HQ)
Your Passport to Peru by Ryan Gale

Uruguay

Country Jumper in Uruguay by Claudia Dobson-Largie
Uruguay by Emily Rose Oachs (Blastoff Readers: Exploring Countries)

Venezuela

Country Jumper in Uruguay by Claudia Dobson-Largie
The People and Culture of Venezuela by Elizabeth Borngraber
Venezuela by Karen Bush Gibson (A Question and Answer Book)
Venezuela by Patrick Merrick (Countries: Faces and Places)
Venezuela by Julie Murray (Explore the Countries)
Venezuela by Kari Schuetz (Exploring Countries)
Venezuela by Terri Willis (Enchantment of the World)
We Visit Venezuela by Douglas Dillon

	The Book You Chose	Date Completed
16.1 Light Reader		
16.2 Interested Reader		
16.3 Avid Reader		
16.4 Committed Reader		
16.5 Enthralled Reader		

Southeast Asia

Challenge 17

Cambodia

Angkat: The Cambodian Cinderella by Jewell Reinhart Coburn

The Caged Birds of Phnom Penh by Frederick Li

Cambodia by Wil Mara (Enchantment of the World)

Cambodia by Adam Markovics (Countries We Come From)

Cambodia by Walter Simmons (Blastoff Readers: Exploring Countries)

Cambodia by Kristine Spanier (All Around the World)

The Cambodian Dancer: Sophany's Gift of Hope by Daryn Reicherter

Country Jumper in Cambodia by Claudia Dobson-Largie

Dara's Clever Trap by Liz Flanagan (Stories from Around the World)

Half Spoon of Rice: A Survival Story of the Cambodian Genocide by Icy Smith

A Path of Stars by Anne Sibley O'Brien

A Song for Cambodia by Michelle Lord

We Visit Cambodia by Claire O'Neal

Indonesia

All About Indonesia: Stories, Songs, Crafts and More by Linda Hibbs

Balinese Children's Favorite Stories by Victor Mason

Country Jumper in Indonesia by Claudia Dobson-Largie

Indonesia by Kristine Spanier (All Around the World)

Indonesia by Robin Lim (Country Explorers)

Indonesia by Tamra Orr (Enchantment of the World)

Indonesia by Tamra Orr (Social Studies Explorers: It's Cool to Learn about Countries)

Indonesia by Lisa Owings (Blastoff Readers: Exploring Countries)

Indonesia by Rachel Rose (Countries We Come From)

Indonesia by Mary Dodson Wade (A Question and Answer Book)

Indonesian Children's Favorite Stories by Joan Suyenaga

The Kids Who Travel the World: Indonesia by Lisa Webb

Komodo! by Peter Sis

My Life in Indonesia by Patience Coster (A Child's Day In…)

Poacher Panic by J. Burchett and S. Vogler (Wild Rescue)

Rainforest Rescue by J. Burchett and S. Vogler (Wild Rescue)

Spotlight on Indonesia by Bobbie Kalman

Tracks of the Tiger by Bear Grylls (Mission: Survival)

Welcome to Indonesia by Patrick Ryan

We Visit Indonesia by Tammy Gagne

Laos

Laos by Adam Markovics (Countries We Come From)

Laos by Emily Rose Oachs (Blastoff Readers: Exploring Countries)

Laos by Kristine Spanier (All Around the World)

Mali Under the Night Sky: A Lao Story of Home by Youme Landowne

Malaysia

The Bee Tree by Stephen Buchmann and Diana Cohn)

Malaysia by Kevin Blake (Countries We Come From)

Malaysia by Michael Burgan (Enchantment of the World)

Malaysia by Lisa Owings (Blastoff Readers: Exploring Countries)

Malaysian Children's Favorite Stories by Kay Lyons

Operation Orangutan by Amandra Lumry (Adventures of Riley)

Thea Stilton and the Rainforest Rescue by Thea Stilton
We Visit Malaysia by John Bankston
Where Are You, Sun Bear? by Eun-mi Choi

Myanmar
Burmese Children's Favorite Stories: Fables, Myths and Fairy Tales by Pascal Khoo Thwe
Hoping for a Home after Myanmar by Ellen Rodger (Leaving My Homeland)
I See the Sun in Myanmar (Burma) by Dedie King
Myanmar by Wil Mar (Enchantment of the World)
Myanmar by Anastasia Vasilyeva (Countries We Come From)
A Refugee's Journey from Myanmar by Ellen Rodger (Leaving My Homeland)

Philippines
All About the Philippines: Stories, Songs, Crafts and Games for Kids by Gidget Roceles Jimenez
The Fabulous Fiestas of the Philippines: A Seek and Find Book by Alexandra Romualdez Broekman
Filipino Children's Favorite Stories: Fables, Myths and Fairy Tales by Liana Romulo
Mango Trees by Tae-yeon Kim (Global Kids Storybooks)
The Myths and Legends of the Philippines: A Seek, Find and Reference Book by Alexandra Romualdez Broekman

Pan de Sal Saves the Day by Norma Olizon-Chikiamco
Philippines by Anne Schraff (Country Explorers)
Philippines by Michael Burgan (Countries of the World)
Philippines by Vicky Franchino (Social Studies Explorers: It's Cool to Learn about Countries)
The Philippines by Suzanne Lieurance (Top Ten Countries of Recent Immigrants)
The Philippines by Holly Longworth (Countries We Come From)
The Philippines by Joanne Mattern (Exploring World Cultures)
The Philippines by Walter Oleksy (Enchantment of the World)
Spotlight on The Philippines by Bobbie Kalman
We Visit the Philippines by John Bankston (Your Land and My Land)
We Were There at the Battle for Bataan by Benjamin Appel

Singapore
Singapore City Trails by Helen Greathead (Lonely Planet Kids)
Singapore by Wil Mara (Enchantment of the World)
Singapore by Lisa Owings (Exploring Countries)
Singapore Children's Favorite Stories by Diane Taylor
We Visit Singapore by John Bankston (Your Land and My Land)

Thailand

All About Thailand: Stories, Songs, Crafts and Games for Kids by Elaine Russell

All Thirteen: The Incredible Cave Rescue of the Thai Boys' Soccer Team by Christina Soontornvat

Aya and Bobby Discover Thailand by Christina Kristoffersson Ameln

The Case of the Silk King by Shannon Gilligan (Choose Your Own Adventure)

Cultural Traditions in Thailand by Molly Aloian

Evie and Andrew's Asian Adventures in Thailand by Katie Do Guthrie

The Floating Field: How a Group of Thai Boys Built Their Own Soccer Field by Scott Riley

A Kid's Guide to Thailand by Jack L. Roberts

Mystery of the Golden Temple by Lisa Travis (Pack-n-Go Girls)

Mystery of the Naga at Night by Lisa Travis (Pack-n-Go Girls)

Silk Umbrellas by Carolyn Marsden

Tara and the Towering Wave: An Indian Ocean Tsunami Survival Story by Cristina Oxtra (Girls Survive)

Thai Children's Favorite Stories: Fables, Myths, Legends and Fairy Tales by Marian D. Toth

Thailand by Madeline Donaldson (Country Explorers)

Thailand by Alex Ericson (Countries: Faces and Places)

Thailand by Mel Friedman (Enchantment of the World)

Thailand by by Lucia Raatma (Social Studies Explorers: It's Cool to Learn about Countries)

Thailand by Walter Simmons (Blastoff Readers: Exploring Countries)

Thailand by Kristine Spanier (All Around the World)

Thailand: The Right Kind of Tiger by Crameye Junker (The Adventurous Mailbox)

Vietnam

Adrift at Sea: A Vietnamese Boy's Story of Survival by Marsha Forchuk Skrypuch with Tuan Ho

All About Vietnam: Projects and Activities for Kids by Phuoc Thi Minh Tran

Children of the Dragon: Selected Tales from Vietnam by Sherry Garland

Cracker! The Best Dog in Vietnam by Cynthia Kadohata

Goodbye, Vietnam by Gloria Whelan

The Journal of Patrick Seamus Flaherty, United States Marine Corps, Khe Sanh, Vietnam, 1968 by Ellen Emerson White (My Name Is America)

The Land I Lost by Quang Nhuong Huynh

Last Airlift: A Vietnamese Orphan's Rescue from War by Marsha Forchuk Skrypuch

Leo Thorsness, Vietnam: Valor in the Sky by Michael P. Spradlin (Medal of Honor)

The Lotus Seed by Sherry Garland

Inside Out and Back Again by Thanhha Lai

Song of the Mekong River by Na-mi Choi (Global Kids Storybooks)

Strays by C. Alexander London (Dog Tags)

Travel to Vietnam by Christine Layton (Searchlight Books: World Traveler)

Vietnam by Mary L. Englar (A Question and Answer Book)

Vietnam by Alison Imbriaco (Top Ten Countries of Recent Immigrants)

Vietnam by Joyce Markovics (Countries We Come From)

Vietnam by Dana Meachen Rau (Social Studies Explorers: It's Cool to Learn about Countries)

Vietnam by Patrick Merrick (Countries: Faces and Places)

Vietnam by Julie Murray (Explore the Countries)

Vietnam by Karen O'Connor (Country Explorers)

Vietnam by Walter Simmons (Blastoff Readers: Exploring Countries)

Vietnam by Kristine Spanier (All Around the World)

Vietnam by Terri Willis (Enchantment of the World)

Vietnam ABCs by Theresa Alberti

Vietnam War (DK Eyewitness)

The Vietnam War by Gary Jeffrey (Graphic Modern History: Cold War Conflicts)

The Vietnam War: An Interactive Modern History Adventure by Michael Burgan (You Choose: Modern History)

Vietnam War Heroes by Allan Zullo (10 True Tales)

Vietnamese Children's Favorite Stories by Phuoc Thi Minh Tran

Water Buffalo Days: Growing Up in Vietnam by Huynh Quang Nhuong

What Was the Vietnam War? by Jim O'Connor (Who HQ)

When Heaven Fell by Carolyn Marsden

	The Book You Chose	**Date Completed**
17.1 Light Reader		
17.2 Interested Reader		
17.3 Avid Reader		
17.4 Committed Reader		
17.5 Enthralled Reader		

United States

Challenge 18

50 Adventures in the 50 States by Kate Siber

All-American Adventure by James Patterson (Treasure Hunters)

The American Story series by Betsy and Giulio Maestro

American Tall Tales by Adrien Stoutenburg

American Tall Tales by Mary Pope Osborne

America's National Parks by Alexa Ward (Lonely Planet Kids)

And Then What Happenened, Paul Revere? by Jean Fritz

Baby-Sitters Club in the U.S.A. by Ann M. Martin (Baby-Sitters Club Super Special)

Birth of the Star-Spangled Banner by Thomas Kingsley Troupe (A Fly on the Wall History)

Capital Mysteries series by Ron Roy

The Case of Capital Intrigue by Carolyn Keene (Nancy Drew)

The Children's Book of America by William J. Bennett

The Counterfeit Constitution Mystery by Carole Marsh (Real Kids, Real Places)

The Creation of the U.S. Constitution by Michael Burgan (Graphic Library)

The Genius Files series by Dan Gutman

The Great Train Mystery by Carole Marsh (Real Kids, Real Places)

Grover Cleveland Again! A Treasury of American Presidents by Ken Burns

Henry Reed's Journey by Keith Robertson

I Can Make This Promise by Christine Day

If America Were a Village by David J. Smith (CitizenKid)

Judy's Journey by Lois Lenski (American Regional)

Midwest by Tamra B. Orr (It's Cool to Learn About the United States)

Minn of the Mississippi by Holling C. Holling

The Mystery in Washington D.C. by Gertrude Chandler Warner (The Boxcar Children)

The National Parks: Discover All 62 National Parks of the United States! (DK)

Northeast by Vicky Franchino (It's Cool to Learn About the United States)

Only in America: The Weird and Wonderful 50 States by Heather Alexander

Out Fifty States by Mark H. Bockenhauer and Stephen F. Cunha (National Geographic)

The Race across America by Geronimo Stilton

The Secret of the Scarlet Hand by Carolyn Keene (Nancy Drew)

Shh! We're Writing the Constitution by Jean Fritz

Skating with the Statue of Liberty by Susan Lynn Meyer

Southwest by Tamra B. Orr (It's Cool to Learn About the United States)

Spotlight on the United States of America by Bobbie Kalman

Thea Stilton and the American Dream by Thea Stilton

This Is America by M. Sasek

Tintin in America by Herge

Ultimate U.S. Road Trip Atlas by Crispin Boyer (National Geographic Kids)

United States by Elden Croy (National Geographic)

United States by Robert Grayson (Countries of the World)

United States by Julie Murray (Explore the Countries)

The United States by Kremena Spengler (A Question and Answer Book)

The United States by Kathryn Stevens (Countries: Faces and Places)

United States Encyclopedia: America's People, Places, and Events (National Geographic)

United States of America by Michael Burgan (Enchantment of the World)

United States of America by Anita Ganeri (Benjamin Blog and His Inquisitive Dog)

United States of America by Katie Marsico (Social Studies Explorers: It's Cool to Learn about Countries)

The United States of America: A State-by-State Guide by Millie Miller and Cyndi Nelson

The U.S. Capital Commotion by Jeff Brown (Flat Stanley's Worldwide Adventures)

Washington D.C. City Trails by Moira Butterfield (Lonely Planet Kids)

Welcome to America, Champ! By Catherine Stier (Tales of the World)

West by Barbara A. Somervill (It's Cool to Learn About the United States)

We the People: The Constitution of the United States by Peter Spier

What Is the Constitution? by Patricia Brenna Demuth (Who HQ)

What Is the Declaration of Independence? by Michael C. Harris (Who HQ)

What's the Big Idea, Ben Franklin? by Jean Fritz

Where Is Mount Rushmore? by True Kelley (Who HQ)

Where Is the Grand Canyon? by Jim O'Connor (Who HQ)

Where Is the Mississippi River? by Dina Anastasio (Who HQ)

Where Is the White House? by Megan Stine (Who HQ)

Where Was Patrick Henry on the 29th of May? by Jean Fritz

The White House Christmas Mystery by Carole Marsh (Real Kids, Real Places)

	The Book You Chose	**Date Completed**
18.1 *Light Reader*		
18.2 *Interested Reader*		
18.3 *Avid Reader*		
18.4 *Committed Reader*		
18.5 *Enthralled Reader*		

China

Challenge 19

Adventures in Ancient China by Linda Bailey (Good Times Travel Agency)

Alvin Ho: Allergic to the Great Wall, the Forbidden Palace, and Other Tourist Attractions by Lenore Look

Anno's China by Mitsumasa Anno

Bronze and Sunflower by Cao Wenxuan

Chee-Lin: A Giraffe's Journey by James Rumford

China by Anita Ganeri (Benjamin Blog and His Inquisitive Dog)

China by Joyce Markovics (Countries We Come From)

China by Joanne Mattern (All Around the World)

China by Julie Murray (Explore the Countries)

China by Emily Rose Oachs (Country Profiles)

China by Nathan Olson (A Question and Answer Book)

China by Pat Ryan (Countries: Faces and Places)

China by Walter Simmons (Blastoff Readers: Exploring Countries)

China by Nel Yomtov (Enchantment of the World)

China, Land of the Emperor's Great Wall by Mary Pope Osborne (Magic Tree House Fact Tracker)

China Through Time (DK)

Chinese Culture by Mary Colson (Global Cultures)

Chinese Dragons by R. A. Montgomery (Choose Your Own Adventure)

Chinese Fairy Tales and Legends by Frederick H. Martens

Chu Ju's House by Gloria Whelan

Country Jumper in China by Claudia Dobson-Largie

The Cricket Warrior: A Chinese Tale by Margaret and Raymond Chang

Day of the Dragon King by Mary Pope Osborne (Magic Tree House)

The Detour of the Elephants by Getrude Chandler Warner (The Boxcar Children)

Earthquake Escape by J. Burchett and S. Vogler (Wild Rescue)

The Flying Chinese Wonders by Jeff Brown (Flat Stanley's Worldwide Adventures)

Great Wall of China by Kristine Spanier (Whole Wide World)

The Great Wall: The Story of Thousands of Miles of Earth and Stone That Turned a Nation Into a Fortress by Elizabeth Mann (Wonders of the World)

Homesick: My Own Story by Jean Fritz

The House of Sixty Fathers by Meindert DeJong

Hu Wan and the Sleeping Dragon by Judy Young

Illustrated Stories from China (Usborne)

A Kid's Guide to China by Jack L. Roberts

Lady of Ch'iao Kuo: Warrior of the South, Southern China, A.D. 531 by Laurence Yep (The Royal Diaries)

Let's Visit Beijing! by Lisa Manzione (The Adventures of Bella and Harry)

Liang's Treasure by Yeo-rim Yun (Global Kids Storybooks)

The Mystery in the Forbidden City by Harper Paris (Greetings from Somewhere)

The Mystery on the Great Wall of China by Carole Marsh (Around the World in 80 Mysteries)

People's Republic of China by Wil Mara (Enchantment of the World)

Red Butterfly by A. L. Sonnichsen

Ruby's Wish by Shirin Yim Bridges

The Silk Route: 7,000 Miles of History by John S. Major

Spring Pearl: The Last Flower by Laurence Yep (Girls of Many Lands)

Starry River of the Sky by Grace Lin

Tiananmen Square: Massacre in China by Wil Mara (Cornerstones of Freedom)

Travel to China by Christine Layton (Searchlight Books: World Traveler)

The Weaving of a Dream by Marilee Heyer

When the Sea Turned to Silver by Grace Lin

Where Is Mount Everest? by Nico Medina (Who HQ)

Where Is the Great Wall? by Patricia Brennan Demuth (Who HQ)

Where the Mountain Meets the Moon by Grace Lin (Who HQ)

Who Was Confucius? by Michael Burgan (Who HQ)

The Year of the Panda by Miriam Schlein

Young Fu of the Upper Yangtze by Elizabeth Foreman Lewis

Your Passport to China by Douglas Hustad (World Passport)

You Wouldn't Want to Work on the Great Wall of China! Defenses You'd Rather Not Build by Jacqueline Morley

	The Book You Chose	**Date Completed**
19.1 Light Reader		
19.2 Interested Reader		
19.3 Avid Reader		
19.4 Committed Reader		
19.5 Enthralled Reader		

Late 1800s in the U.S.

Challenge 20

Post-Civil War

All Different Now by Angela Johnson

The Assassination of Abraham Lincoln by Jessica Gunderson (Days That Changed America)

The Assassination of Abraham Lincoln by Kay Melchisedech Olson (Graphic Library)

The Buffalo Soldier by Sherry Garland

Crow by Barbara Wright

Dark Sky Rising: Reconstruction and the Dawn of Jim Crow by Henry Louis Gates, Jr.

Days of Jubilee: The End of Slavery in the United States by Patricia C. and Fredrick L. McKissack

Emma Eileen Grove, Mississippi, 1865 by Kathleen Duey (American Diaries)

Forty Acres and Maybe a Mule by Harriette Gillem Robinet

I Thought My Soul Would Rise and Fly by Joyce Hansen (Dear America)

Journey to a Promised Land: A Story of the Exodusters by Allison Lassieur (I Am America)

The Reconstruction Amendments by Michael Burgan (We the People)

Reconstruction Junction by Bentley Boyd (Chester the Crab Comix with Content)

Run Away Home by Patricia C. McKissack

Shades of Gray by Carolyn Reeder

Storm Warriors by Elisa Carbone

The Story of Juneteenth: An Interactive History Adventure by Steven Otfinoski (You Choose: History)

Tracking an Assassin! by Nel Yomtov (Nickolas Flux History Chronicles)

Whistler in the Dark by Kathleen Ernst (History Mysteries)

Settlers / Wild West

Away West by Patricia McKissack (Scraps of Time)

The Battle of the Little Bighorn by Gary Jeffrey (Graphic History of the American West)

Behind the Masks: The Diary of Angeline Reddy, Bodie, California, 1880 by Susan Patron (Dear America)

Brave Buffalo Fighter by John D. Fitzgerald

Buffalo Soldiers: Heroes of the American West by Brynn Baker (Military Heroes)

Can You Survive the Schoolchildren's Blizzard? by Ailynn Collins (You Choose: Disasters in History)

Cowboys on the Western Trail: The Cattle Drive Adventures of Joshua McNabb and Davy Bartlett by Eric Oatman

Ellen Elizabeth Hawkins: Texas, 1886 by Kathleen Duey (American Diaries)

I Survived the Children's Blizzard, 1888 by Lauren Tarshis

The Journal of Joshua Loper: A Black Cowboy, The Chisolm Trail, 1871 by Walter Dean Myers (My Name Is America)

Journey to a Promised Land: A Story of the Exodusters by Allison Lassieur (I Am America)

Land of the Buffalo Bones: The Diary of Mary Ann Elizabeth Rodgers, An English Girl in Minnesota, New Yeovil, Minnesota, 1873 by Marion Dean Bauer (Dear America)

Kirsten series by Janet Shaw (American Girl)

Meg's Prairie Diary series by Kate McMullan (My America)

Miranda's Last Stand by Gloria Whelan

My Face to the Wind: The Diary of Sarah Jane Price, A Prairie Teacher, Broken Bow, Nebraska, 1881 by Jim Murphy (Dear America)

On the Banks of Plum Creek by Laura Ingalls Wilder

The Prairie Adventure of Sarah and Annie, Blizzard Survivors by Marty Rhodes Figley

The Quilt Walk by Sandra Dallas

The Railroad, the Telegraph, and Other Technologies by Xina M. Uhl (Westward Expansion: America's Push to the Pacific)

The Runaway Friend: A Kirsten Mystery by Kathleen Ernst (American Girl)

Sarah, Plain and Tall by Patricia McLachlan

West to a Land of Plenty: The Diary of Teresa Angelino Viscardi, New York to Idaho Territory, 1883 by Jim Murphy (Dear America)

We Were There on the Chisholm Trail by Ross McLaury Taylor

Wild Bill Hickok Tames the Wild West by Stewart H. Holbrook

The Wild West: Spies, Secret Missions, and Hidden Facts by Stephanie Bearce

Great Chicago Fire

Cinders by Kate Klimo (Horse Diaries)

Down the Rabbit Hole: The Diary of Pringle Rose, Chicago, Illinois, 1871 by Susan Campbell Bartoletti (Dear America)

Emmi in the City: A Great Chicago Fire Survival Story by Salima Alikhan (Girls Survive)

The Great Chicago Fire: All Is Not Lost by Steven Otfinoski (Tangled History)

The Great Chicago Fire of 1871 by Kay Melchisedech Olson (Graphic Library)

The Great Chicago Fire: Rising from the Ashes by Kate Hannigan (History Comics)

The Great Fire by Jim Murphy

I Survived the Great Chicago Fire 1871 by Lauren Tarshis

Sparky by Kate Klimo

Surviving the Great Chicago Fire by Joann Cleland (Eye on History)

What Was the Great Chicago Fire? by Janet B. Pascal (Who HQ)

	The Book You Chose	Date Completed
20.1 Light Reader		
20.2 Interested Reader		
20.3 Avid Reader		
20.4 Committed Reader		
20.5 Enthralled Reader		

Early 1900s in the U.S.

Challenge 21

San Francisco Earthquake

Can You Survive the Great San Francisco Earthquake? by Ailynn Collins (You Choose: Disasters in History)

A City Tossed and Broken: The Diary of Minnie Bonner, San Francisco, California, 1906 by Judy Blundell (Dear America)

The Earth Dragon Awakes: The San Francisco Earthquake of 1906 by Laurence Yep

Earthquake! A Story of the San Francisco Earthquake by Kathleen V. Kudlinski (Once Upon America)

Earthquake at Dawn by Kristiana Gregory

Earthquake in the Early Morning by Mary Pope Osborne (Magic Tree House)

Earthquake: San Francisco, 1906 by Kathleen Duey and Karen A. Bale (Survivors)

Earthquake Shock by Marlane Kennedy (Disaster Strikes)

Escape from the Great Earthquake by Kate Messner (Ranger in Time)

I Survived the San Francisco Earthquake by Lauren Tarshis

Lizzie Newton and the San Francisco Earthquake by Stephen Krensky (History Speaks)

Quake! Disaster in San Francisco, 1906 by Gail Langer Karwoski

The San Francisco Earthquake of 1906 by Marcia Amidon Lusted (Perspectives Library)

Surviving the San Francisco Earthquake by Joann Cleland (Eye on History)

What Was the San Francisco Earthquake? by Dorothy Hoobler

When the Earth Dragon Trembled: A Story of Chinatown during the San Francisco Earthquake and Fire by Judy Dodge Cummings (I Am America)

Immigrants

At Ellis Island: A History in Many Voices by Louise Peacock

Dreams in the Golden Country: The Diary of Zipporah Feldman, a Jewish Immigrant Girl, New York City, 1903 by Kathryn Lasky (Dear America)

Ellis Island by Elaine Landau (A True Book)

Ellis Island by Melissa McDaniel (Cornerstones of Freedom)

Ellis Island: An Interactive History Adventure by Michael Burgan (You Choose: History)

Emma's New Beginning by Jessica Gunderson

Hannah's Journal: The Story of an Immigrant Girl by Marissa Moss

In the Shadow of Lady Liberty: Immigrant Stories from Ellis Island by Danny Kravitz

The Journal of Otto Peltonen: A Finnish Immigrant by William Durbin (My Name Is America)

Journey to Ellis Island: How My Father Came to America by Carol Bierman

Nell Dunne: Ellis Island, 1904 by Kathleen Duey (American Diaries)

The Orphan of Ellis Island: A Time-Travel Adventure by Elvira Woodruff

Sofia's Immigrant Diary series by Kathryn Lasky (My America)

We Came through Ellis Island: The Immigrant Adventures of Emma Markowitz by Gare Thompson (National Geographic: I Am American)

What Was Ellis Island? by Patricia Brenna Demuth (Who HQ)

Great Migration

Color Me Dark by Patricia McKissack (Dear America)

The Great Migration by Duchess Harris (Freedom's Promise)

The Great Migration: Journey to the North by Eloise Greenfield

The Harlem Renaissance by Duchess Harris (Freedom's Promise)

The Harlem Renaissance: An Interactive History Adventure by Allison Lassieur (You Choose: History)

Moving North: African Americans and the Great Migration, 1915–1930 by Monica Halpern

Moving North: The Johnson Family in the Great Migration by Mary J. Grant

Overground Railroad by Lesa Cline-Ransome

Women's Suffrage

Francesca Vigiluccie: Washington, D.C. 1913 by Kathleen Duey (American Diaries)

National Woman's Party Fight for Suffrage by Emily Beth Sohn (Graphic Library)

Rightfully Ours: How Women Won the Vote by Kerrie Logan Hollihan

Secrets on 26th Street by Elizabeth McDavid Jones (History Mysteries)

A Time for Courage: The Suffragette Diary of Kathleen Bowen, Washington, D.C. 1917, by Kathryn Lasky (Dear America)

Women's Right to Vote by Kate Messner

Labor Issues

The 1899 Newsboys' Strike by Nel Yomtov (Graphic Library)

Annie Shapiro and the Clothing Workers' Strike by Marlene Targ Brill (History Speaks)

The Child Labor Reform Movement: An Interactive History Adventure by Steven Otfinoski (You Choose: History)

Factory Girl by Barbara Greenwood

Finder: Coal Mine Dog by Alison Hart (Dog Chronicles)

Fire at the Triangle Factory by Holly Littlefield (On My Own)

The Haymarket Square Tragedy by Michael Burgan (We the People)

Hear My Sorrow: The Diary of Angela Denoto, a Shirtwaist Worker, New York City, 1909 by Deborah Hopkinson (Dear America)

Lucy Fights the Flames: A Triangle Shirtwaist Factory Survival Story by Julie Gilbert (Girls Survive)

The Rooftop Adventure of Minnie and Tessa, Factory Fire Survivors by Holly Littlefield (History's Kid Heroes)

The Triangle Shirtwaist Factory Fire by Jessica Sarah Gunderson (Graphic Library)

The Triangle Shirtwaist Factory Fire by Rachel A. Bailey (Perspectives Library)

Titanic

Can You Survive the Titanic? An Interactive Survival Adventure by Allison Lassieur (You Choose: Survival)

Disaster on the Titanic by Kate Messner (Ranger in Time)

Escape This Book! Titanic by Bill Doyle

Escaping Titanic: A Young Girl's True Story of Survival by Marybeth Lorbiecki

I Survived the Sinking of the Titanic 1912 by Lauren Tarshis

Kaspar the Titanic Cat by Michael Marpurgo

The Mystery of the Titanic: A Historical Investigation for Kids by Kelly Milner Halls

Noelle at Sea: A Titanic Survival Story by Nikki Shannon Smith (Girls Survive)

The Sinking of the Titanic by Marcia Amidon Lusted (Perspectives Library)

The Sinking of the Titanic by Matt Doeden (Graphic Library)

Sunny by Kate Klimo

Smooth Sea and a Fighting Chance: The Story of the Sinking Titanic by Steven Otfinoski (Tangled History)

The Titanic by Peter Benoit (Cornerstones of Freedom)

Titanic by Emma Carlson Berne (American Girl: Real Stories From My Time)

The Titanic by Kate Messner

Titanic (DK Eyewitness)

The Titanic: An Interactive History Adventure by Bob Temple (You Choose: History)

Titanic Disaster! by Nel Yomtov (Nickolas Flux History Chronicles)

Titanic Q&A: 175+ Fascinating Facts for Kids by Mary Montero (History Q&A)

The Titanic Sinks by Thomas Conklin

Titanic: Truth and Rumors by Michael Burgan (Edge Books)

Voices of the Titanic by Mary Montero

Voyage on the Great Titanic by Ellen Emerson White (Dear America)

What Was the Titanic? by Stephanie Sabol

Your Life as a Cabin Attendant on the Titanic by Jessica Gunderson (The Way It Was)

	The Book You Chose	Date Completed
21.1 Light Reader		
21.2 Interested Reader		
21.3 Avid Reader		
21.4 Committed Reader		
21.5 Enthralled Reader		

Central America

Challenge 22

Belize

Anteater Adventure by Kama Einhorn (True Tales of Rescue)
Country Jumper in Belize by Claudia Dobson-Largie

Costa Rica

Costa Rica by Jim Bartell (Exploring Countries)
Costa Rica by Elizabeth Raum (Countries Around the World)
Costa Rica by Tracey West (Country Explorer)
Costa Rica by Nel Yomtov (Enchantment of the World)
Country Jumper in Costa Rica by Claudia Dobson-Largie
The Forever Forest: Kids Save a Tropical Forest by Kristin Joy Pratt-Serafini
Handle with Care: An Unusual Butterfly Journey by Loree Griffin Burns
A Kid's Guide to Costa Rica by Jack L. Roberts and Michael Owens
The Scarlet Macaw Scandal by Carolyn Keene (Nancy Drew Girl Detective)
Sophie Washington: Mission Costa Rica by Tonya Duncan Ellis
Trails of Treachery by Carolyn Keene (Nancy Drew Girl Detective)

El Salvador

Country Jumper in El Salvador by Claudia Dobson-Largie
El Salvador by Chris Bowman (Country Profiles)
El Salvador by Kathleen W. Deady (A Question and Answer Book)
El Salvador by James M. Deem (Top Ten Countries of Recent Immigrants)
El Salvador by Joanne Mattern (All Around the World)
El Salvador by Marion Morrison (Enchantment of the World)
El Salvador by Walter Simmons (Exploring Countries)
Hoping for a Home after El Salvador by Linda Barghoorn (Leaving My Homeland)
A Refugee's Journey from El Salvador by Linda Barghoorn (Leaving My Homeland)
Your Passport to El Salvador by Sarah Cords

Guatemala

Country Jumper in Guatemala by Claudia Dobson-Largie
Elena's Story by Nancy Shaw (Tales of the World)
Guatemala by Anita Croy (Countries of the World)
Guatemala by Mary Englar (A Question and Answer Book)
Guatemala by Marion Morrison (Enchantment of the World)
Guatemala by Elma Schemenauer (Countries: Faces and Places)
Guatemala by Kari Schuetz (Exploring Countries)
Libertad by Alma Fullerton
Mayan Folktales by James D. Sexton
The Most Beautiful Place in the World by Ann Cameron
A Refugee's Journey from Guatemala by Heather Hudak (Leaving My Homeland)
Returning to Guatemala by Heather C. Hudak (Leaving My Homeland)
Tikal: The Center of the Maya World by Elizabeth Mann (Wonders of the World)
Your Passport to Guatemala by Nancy Dickmann

Honduras

Country Jumper in Honduras by Claudia Dobson-Largie

The Good Garden by Katie Smith Milway

Honduras by Ellen Frazel (Exploring Countries)

Honduras by Sara Louise Kras (Enchantment of the World)

Honduras by Patrick Merrick (Countries: Faces and Places)

Secrets of the Lost City: A Scientific Adventure in the Honduran Rain Forest by Sandra Markle

Mexico

The Amazing Mexican Secret by Jeff Brown (Flat Stanley's Worldwide Adventures)

Basil in Mexico by Eve Titus (The Great Mouse Detective)

Becoming Naomi Leon by Pam Munoz Ryan

The Clue of the Black Keys by Carolyn Keene (Nancy Drew)

The Corn Grows Ripe by Dorothy Rhoads

Dancing Home by Alma Flor Ada

The Day It Snowed Tortillas: Folktales Told in Spanish and English by Joe Hayes

Elena by Diane Stanley

Explore Mexico: A Coco Discovery Book by Lars Ortiz

Folktales of Mexico: Horse Hooves and Chicken Feet by Neil Philip

The Happy Hollisters and the Mystery of the Mexican Idol by Jerry West

The Hungry Wolf: A Tale from Mexico by Lari Don (Stories from Around the World)

Immigrants from Mexico and Central America by Emma Carlson Berne (Fact Finders: Immigration Today)

A Kid's Guide to Mexico by Jack L. Roberts

Lady of Palenque: Flower of Bacal, Mesoamerica, A.D. 749 by Anna Kirwan (The Royal Diaries)

Made in Mexico by Peter Laufer and Susan Roth (National Geographic)

Meet Our New Student from Mexico by Tamra Orr

Mexican Culture by Lori McManus (Global Cultures)

Mexico by Mary Berendes and R. Conrad Stein (Countries: Faces and Places)

Mexico by Jessica Dean (All Around the World)

Mexico by Anita Ganeri (Benjamin Blog and His Inquisitive Dog)

Mexico by Beth Gruber (Countries of the World)

Mexico by Fran Hodgkins (A Question and Answer Book)

Mexico by Suzanne Lieurance (Top Top Countries of Recent Immigrants)

Mexico by Jessica Rudolph (Countries We Come From)

Mexico by Colleen Sexton (Exploring Countries)

Mexico by Barbara A. Somervill (Social Studies Explorers: It's Cool to Learn about Countries)

Mexico by Sarah Tieck (Explore the Countries)

Mystery in Mayan Mexico by Marcia Wells (Eddie Red, Undercover)

Mystery of the Disappearing Dolphin by Janelle Diller (Pack-n-Go Girls)

Mystery of the Thief in the Night by Janelle Diller (Pack-n-Go Girls)

Nacar: The White Deer by Elizabeth Borton de Trevino

P Is for Pinata: A Mexico Alphabet by Tony Johnston

Shadow of the Shark by Mary Pope Osborne (Magic Tree House)

Soccer on Sunday by Mary Pope Osborne (Magic Tree House)
Spotlight on Mexico by Bobbie Kalman
Travel to Mexico by Matt Doeden (Searchlight Books: World Traveler)
We Visit Mexico by Tammy Gagne

Nicaragua

Meet Our New Student from Nicaragua by John A. Torres
Nicaragua by Wil Mara (Enchantment of the World)
Nicaragua by Lisa Owings (Exploring Countries)
Nicaragua by Charles J. Shields (Central America Today)

Panama

The Case of the Vanishing Golden Frogs by Sandra Markle
Delta Force: Hostage in Panama! by Sarah Eason (Mission: Special Ops)
Panama by Heather Adamson (Exploring Countries)
Panama by Jean F. Blashfield (Enchantment of the World)
Panama by Kristine Spanier (All Around the World)
The Panama Canal: The Story of How a Jungle Was Conquered and the World Was Made Smaller by Elizabeth Mann (Wonders of the World)
What Is the Panama Canal? by Janet B. Pascal (Who HQ)

	The Book You Chose	**Date Completed**
22.1 Light Reader		
22.2 Interested Reader		
22.3 Avid Reader		
22.4 Committed Reader		
22.5 Enthralled Reader		

World War I

Challenge 23

Many titles duplicated in the country listing:

At Battle in World War I: An Interactive Battlefield Adventure by Allison Lassieur (You Choose: Battlefields)

Anastasia: The Last Grand Duchess by Carolyn Meyer (The Royal Diaries) (Russia)

Archie's War by Marcia Williams (England)

Darling: Mercy Dog of World War I by Alison Hart (Dog Chronicles)

Edith Cavell: Nurse Hero by Terri Arthur and Jaclyn Taylor

Everything World War I by Karen L. Kenney

Gallipoli and the Southern Theaters by Gary Jeffrey (Graphic Modern History: World War I)

Harlem Hellfighters: African-American Heroes of World War I by John Micklos, Jr. (Military Heroes)

Lawrence of Arabia and the Middle East and Africa by Gary Jeffrey (Graphic Modern History: World War I)

Like the Willow Tree by Lois Lowry (Dear America)

The Night Flyers by Elizabeth McDavid Jones (History Mysteries)

The Night the Bells Rang by Natalie Kinsey-Warnock

On the Eastern Front by Gary Jeffrey (Graphic Modern History: World War I)

On the Western Front by Gary Jeffrey (Graphic Modern History: World War I)

One-of-a-Kind Mallie by Kimberly Brubaker Bradley

Rags: Hero Dog of WWI by Margot Theis Raven (France)

Sergeant Stubby: Hero Pup of World War I by Laurie Calkhoven (G.I. Dogs)

Shooting at the Stars: The Christmas Truce of 1914 by John Hendrix (France)

The Singing Tree by Kate Seredy (Hungary)

The Sinking of the Lusitania: An Interactive History Adventure by Steven Otfinoski (You Choose: History)

Spies of World War I: An Interactive Espionage Adventure by Elizabeth Raum (You Choose: Spies)

Stranger on the Home Front: A Story of Indian Immigrants and World War I by Maya Chhabra (I Am America)

Stubby by Kate Klimo

Stubby the Dog Soldier: World War I Hero by Blake Hoena (Animal Heroes)

Treaties, Trenches, Mud, and Blood by Nathan Hale (Hazardous Tales)

True Stories of World War I by Nel Yomtov

War at Sea by Gary Jeffrey (Graphic Modern History: World War I)

War Horse by Michael Morpurgo

War in the Air by Gary Jeffrey (Graphic Modern History: World War I)

We Were There with the Lafayette Escadrille by Clayton and K.S. Knight

Winnie's Great War by Lindsay Mattick and Josh Greenhut

World War I (DK Eyewitness)

World War I by Joe Giorello (Great Battles for Boys)

World War I by Josh Gregory (Cornerstones of Freedom)

World War I: An Interactive History Adventure by Gwyneth Swain (You Choose: History)

World War I: Spies, Secret Missions, and Hidden Facts by Stephanie Bearce

The World War I Web by Bentley Boyd (Chester the Crab Comix with Content)

The World Wars by Paul Dowswell

	The Book You Chose	**Date Completed**
23.1 *Light Reader*		
23.2 *Interested Reader*		
23.3 *Avid Reader*		
23.4 *Committed Reader*		
23.5 *Enthralled Reader*		

Fantasy / Sci-Fi

Challenge 24

100 Cupboards series by N. D. Wilson
Andrew and the Firedrake by Douglas Wilson
At the Back of the North Wind by George MacDonald
Beauty by Robin McKinley
Beyonders trilogy by Brandon Mull
The Borrowers by Mary Norton
Boys of Blur by N.D. Wilson
Brave Red, Smart Frog: A New Book of Old Tales by Emily Jenkins
Chronicle of the Dark Star trilogy by Kevin Emerson
The Chronicles of Narnia series by C.S. Lewis
Circus Mirandus by Cassie Beasley
Clever Jack Takes the Cake by Candace Fleming
The Dark Is Rising series by Susan Cooper
The Dragonfly Pool by Eva Ibbotsen
Ella Enchanted by Gail Carson Levine
Freaky Friday by Mary Rodgers
Fairy Tale Comics by Chris Duff
Floors by Patrick Carman
Gregor the Overlander series by Suzanne Collins
Guardians of Ga'hoole series by Kathryn Lasky

Harry Potter and the Sorcerer's Stone by J.K. Rowling
The Hobbit by J.R.R. Tolkien
The Legend of the Lady's Slipper by Kathy-jo Wargin
The Lighthouse between the Worlds by Melanie Crowder
Miss Pickerell series by Ellen MacGregor
The Mushroom Planet series by Eleanor Cameron
The Ordinary Princess by M.M. Kaye
Oz series by L. Frank Baum
The Princess and the Goblin by George MacDonald
Princess Sonora and the Long Sleep by Gail Carson Levine
Redwall series by Brian Jacques
The Rise and Fall of Mount Majestic by Jennifer Trafton
The Secret Keepers by Trenton Lee Stewart
The Ship of Stolen Words by Fran Wilde
The Tale of Despereaux by Kate diCamillo
The Thirteen Clocks by James Thurber
Twig by Elizabeth Orton Jones
The Unwanteds series by Lisa McMann
Wilderking trilogy by Jonathan Rogers
The Wolves of Willoughby Chase by Joan Aiken
A Wrinkle in Time by Madeleine L'Engle

	The Book You Chose	Date Completed
24.1 *Light Reader*		
24.2 *Interested Reader*		
24.3 *Avid Reader*		
24.4 *Committed Reader*		
24.5 *Enthralled Reader*		

Great Depression

Challenge 25

Agnes May Gleason: Walsenburg, Colorado, 1933 by Kathleen Duey (American Diaries)

Blue Willow by Doris Gates

Bud, Not Buddy by Christopher Paul Curtis

Born and Bred in the Great Depression by Jonah Winter

Children of the Dust Bowl: The True Story of the School at Weedpatch Camp by Jerry Stanley

Christmas After All: The Diary of Minnie Swift, Indianapolis, Indiana, 1932 by Kathryn Lasky (Dear America)

The Dust Bowl by Christine Zuchora-Walske (Perspectives Library)

The Dust Bowl: An Interactive History Adventure by Allison Lassieur (You Choose: History)

Esperanza Rising by Pam Muñoz Ryan

The Everlasting Now by Sara Harrell Banks

Full of Beans by Jennifer L. Holm

The Great Depression by Melissa McDaniel (Cornerstones of Freedom)

The Great Depression for Kids: Hardship and Hope in 1930s America by Cheryl Mullenbach

The Hindenburg Disaster by Matt Doeden (Graphic Library)

The Home-Run King by Patricia McKissack (Scraps of Time)

Hoping for Rain: The Dust Bowl Adventures of Patty and Earl Buckler by Kate Connell (National Geographic (I Am American)

If the Fire Comes: A Story of Segregation during the Great Depression by Tracy Daley (I Am America)

I Survived the Hindenburg Disaster by Lauren Tarshis

A Jar of Dreams by Yoshiko Uchida

The Journal of C.J. Jackson: A Dust Bowl Migrant, Oklahoma to California, 1935 by William Durbin (My Name is America)

A Letter to Mrs. Roosevelt by C. Coco De Young

The Lucky Star by Judy Young

Lucky's Mountain by Dianne Maycock (Orca Young Readers)

The Mighty Miss Malone by Christopher Paul Curtis

Mirror, Mirror on the Wall by Barry Deneberg (Dear America)

Mississippi Morning by Ruth Vander Zee

A Nation's Hope by Matt de la Peña

The Rescue Adventure of Stenny Green, Hindenburg Crash Eyewitness by Candice Ransom

Risky Chance by Alison Hart (Horse Diaries)

R My Name Is Rachel by Patricia Reilly Giff

Rose's Journal: The Story of a Girl in the Great Depression by Marissa Moss

Secret Signs by Jacqueline Guest (Orca Young Readers)

Stella by Starlight by Sharon M. Draper

Survival in the Storm: The Dust Bowl Diary of Grace Edwards, Dalhart, Texas, 1935 by Katelan Janke (Dear America)

Surviving the Dust Bowl by Joann Cleland (Eye on History)

Turtle in Paradise by Jennifer L. Holm

Under a Living Sky by Joseph Simons (Orca Young Readers)

Voices of the Dust Bowl by Sherry Garland

	The Book You Chose	Date Completed
25.1 *Light Reader*		
25.2 *Interested Reader*		
25.3 *Avid Reader*		
25.4 *Committed Reader*		
25.5 *Enthralled Reader*		

Northern Europe

Challenge 26

Denmark

Anno's Denmark by Mitsumasa Anno

Country Jumper in Denmark by Claudia Dobson-Largie

The Crow–Girl by Bodil Bredsdorff

Denmark by Julie Murray (Explore the Countries)

Denmark by R. Conrad Stein (Enchantment of the World)

Denmark by Derek Zobel (Exploring Countries)

Favorite Fairy Tales Told in Denmark by Victoria Haviland

The Happy Hollisters and the Mystery of the Little Mermaid by Jerry West

Sticks across the Chimney by Nora Burglon

A Time to Be Brave by Joan Betty Stuchner (Stepping Stones)

The Yellow Star: The Legend of King Christian X of Denmark by Carmen Agra Deedy

Finland

Country Jumper in Finland by Claudia Dobson-Largie

Finland by Geri Clark (Enchantment of the World)

Finland by Donald B. Lemke (A Question and Answer Book)

Finland by Kristine Spanier (All Around the World)

Finland by Megan Borgert-Spaniol (Exploring Countries)

Finland: The Mysterious Triplets by Crameye Junker (The Adventurous Mailbox)

An Illustrated Kalevala: Myths and Legends from Finland by Kirsti Makinen

Tales from a Finnish Tupa by James Cloyd Bowman

Greenland

Escape Greenland by Ellen Prager (The Wonder List Adventures)

First Light by Rebecca Stead

Greenland by Ruth Bjorklund (Enchantment of the World)

Greenland by David C. King (Cultures of the World)

Greenland by Patti Wheeler and Keith Hemstreet (Travels with Gannon and Wyatt)

Who Was Leif Erikson? by Nico Medina (Who HQ)

Iceland

The Arctic Patrol Mystery by Franklin W. Dixon (Hardy Boys)

Country Jumper in Iceland by Claudia Dobson-Largie

The Falcon's Feather by Trudi Trueit (Explorer Academy)

The Happy Hollisters and the Mystery of the Midnight Trolls by Jerry West

Iceland by Jennifer A. Miller (Country Explorers)

Iceland by Lisa Owings (Exploring Countries)

Iceland by Barbara A. Somervill (Enchantment of the World)

A Kid's Guide to Iceland by Jack L. Roberts and Michael Owens

Life on Surtsey: Iceland's Upstart Island by Loree Griffin Burns (Scientists in the Field)

Mystery of the Hidden Elves by Gertrude Chandler Warner (The Boxcar Children)

Puffling Patrol by Ted and Betsy Lewin

Thea Stilton and the Frozen Fiasco by Thea Stilton

Top Secret Smackdown by Mac Barnett (Mac B., Kid Spy)

Norway

Adventures with Waffles by Maria Parr

Arne and the Christmas Star by Alta Halverson Seymour

Astrid the Unstoppable by Maria Parr

Children of the Northlights by Ingri and Edgar Parin d'Aulaire

The Christmas Star by Alta Halverson Seymour

D'Aulaire's Book of Norwegian Folktales by Ingri and Edgar Parin d'Aulaire

Far North by Jan Reynolds (Vanishing Cultures)
A Grandma for Christmas by Alta Halverson Seymour
Happy Times in Norway by Sigrid Undset
My Grandmother Ironed the King's Shirts by Torill Kove
Nordic Tales: Folktales from Norway, Sweden, Finland, Iceland, and Denmark by Ulla Thynell
Norway by Deborah Kopka (Country Explorers)
Norway by Wil Mara (Enchantment of the World)
Norway by Julie Murray (Explore the Countries)
Norway by Kristine Spanier (All Around the World)
Norway by Derek Zobel (Exploring Countries)
Ola by Ingri and Edgar Parin d'Aulaire
Sigurd and His Brave Companions by Sigrid Undset
Sister Bear: A Norse Tale by Jane Yolen
Snow Treasure by Marie McSwigan
The Terrible Troll–Bird by Ingri and Edgar d'Aulaire
You Wouldn't Want to Be a Viking Explorer! by Andrew Langley

Sweden

Call across the Sea by Kathy Kacer (The Heroes Quartet)
The Children of Noisy Village by Astrid Lindgren

The Christmas Camera by Alta Halverson Seymour
Cultural Traditions in Sweden by Natalie Hyde
Flicka, Ricka, Dicka series by Maj Lindman
The Gate Swings In: A Story of Sweden by Nora Burglon
Happy Times in Noisy Village by Astrid Lindgren
Karl, Get Out of the Garden! Carolus Linnaeus and the Naming of Everything by Anita Sanchez
Kristina: The Girl King, Sweden, 1638 by Carolyn Meyer (The Royal Diaries)
Pippi Longstocking series by Astrid Lindgren
Queen Christina of Sweden by Joanne Mattern
Snipp, Snapp, Snurr series by Maj Lindman
The Snow Queen by Hans Christian Andersen, illustrated by Bagram Ibatoulline
Sweden by Amy Rechner (Country Profiles)
Sweden by Ann Heinrichs (Enchantment of the World)
Sweden by Charles Phillips (Countries of the World)
Sweden by Jessica Dean (All Around the World)
Sweden by Joanne Mattern (Exploring World Cultures)
Sweden by Julie Murray (Explore the Countries)
Sweden by Rachel Grack (Exploring Countries)
Swedish Fairy Tales illustrated by John Bauer

	The Book You Chose	**Date Completed**
26.1 Light Reader		
26.2 Interested Reader		
26.3 Avid Reader		
26.4 Committed Reader		
26.5 Enthralled Reader		

Nazi Invasion / Holocaust

Challenge 27

Air Raid Search and Rescue by Marcus Sutter (Soldier Dogs)

Benno and the Night of Broken Glass by Meg Wiviott

Black Radishes by Susan Lynn Meyer

The Butterfly by Patricia Polacco

Call across the Sea by Kathy Kacer

Catherine's War by Julia Billet

The Cats in Kraskinski Square by Karen Hesse

The Champion of Children: The Story of Janusz Korczak by Tomek Bogacki

The Devil in Vienna by Doris Orgel (Austria)

Don't Tell the Nazis by Marsha Forchuk Skrypuch

Eli Remembers by Ruth Vander Zee

Faraway Home by Marilyn Taylor

A Faraway Island by Annika Thor

Fight for Survival: The Story of the Holocaust by Jessica Freeburg (Tangled History)

Genevieve's War by Patricia Reilly Giff

The Greatest Skating Race by Louise Borden

Hedy's Journey: The True Story of a Hungarian Girl Fleeing the Holocaust by Michelle Bisson

A Hero and the Holocaust: The Story of Janusz Korczak and His Children by David A. Adler

Hettie and the London Blitz: A World War II Survival Story by Jenni L. Walsh (Girls Survive)

Hiding from the Nazis by David A. Adler

Hunger Winter: A World War II Novel by Rob Currie

I Survived the Nazi Invasion, 1944 by Lauren Tarshis

Jacob's Rescue by Malka Drucker

Jars of Hope: How One Woman Helped Save 2,500 Children during the Holocaust by Jennifer Roy

The Journey That Saved Curious George: The True Wartime Escape of Margret and H.A. Rey by Louise Borden

Lily by Whitney Sanderson (Horse Diaries)

The Little Riders by Margaretha Shemin

Louder Than Words by Kathy Kacer (The Heroes Quartet)

Michael at the Invasion of France, 1943 by Laurie Calkhoven (Boys of Wartime)

Miep and the Most Famous Diary: The Woman Who Rescued Anne Frank's Diary by Meeg Pincus

The Night Crossing by Karen Ackerman

The Night Spies by Kathy Kacer

Passage to Freedom by Ken Mochizuki

Peggy's Letters by Jacqueline Halsey

A Place to Hang the Moon by Kate Albus

Rescue by Jennifer A. Nielsen

Rip to the Rescue by Miriam Halahmy

Ruth and the Night of Broken Glass: A World War II Survival Story by Emma Carlson Berne (Girls Survive)

The Secret of Gabi's Dresser by Kathy Kacer

Snow Treasure by Marie McSwigan

A Time to Be Brave by Joan Betty Stuchner (Stepping Stones)

Trapped in Hitler's Web by Marsha Forchuk Skrypuch

Twenty and Ten by Claire Hutchet Bishop

The Watcher by Joan Hiatt Harlow

A Whale in Paris by Daniel Presley and Claire Polders

When We Were Shadows by Janet Wees

Who Was Anne Frank? by Ann Abramson (Who HQ)

The Winged Watchman by Hilda Van Stockum

The Wren and the Sparrow by J. Patrick Lewis

The Yellow Star: The Legend of King Christian X of Denmark by Carmen Agra Deedy

	The Book You Chose	**Date Completed**
27.1 *Light Reader*		
27.2 *Interested Reader*		
27.3 *Avid Reader*		
27.4 *Committed Reader*		
27.5 *Enthralled Reader*		

World War II

Challenge 28

Note: Many titles duplicated in the country lists.

World War II Overview

See Inside the Second World War by Rob Lloyd Jones

True Stories of World War II by Terry Lee Collins

U.S. Ghost Army: The Master Illusionists of World War II by Nel Yomtov (Graphic Library)

World War II (DK Eyewitness)

World War II by R. Conrad Stein (Cornerstones of Freedom)

World War II: An Interactive History Adventure by Elizabeth Raum (You Choose: History)

World War II for Kids: A History with 21 Activities by Richard Panchyk

World War II series by Chris Lynch

World War II: Spies, Secret Missions, and Hidden Facts by Stephanie Bearce

World War 2 Tales by Bentley Boyd (Chester the Crab Comix with Content)

World War II Battles

At Battle in World War II by Matt Doeden (You Choose: Battlefields)

Battle for the Atlantic by Gary Jeffrey (Graphic Modern History: World War II)

Battle of the Bulge by Marcus Sutter (Soldier Dogs)

The Battle of the Bulge: Nazi Germany's Final Attack on the Western Front by Michael Burgan (Tangled History)

Jack Montgomery, World War II: Gallantry at Anzio by Michael P. Spradlin (Medal of Honor)

Night Witches: A Novel of World War II by Kathryn Lasky

North Africa and the Mediterranean by Gary Jeffrey (Graphic Modern History: World War II)

Raid of No Return by Nathan Hale (Hazardous Tales)

The Western Front by Gary Jeffrey (Graphic Modern History: World War II)

We Were There at the Battle for Bataan by Benjamin Appel

We Were There at the Battle of Britain by Clayton and K.S. Knight

We Were There at the Battle of the Bulge by David Shepherd

WW2 Europe by Joe Giorello (Great Battles for Boys)

D-Day

D–Day Battle on the Beach by Kate Messner (Ranger in Time)

D–Day: June 6, 1944 by Agnieszka Jozefina Biskup (24-Hour History)

D–Day Landings by Richard Platt (DK Readers)

I Survived the Battle of D–Day 1944 by Lauren Tarshis

Resist: A Story of D–Day by Alan Gratz

Turning Point: The Story of the D–Day Landings by Michael Burgan (Tangled History)

Victory at Normandy by Marcus Sutter (Soldier Dogs)

We Were Heroes: The Journal of Scott Pendleton Collins, a World War II Soldier, Normandy, France, 1944 by Walter Dean Myers (My Name Is America)

We Were There at the Normandy Invasion by Clayton Knight

What Was D–Day? by Patricia Brennan Demuth (Who HQ)

World War II Espionage

Chester Nez and the Unbreakable Code: A Navajo Code Talker's Story by Joseph Bruchac

Navajo Code Talkers by Nathan Aaseng

Navajo Code Talkers by Blake Hoena (Graphic Library)

Navajo Code Talkers: Secret American Indian Heroes of World War II by Brynn Baker (Military Heroes)

The Secret War by Gary Jeffrey (Graphic Modern History: World War II)

The Spy Who Came In from the Sea by Peggy Nolan

Stealing Nazi Secrets in World War II: An Interactive Espionage Adventure by Elizabeth Raum (You Choose: Spies)

World War II Spies: An Interactive History Adventure by Michael Burgan (You Choose)

World War II Home Front

Blue by Joyce Moyer Hostetter (Bakers Mountain Stories)

Clues in the Shadows: A Molly Mystery by Kathleen Ernst (American Girl)

Don't Talk to Me about the War by David A. Adler

Five for Victory by Hilda van Stockum (The Mitchells)

Heroes on the Home Front by Marcus Sutter (Soldier Dogs)

Josie Poe: Palouse, Washington, 1943 by Kathleen Duey (American Diaries)

Lily's Crossing by Patricia Reilly Giff

My Secret War: The World War II Diary of Madeline Beck, Long Ilsand, New York, 1941 by Mary Pope Osborne (Dear America)

Summer of the War by Gloria Whelan (USA)

Voices at Whisper Bend by Katherine Ayres (History Mysteries)

World War II on the Home Front: An Interactive History Adventure by Martin Gitlin (You Choose: History)

World War II U.S. Homefront by Martin Gitlin (Perspectives Library)

Pearl Harbor

Alice on the Island: A Pearl Harbor Survival Story by Mayumi Shimose Poe (Girls Survive)

The Attack on Pearl Harbor by Katherine Krieg (Perspectives Library)

Attack on Pearl Harbor by Kate Messner (Ranger in Time)

The Attack on Pearl Harbor by Christy Serrano (Days That Changed America)

The Attack on Pearl Harbor by Jane Sutcliffe and Bob Lentz (Graphic Library)

Attack on Pearl Harbor by Marcus Sutter (Soldier Dogs)

The Attack on Pearl Harbor by Nel Yomtov (24-Hour History)

The Attack on Pearl Harbor: An Interactive History Adventure by Allison Lassieur (You Choose: History)

Day of Infamy: The Story of the Attack on Pearl Harbor by Steven Otfinoski (Tangled History)

Early Sunday Morning: The Pearl Harbor Diary of Amber Billows, Hawaii, 1941 by Barry Denenberg (Dear America)

Heroes of Pearl Harbor by Allan Zullo (10 True Tales)

I Survived the Bombing of Pearl Harbor, 1941 by Lauren Tarshis

My Friend the Enemy by J.D. Cheaney

Pearl Harbor by Kate Messner (History Smashers)

Pearl Harbor by Nancy Ohlin (Blast Back)

Pearl Harbor by Jennifer Swanson (American Girl: Real Stories From My Time)

Pearl Harbor Is Burning! A Story of World War II by Kathleen V. Kudlinski (Once Upon America)

Surprise Attack! by Terry Collins (Nickolas Flux History Chronicles)

We Were There at Pearl Harbor by Felix Sutton

What Was Pearl Harbor? by Patricia Brennan Demuth (Who HQ)

Prisoners of War and Internment Camps

Baseball Saved Us by Ken Mochizuki

Dash by Kirby Larson (Dogs of World War II)

Dust of Eden by Mariko Nagai

A Diamond in the Desert by Kathryn Fitzmaurice

The Endless Steppe by Esther Hautzig

The Fences between Us by Kirby Larson (Dear America)

Japanese American Internment: Prisoners in Their Own Land by Steven Otfinoski (Tangled History)

The Japanese Internment Camps by Rachel A. Bailey (Perspectives Library)

The Journal of Ben Uchida: Citizen 13559 by Barry Denenberg (My Name Is America)

Judy: Prisoner of War by Laurie Calkhoven (G.I. Dogs)

Lines We Draw: A Story of Imprisoned Japanese Americans by Camellia Lee (I Am America)

Nazi Prison Camp Escape by Michael Burgan (Great Escapes)

The Reunion by Jacqueline Pearce (Orca Young Readers)

Stealing Home by J. Torres and David Namisato

World War II and the War in the Pacific

The Battle of Iwo Jima: Turning the Tide of War in the Pacific by Steven Otfinoski (Tangled History)

The Dropping of the Atomic Bombs by Roberta Baxter (Perspectives Library)

Hiroshima and Nagasaki: The Atomic Bombings That Shook the World by Michael Burgan (Tangled History)

The House of Sixty Fathers by Meindert DeJong

Lost in the Pacific, 1942: Not a Drop to Drink by Tod Olson

Secret Mission: Guam by Marcus Sutter (Soldier Dogs)

Shipwreck on the High Seas by Marcus Sutter (Soldier Dogs)

War in the Pacific by Gary Jeffrey (Graphic Modern History: World War II)

WW2 in the Pacific by Joe Giorello (Great Battles for Boys)

	The Book You Chose	**Date Completed**
28.1 Light Reader		
28.2 Interested Reader		
28.3 Avid Reader		
28.4 Committed Reader		
28.5 Enthralled Reader		

The Cold War

Challenge 29

The Berlin Wall: An Interactive Modern History Adventure by Matt Doeden (You Choose: Modern History)

Breaking Stalin's Nose by Eugene Yelchin

Captive Witness by Carolyn Keene (Nancy Drew)

Charlie and Pushinka by Brandon Smith

Cold War Correspondent: A Korean War Tale by Nathan Hale (Hazardous Tales)

The Cold War: Secrets, Special Missions, and Hidden Facts about the CIA, KGB, and MI6 by Stephanie Bearce (Top Secret Files of History)

The Cuban Missile Crisis by Gary Jeffrey (Graphic Modern History)

Drive by Joyce Moyer Hostetter (Bakers Mountain Stories)

The End of the Cold War by Kate Riggs (Turning Points)

Escape from East Berlin by Andy Marino

Great Escapes Over the Berlin Wall by Daniel Goebel

I Am David by Ann Holm

Mac Saves the World by Mac Barnett (Mac B., Kid Spy)

A Night Divided by Jennifer Nielsen

Over and Out by Jenni L. Walsh

The Spy Catchers of Maple Hill by Megan Frazer Blakemore

Spy Runner by Eugene Yelchin

We Were There at the Opening of the Atomic Era by James Munves

What Was the Berlin Wall? by Nico Medina (Who HQ)

Where Is Area 51? by Paula K. Manzaanero (Who HQ)

Which Way Is Home? by Maria Kiely

White Sands, Red Menace by Ellen Klages

Who Was Fidel Castro? by Sarah Fabiny (Who HQ)

	The Book You Chose	Date Completed
29.1 Light Reader		
29.2 Interested Reader		
29.3 Avid Reader		
29.4 Committed Reader		
29.5 Enthralled Reader		

Space Exploration

Challenge 30

The 100 Year Starship by Mae Jemison (A True Book)

The Apollo 11 Moon Landing by Amy Maranville (Days That Changed America)

The Apollo 11 Moon Landing by Nel Yomtov (24-Hour History)

Apollo 11 Q&A: 175+ Fascinating Facts for Kids by Kelly Milner Halls (History Q&A)

Apollo 13: How Three Brave Astronauts Survived a Space Disaster by Kathleen Weidner Zoehfeld (Totally True Adventures)

Astronaut Mae Jemison by Allison Lassieur (STEM Trailblazer Bios)

Audrey and Apollo 11 by Rebecca Rissman (Smithsonian)

Blast Off! How Mary Sherman Morgan Fueled America Into Space by Suzanne Slade

Buzz Aldrin: Pioneer Moon Explorer by Jessie Alkire (Space Crusaders)

Dr. Mae Jemison: Brave Rocketeer by Heather Alexander (VIP)

Exploring Space by Steve Parker (100 Facts)

The Extraordinary Life of Neil Armstrong by Martin Howard (Extraordinary Lives)

The First Moon Landing by Thomas K. Adamson (Graphic Library)

The Girl Who Could Dance in Outer Space: An Inspirational Tale about Mae Jemison by Maya Cointreau

Houston, We've Had a Problem: The Story of the Apollo 13 Disaster by Rebecca Rissman (Tangled History)

I Love You, Michael Collins by Lauren Baratz-Logsted

Laika the Space Dog by Jeni Wittrock (Animal Heroes)

Lost in Outer Space: The Incredible Journey of Apollo 13 by Tod Olson

The Man Who Went to the Far Side of the Moon: The Story of Apollo 11 Astronaut Michael Collins by Bea Uusma Schyffert

Michael Collins: Forgotten Astronaut by James Buckley (Discovering History's Heroes)

The Mission Possible Mystery at Space Center Houston by Carole Marsh (Real Kids, Real Places)

Moon Shot: The Flight of Apollo 11 by Brian Floca

Neil Armstrong by Tim Goss (Trailblazers of the Modern World)

Neil Armstrong: First Man on the Moon! by James Buckley, Jr. (Show Me History)

Neil Armstrong: First Man on the Moon by Alex Woolf (Trailblazers)

Neil Armstrong: Man on the Moon by Tamara Hollingsworth (Social Studies Readers)

Neil Armstrong: Young Flyer by Montrew Dunham (Childhood of Famous Americans)

The Race to Space: From Sputnik to the Moon Landing and Beyond by Clive Gifford

The Race to the Moon: An Interactive History Adventure by Allison Lassieur (You Choose: History)

The Race to Space: Countdown to Liftoff by Erik Slader and Ben Thompson (Epic Fails)

Reaching for the Moon by Buzz Aldrin

The Space Race by Peter Benoit (Cornerstones of Freedom)

Team Moon: How 400,000 People Landed Apollo 11 on the Moon by Catherine Thimmesh

To the Moon and Back by Buzz Aldrin with Marianne J. Dyson (National Geographic)

When Neil Armstrong Built a Wind Tunnel by Mark Weakland

Who Was Neil Armstrong? by Roberta Edwards (Who HQ)

	The Book You Chose	Date Completed
30.1 *Light Reader*		
30.2 *Interested Reader*		
30.3 *Avid Reader*		
30.4 *Committed Reader*		
30.5 *Enthralled Reader*		

Civil Rights Movement

Challenge 31

Abby Takes a Stand by Patricia McKissack (Scraps of Time)

The Assassination of Martin Luther King, Jr. by Terry Collins (24-Hour History)

Birmingham 1963: How a Photograph Rallied Civil Rights Support by Shelley Tougas

Boycott Blues: How Rosa Parks Inspired a Nation by Andrea Davis Pinkney

Breaking Barriers: The Story of Jackie Robinson by Michael Burgan (Tangled History)

Child of the Dream: A Memoir of 1963 by Sharon Robinson

The Civil Rights Movement by Jennifer Zeiger (Cornerstones of Freedom)

The Civil Rights Movement: An Interactive History Adventure by Heather Adamson (You Choose: History)

Cracking the Wall: The Struggles of the Little Rock Nine by Eileen Lucas

Daisy Bates and the Little Rock Nine by Harris Duchess

Don't Know Much about Martin Luther King, Jr. by Kenneth C. Davis

Don't Know Much about Rosa Parks by Kenneth C. Davis

The Extraordinary Life of Rosa Parks by Sheila Kanani (Extraordinary Lives)

A Girl Named Rose: The True Story of Rosa Parks by Denise Lewis Patrick (American Girl)

The Highest Tribute: Thurgood Marshall's Life, Leadership, and Legacy by Kekla Magoon

I Have a Dream: The Story of Martin Luther King by Margaret Davidson

Ida B. Wells: Fighter for Justice by Diane Bailey

Ida B. Wells: Let the Truth Be Told by Walter Dean Myers

Ida B. Wells: Mother of the Civil Rights Movement by Dennis Brindell Fradin and Judith Bloom Fradin

The Liberation of Gabriel King by K.L. Going

The Lions of Little Rock by Kristin Levine

Little Rock Girl 1957: How a Photograph Changed the Fight for Integration by Shelley Tougas

Little Rock Nine by Marshall Poe (Turning Points)

The Little Rock Nine and the Fight for Equal Education by Gary Jeffrey (Graphic History of the Civil Rights Movement)

Lunch Counter Sit-Ins: How Photographs Helped Foster Peaceful Civil Rights Protests by Danielle Smith-Llera

March Forward, Girl: From Young Warrior to Little Rock Nine by Melba Pattillo Beals

The March on Washington by Bonnie Bader (American Girl: Real Stories from My Time)

The March on Washington by Margeaux Weston (Days That Changed America)

Martin Luther King, Jr. by Adele Q. Brown (Trailblazers of the Modern World)

Martin Luther King, Jr. by Laurie Calkhoven (DK Life Stories)

Martin Luther King, Jr. and the March on Washington by Gary Jeffrey (Graphic History of the Civil Rights Movement)

Martin Luther King, Jr.: Fighting for Civil Rights by Christine Platt (Trailblazers)

Martin Luther King, Jr.: Great Civil Rights Leader by Jennifer Lee Fandel (Graphic Library)

Martin Luther King, Jr.: Voice for Equality! by James Buckley, Jr. (Show Me History)

Martin Luther King, Jr.: Young Man with a Dream by Dharathula H. Millender (Childhood of Famous Americans)

The Montgomery Bus Boycott by Martin Gitlin (Perspectives Library)

Nobody Gonna Turn Me 'Round: Stories and Songs of the Civil Rights Movement by Doreen Rappaport

A Picture Book of Martin Luther King, Jr. by David A. Adler

A Picture Book of Rosa Parks by David A. Adler

A Picture Book of Thurgood Marshall by David A. Adler

A Place to Land: Martin Luther King, Jr. and the Speech That Inspired a Nation by Barry Wittenstein

Remember Little Rock: The Time, the People, the Stories by Paul Robert Walker

Rosa by Nikki Giovanni

Rosa Parks and the Montgomery Bus Boycott by Gary Jeffrey (Graphic History of the Civil Rights Movement)

Rosa Parks and the Montgomery Bus Boycott by Connie Rose Miller

Rosa Parks: Civil Rights Pioneer by Karen Kellaher

Rosa Parks: Young Rebel by Kathleen Kudlinski

The School Is Not White! A True Story of the Civil Rights Movement by Doreen Rappaport

The Selma Marches for Civil Rights: We Shall Overcome by Steven Otfinoski (Tangled History)

Sit-In: How Four Friends Stood Up by Sitting In by Andrea Davis Pinkney

The Story of Thurgood Marshall: Justice for All by Joe Arthur

Through My Eyes by Ruby Bridges

Thurgood by Jonah Winter

Thurgood Marshall by Geoffrey M. Horn

Thurgood Marshall by Teri Kanefield

Thurgood Marshall by Kristin Kemp

Thurgood Marshall and the Supreme Court by Deborah Kent

Thurgood Marshall: The Supreme Court Rules on "Separate But Equal" by Gary Jeffrey (Graphic History of the Civil Rights Movement)

Thurgood Marshall: Young Justice by Montrew Dunham

Twelve Days in May: Freedom Ride 1961 by Larry Dane Brimner

The Voting Rights Act of 1965: An Interactive History Adventure by Michael Burgan (You Choose: History)

The Watsons Go to Birmingham, 1963 by Christopher Paul Curtis

Who Was Ida B. Wells? by Sarah Fabiny (Who HQ)

Who Was Martin Luther King, Jr.? by Bonnie Bader (Who HQ)

Who Was Rosa Parks? by Yona Zeldis McDonough (Who HQ)

With the Might of Angels: The Diary of Dawnie Rae Johnson, Hadley, Virginia, 1954 by Andrea Davis Pinkney (Dear America)

Yours for Justice, Ida B. Wells: The Daring Life of a Crusading Journalist by Philip Dray

	The Book You Chose	Date Completed
31.1 Light Reader		
31.2 Interested Reader		
31.3 Avid Reader		
31.4 Committed Reader		
31.5 Enthralled Reader		

Health

Challenge 32

100 Things to Know about Food (Usborne)

100 Things to Know about the Human Body (Usborne)

The 1918 Flu Pandemic by Katherine Krohn (Graphic Library)

The 1918 Flu Pandemic: Core Events of a Worldwide Outbreak by John Micklos, Jr. (What Went Wrong)

All in a Day's Work: ER Doctor by Diana Herweck

Are You What You Eat? A Guide to What's On Your Plate and Why (DK)

The Berenstain Bears and the Drug-Free Zone by Stan and Jan Berenstain

The Black Death by Jim Ollhoff

The Boy Who Saved Cleveland by James Cross Giblin

The Boy's Body Book by Kelli Dunham (for boys)

Can You Survive the 1918 Flu Pandemic? by Matthew K. Manning (You Choose: Disasters in History)

The Care and Keeping of You by Valorie Schaefer (American Girl) (for girls)

The Case of the Measled Cowboy by John R. Erickson (Hank the Cowdog)

The Chocolate Touch by Patrick Skene Catling

Daisy and the Deadly Flu: A 1918 Influenza Survival Story by Julie Gilbert (Girls Survive)

The Dangers of Alcohol by Kristin Thiel

The Dangers of Illegal Drugs by Christine Honders

The Dangers of Marijuana by Jodyanne Benson

The Dangers of Prescription Drugs by Kristin Thiel

The Dangers of Tobacco by Jenna Tolli

Decoding Genes by Amber J. Keyser (Max Axiom)

Feeling Better: A Kid's Book about Therapy by Rachel Rashkin

The Feelings Book: The Care and Keeping of Your Emotions by Lynda Madison (American Girl) (for girls)

Feelings: Everything You Need to Know about Your Emotions by Cara Natterson (Guy Stuff) (for boys)

Food and Nutrition for Every Kid by Janice VanCleave

The Germ Detectives by Jim Ollhoff

Get Well Soon, Mallory! by Ann M. Martin (The Baby-Sitters Club)

Head to Toe Science: Over 40 Eye-Popping, Spine-Tingling, Heart-Pounding Activities That Teach Kids about the Human Body by Jim Wiese

Human Body (DK Eyewitness)

Human Body (DK Pocket Genius)

The Human Life Cycle by Jennifer Prior

Inside My Body series by Jody Jensen Shaffer

Jessi and the Awful Secret by Ann M. Martin (The Baby-Sitters Club)

A Journey through the Digestive System by Emily Sohn (Max Axiom)

Malaria by Jim Ollhoff

Maria and the Plague: A Black Death Survival Story by Natasha Deen (Girls Survive)

Medical Breakthroughs by Gary Jeffrey (Graphic Discoveries)

Mimi's Village and How Basic Health Care Transformed It by Katie Smith Milway

Penny from Heaven by Jennifer L. Holm

Plagues: The Microscopic Battlefield by Falynn Koch (Science Comics)

Sadako and the Thousand Paper Cranes by Eleanor Coerr

Slow Down: 50 Mindful Moments in Nature by Rachel Williams

Smallpox by Jim Ollhoff

Small Steps: The Year I Got Polio by Peg Kehret

A Smart Girl's Guide: Sports and Fitness by Therese Kauchak Maring
Straight Talk: Drugs and Alcohol by Stephanie Paris
Straight Talk: The Truth about Food by Stephanie Paris
Strange But True: Gross Anatomy by Timothy J. Bradley
Sunny Side Up by Jennifer L. Holm
The Truth about Stacey by Ann M. Martin (The Baby-Sitters Club)

Ultimate Body-pedia by Christina Wilsdon
Understanding Myself: A Kid's Guide to Intense Emotions and Strong Feelings by Mary C. Lamia
Understanding Viruses by Agnieszka Biskup (Max Axiom)
What's Drug Abuse? by Richard Alexander

	The Book You Chose	Date Completed
32.1 *Light Reader*		
32.2 *Interested Reader*		
32.3 *Avid Reader*		
32.4 *Committed Reader*		
32.5 *Enthralled Reader*		

1970s-1990s in the U.S.

Challenge 33

The 1980 U.S. Olympic Boycott by Martin Gitlin (Perspectives Library)

Basher Five-Two by Scott O'Grady with Michael French

The Blackbird Girls by Anne Blankman

Brave Bird at Wounded Knee: A Story of the Protest on the Pine Ridge Indian Reservation by Rachel Bithell (I Am America)

The Challenger Disaster: Tragedy in the Skies by Pranas T. Naujokaitis (History Comics)

The Challenger Explosion by Heather Adamson (Graphic Library)

The Challenger Explosion: Core Events of a Space Tragedy by John Micklos, Jr. (What Went Wrong)

Chernobyl by Nikole Brooks Bethea (Man-Made Disasters)

Dogs of the Deadlands by Anothony McGowan

The Eruption of Mount St. Helens by Thomas K. Adamson (Deadly Disasters)

Escape From Chernobyl by Andy Marino

Fatal Faults: The Story of the Challenger Explosion by Eric Braun (Tangled History)

A Girl Named Disaster by Nancy Farmer

I Survived the Eruption of Mount St. Helens 1980 by Lauren Tarshis

Maribel Versus the Volcano: A Mount St. Helens Survival Story by Sarah Hannah Gomez (Girls Survive)

The Mount Everest Disaster of 1996 by Cindy L. Rodriguez (Graphic Library)

Playing Atari with Saddam Hussein by Jennifer Roy

The Volcano Disaster by Peg Kehret

	The Book You Chose	Date Completed
33.1 Light Reader		
33.2 Interested Reader		
33.3 Avid Reader		
33.4 Committed Reader		
33.5 Enthralled Reader		

21st Century in the U.S.

Challenge 34

The 9/11 Terrorist Attacks by Amy Maranville (Days That Changed America)

America Is Under Attack: The Day the Towers Fell by Don Brown (Actual Times)

The Boston Marathon Bombing: Running for Their Lives by Blake Hoena (Tangled History)

Captain Sully's River Landing: The Hudson Hero of Flight 1549 by Steven Otfinoski (Tangled History)

Collapse and Chaos: The Story of the 2010 Earthquake in Haiti by Jessica Freeburg (Tangled History)

Escape from the Twin Towers by Kate Messner (Ranger in Time)

Finding Someplace by Denise Lewis Patrick

Ground Zero: A Novel of 9/11 by Alan Gratz

Ground Zero: How a Photograph Sent a Message of Hope by Don Nardo

Hurricane Katrina by Peter Benoit (A True Book: Disasters)

Hurricane Katrina: An Interactive Modern History Adventure by Blake Hoena (You Choose: Modern History)

Hurricane Katrina Rescue by Kate Messner (Ranger in Time)

I Escaped the California Camp Fire by SD Brown and Scott Peters

I Escaped the Grizzly Maze by Ellie Crowe and Scott Peters

I Survived Hurricane Katrina 2005 by Lauren Tarshis

I Survived the Attacks of September 11, 2001 by Lauren Tarshis

I Survived the California Wildfires, 2018 by Lauren Tarshis

I Survived the Japanese Tsunami, 2011 by Lauren Tarshis

I Survived the Joplin Tornado, 2011 by Lauren Tarshis

Impact: The Story of the September 11 Terrorist Attacks by Matt Doeden (Tangled History)

The Making of the Social Network: An Interactive Modern History Adventure by Michael Burgan (You Choose: Modern History)

Nine, Ten: A September 11 Story by Nora Raleigh Baskin

Saved by the Boats: The Heroic Sea Evacuation of September 11 by Julie Gassman

Shooting Kabul by N. H. Senzai

Swept Away: The Story of the 2011 Japanese Tsunami by Rebecca Rissman (Tangled History)

Tara and the Towering Wave: An Indian Ocean Tsunami Survival Story by Cristina Oxtra (Girls Survive)

Titan and the Wild Boars: The True Cave Rescue of the Thai Soccer Team by Susan Hood and Pathana Sornhiran

Total Devastation: The Story of Hurricane Katrina by Michael Burgan (Tangled History)

Towers Falling by Jewell Parker Rhodes

What Was Hurricane Katrina? by Robin Koontz (Who HQ)

What Were the Twin Towers? by Jim O'Connor (Who HQ)

	The Book You Chose	Date Completed
34.1 Light Reader		
34.2 Interested Reader		
34.3 Avid Reader		
34.4 Committed Reader		
34.5 Enthralled Reader		

Caribbean Islands

Challenge 35

Antigua and Barbuda

Antigua and Barbuda by Sara Louise Kras (Cultures of the World)

Country Jumper in Antigua and Barbuda by Claudia Dobson-Largie

Honey Dew's Carnival Fever by Cray Mahalia Francis

Aruba

Country Jumper in Aruba by Claudia Dobson-Largie

The Bahamas

The Bahamas by Martin Hintz (Enchantment of the World)

Country Jumper in The Bahamas by Claudia Dobson-Largie

The Island of Lost Horses by Stacy Gregg

The Misadventures of Maria the Hutia by Ron Shaklee

Cuba

Country Jumper in Cuba by Claudia Dobson-Largie

Cuba by Anna Cavallo (Country Explorers)

Cuba by Muriel L. Dubois (A Question and Answer Book)

Cuba by Lisa Harkrader (Top Ten Countries of Recent Immigrants)

Cuba by Deborah Kent (Enchantment of the World)

Cuba by Joanne Mattern (All Around the World)

Cuba by Julie Murray (Explore the Countries)

Cuba by Amy Rechner (Country Profiles)

Cuba by Walter Simmons (Exploring Countries)

Cuba by Kathryn Stevens (Countries: Faces and Places)

Island Treasures: Growing Up in Cuba by Alma Flor Ada

My Havana: Memories of a Cuban Boyhood by Rosemary Wells with Secundino Fernandez

The People and Culture of Cuba by Melissa Rae Shofner

Travels in Cuba by Marie-Louise Gay and David Homel

We Visit Cuba by Kathleen Tracy

Where the Flame Trees Bloom by Alma Flor Ada

Who Was Fidel Castro? by Sarah Fabiny (Who HQ)

Under the Royal Palms by Alma Flor Ada

Dominican Republic

The Color of My Words by Lynn Joseph

Country Jumper in the Dominican Republic by Claudia Dobson-Largie

Dominican Republic by Barbara R. Rogers and Lura Rogers Seavey (Enchantment of the World)

Dominican Republic by Jessica Dean (All Around the World)

The Dominican Republic by Mary Dodson Wade (A Question and Answer Book)

The Dominican Republic by Pat McCarthy (Top Ten Countries of Recent Immigrants)

The Dominican Republic by Walter Simmons (Exploring Countries)

Growing Up Pedro by Matt Tavares

How Tia Lola Came to (Visit) Stay by Julia Alvarez

The People & Culture of the Dominican Republic by Ian Emminizer

We Visit the Dominican Republic by John A. Torres

Haiti

Anacaona: Golden Flower by Edwidge Danticat (The Royal Diaries)

Blades of Freedom: A Tale of Haiti, Napoleon, and the Louisiana Purchase by Nathan Hale (Hazardous Tales)

Collapse and Chaos: The Story of the 2010 Earthquake in Haiti by Jessica Freeburg (Tangled History)

Country Jumper in Haiti by Claudia Dobson-Largie

Haiti by Jim Bartell (Exploring Countries)

Haiti, continued

Haiti by Clara Bennington (All Around the World)
Haiti by June Preszler (A Question and Answer Book)
Haiti by Elma Schemenauer (Countries: Faces and Places)
Haiti by Nel Yomtov (Enchantment of the World)
Meet Our New Student from Haiti by John A. Torres

Jamaica

Country Jumper in Jamaica by Claudia Dobson-Largie
Cultural Traditions in Jamaica by Lynn Peppas
Jamaica by Mary Berendes (Countries: Faces and Places)
Jamaica by Ruth Bjorklund (Enchantment of the World)
Jamaica by Michael Capek (Country Explorers)
Jamaica by Lisa Owings (Exploring Countries)
Jamaica by Kristine Spanier (All Around the World)
Let's Visit Jamaica by Frances Wilkins
My Life in Jamaica by Patience Coster (A Child's Day In…)
The Mysterious Cavern by Franklin W. Dixon (Hardy Boys)
When Life Gives You Mangos by Kereen Getten
Yes, I Can! The Story of the Jamaican Bobsled Team by Devon Harris

Puerto Rico

The Happy Hollisters at Lizard Cove by Jerry West
Juan and Chico's Wintry Puerto Rico Adventure by Gerard Aflague
A Kid's Guide to Puerto Rico by Jack L. Roberts
Marcus Vega Doesn't Speak Spanish by Pablo Cartaya

My Name Is Maria Isabel by Alma Flor Ada
Taino Tales: The Secret of the Hummingbird by Vicky Weber
We Visit Puerto Rico by John A. Torres

St. Lucia

The Secret of Skeleton Reef by Franklin W. Dixon (Hardy Boys)
St. Lucia: The Land and the People by Daniel Gilpin
Telling Tales from Saint Lucia by Nahdjla Bailey

Trinidad and Tobago

Trinidad and Tobago by Sean Sheehan (Cultures of the World)
A Wave in Her Pocket: Stories from Trinidad by Lynn Joseph

Virgin Islands

Alexander Hamilton: Little Lion by Ann Hood (The Treasure Chest)
Escape from Fear by Gloria Skurzynsk (Mysteries in Our National Parks)
Hurricane Child by Kacen Callender
The Lizard Lady by Jennifer Keats Curtis and Nicole F. Angeli (Working with Scientists)
My Name Is Not Angelica by Scott O'Dell
Trouble in Paradise by Franklin W. Dixon (Hardy Boys Undercover Brothers)

	The Book You Chose	**Date Completed**
35.1 *Light Reader*		
35.2 *Interested Reader*		
35.3 *Avid Reader*		
35.4 *Committed Reader*		
35.5 *Enthralled Reader*		

Travel/Transportation

Challenge 36

125 Wacky Roadside Attractions (National Geographic Kids)

50 Adventures in the 50 States by Kate Siber

The 50 States by Gabrielle Balkan

Amelia's Are-We-There-Yet Longest Ever Car Trip by Marissa Moss

Around the World in 50 Ways by Dan Smith (Lonely Planet)

Baby-Sitters Club in the U.S.A. by Ann M. Martin (Baby-Sitters Club Super Special)

Barfing in the Backseat by Henry Winkler (Hank Zipzer)

Bus Station Mystery by Gertrude Chandler Warner (The Boxcar Children)

Car (DK Eyewitness)

Cars (DK Pocket Genius)

Cars: Engines That Move You by Dan Zettwoch (Science Comics)

Charting the World: Geography and Maps from Cave Paintings to GPS by Richard Panchyk

Coast to Coast by Betsy Byars

The Genius Files series by Dan Gutman

The Great Train Mystery by Carole Marsh (Real Kids, Real Places)

Henry Reed's Journey by Keith Robertson

Judy's Journey by Lois Lenski

Kristy and the Mystery Train by Ann M. Martin (Baby-Sitters Club Mysteries)

Moving and Grooving by Bentley Boyd (Chester the Crab Comix with Content)

Paddle-to-the-Sea by Holling Clancy Holling

The Race across America by Geronimo Stilton

The Race around the World: How Nellie Bly Chased an Impossible Dream by Nancy Castaldo

The Red Trailer Mystery by Julie Campbell (Trixie Belden)

Road Trip by Gary Paulsen

Ruth and the Green Book by Calvin Alexander Ramsey

Talkin' about Bessie: The Story of Aviator Elizabeth Coleman by Nikki Grimes

Train (DK Eyewitness)

The Travel Book by Malcolm Croft (Lonely Planet)

The Twenty-One Balloons by William Pene Du Bois

Ultimate U.S. Road Trip Atlas (National Geographic Kids)

Wagons Ho! by George Hallowell and Joan Holub

Walk Two Moons by Sharon Creech

	The Book You Chose	**Date Completed**
36.1 *Light Reader*		
36.2 *Interested Reader*		
36.3 *Avid Reader*		
36.4 *Committed Reader*		
36.5 *Enthralled Reader*		

Book Awards & Party

Do This As Soon As You Finish Your Reading Challenge

Grab your child's completed reading log and help him fill out the awards page (opposite page) to give his best and worst books an official award and mark them as most memorable this year.

Encourage him not to agonize over "was this one really the best..." but to go with his general impressions or write down all the contenders.

Send us a copy of this at books@timberdoodle.com, and we'll be thrilled to credit you 50 Doodle Dollar Reward points (worth $2.50 off your next order) as our thank-you for taking the time to share. We'll also congratulate your child on a job so well done!

Bonus Idea

Have an awards ceremony night all about one of the books on your list! You'll get the most specific ideas by searching online for "book I picked theme party," but here are some things to think through as you get started.

Food: How can you tie the menu to the theme? A book like *Green Eggs and Ham* or *Pancakes for Breakfast* is easy—just replicate the food in the book! If you're working with a book that doesn't feature food directly, there are a few options. Perhaps the book featured a construction crew; you could all eat from "lunchboxes" tonight or set up your kitchen to masquerade as a food truck. Or if you're reading a book about the pioneers, do a little research and eat frying pan bread, beans, venison, and cornmeal mush.

You could also take the food you would normally eat and reshape it to match your story. For instance, sandwiches can be cut into ships, round apple slices can be life preservers, crackers can be labeled "hardtack," and you're well on your way to a party featuring your favorite nautical tale.

Don't forget the setting. As ridiculous as it sounds, eating dinner by (battery-operated!) lantern light under your table draped with blankets will make that simple camping tale an experience your family will be recalling for years to come.

Or perhaps some handmade red table fans, softly playing traditional Chinese music, and a red tablecloth would provide the perfect backdrop for the story about life in China.

The more senses you use, the more memorable you make this experience. Use appropriate background music, diffuse peppermint oil to make it smell like Christmas, dim the lights, eat at the top of the swing set, or whatever would set this apart from a regular night and make it just a bit more exciting.

Don't get trapped in either the "we must do this tonight" mode or the "we can't do this because it won't be perfect" mode. Allowing your child to spend a few days creating decorations and menus is wonderful! Doing it today because it's the only free night on the horizon even though you can only integrate a few ideas into the preset menu? Also amazing! Your goal is to value the book and make some fun memories.

Book Awards of

_____
(YOUR CHILD'S NAME HERE)   (YEAR HERE)

I READ _____ BOOKS FROM THE READING CHALLENGE THIS YEAR!

FUNNIEST BOOK:
_____

MOST MEMORABLE BOOK:
_____

BOOK I READ THE MOST TIMES:
_____

BOOK I ENJOYED THE LEAST:
_____

TEACHER'S FAVORITE BOOK:
_____

BOOK I MOST WISH WAS A SERIES:
_____

CHOOSE YOUR OWN AWARD:
_____

When You're Done Here

Your Top 4 FAQ about Next Year

Things to Think through as You Anticipate Fifth Grade

So you're finishing up fourth grade already? How has it gone for you? Really, we'd love to know! (Plus, you get reward points for your review.) Just jump over to the Fourth-Grade Curriculum page on our website and scroll down to submit a review.

As you look toward next year, there are a few things that you may want to know.

1. When Can We See the New Kits?

New kits usually release in April. Check our Facebook page or give us a call for this year's projection, but it's always in the spring and usually mid-April.

2. Free Customization

If your child has raced ahead in some subjects this year, or if you need to go back and fill in some gaps, or if you don't need more Math-U-See blocks, you'll be thrilled to know that you can customize your kit next year. You'll find full details on our website, but know that customization is free and can often be completed online if you prefer to DIY.

3. Do I Need to Take the Summer Off?

Some students finish a grade with an eager passion to jump right into the next grade, and parents contact us asking if that's OK or if they should take some time off so the child doesn't burn out. We are year-round homeschoolers, so we would definitely be fans of jumping into the next grade!

However, the truth is that this is your decision. We can tell you that a long break can quench the thirst for knowledge, and that's why our family typically moves right into the next grade. However, sometimes a little suspense makes the year begin with beautiful anticipation. If you have a crazy summer planned, it can be ideal to set school aside and enjoy the season!

If you decide to start early, you could consider saving 1 or 2 items for your official start date so that there is still some anticipation.

4. Can I Refill This Kit for My Next Child?

Absolutely! Each year's Additional Student Kit reflects the current year's kit (so the 2024-2025 Elite Curriculum Kit and the 2024-2025 Additional Student Kit correlate). If you loved it just the way it was, refill it now before we swap things around for next year. Or, if you prefer, wait for the new kits to launch and then let our team help you figure out what tweaks (if any) need to be made.

We're Here to Help!

If you have other questions for us, want to share additional feedback, or would like to get in touch for some other reason, don't hesitate to drop us a line or give us a call. (FYI, we also have online chat on our website if that's easier for you.)

mail@Timberdoodle.com
800-478-0672

Doodle Dollar Reward Points

What They Are, How They Work, and Where to Find Them

If you're one of our Charter School BFFs, we just want to give you a heads up that the following information doesn't really apply to you. Doodle Dollars are earned on individual prepaid orders (credit cards or online payment plans are fine) and sadly don't apply to purchase orders or school district orders.

Now, with that out of the way, here's the good news. Almost any item you order directly from us earns you reward points!

You will earn 1 point for every $1 you spend.
20 points = $1 off a future order!

Some families prefer to use this money as they go, while others save it up for Christmas or for those midyear purchases that just weren't in the budget.

Can I Earn More Points?

Absolutely! Review your purchases on Timberdoodle.com to earn points. Add pictures for even more points!

What Can I Spend My Points On?

Anything on our website. These reward points act as a gift certificate to be used on anything you like.

How Do I Get to My Points?

The simplest way is to look for the teal Doodle Dollars pop-up in the lower left corner of our website. Click it, log in, then click "All Rewards" > "Redeem" and drag the slider to choose how many points to cash out. You'll immediately be issued a gift certificate to apply to your order. If you run into any challenges, please let our team know, and we will be thrilled to assist you.

Check our website for the latest information on reward points:
www.Timberdoodle.com/doodledollars

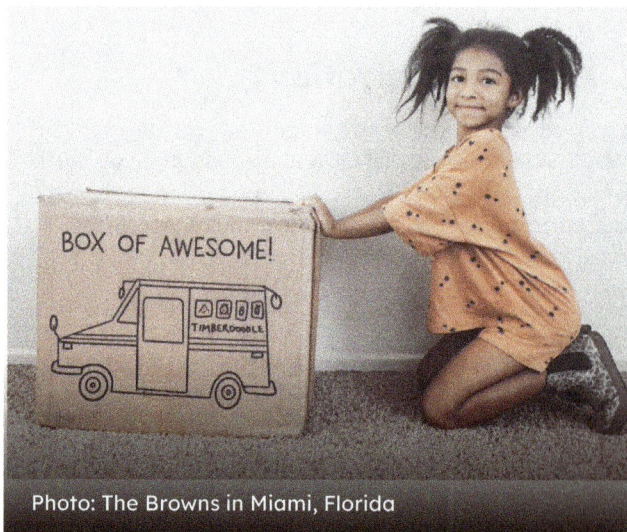

Photo: The Browns in Miami, Florida

Printed in the USA
CPSIA information can be obtained
at www.ICGtesting.com
CBHW080543160424
6992CB00002B/11